CHARLES X'S WARS

Volume 2 – The Wars in the East, 1655–1657

Michael Fredholm von Essen

'This is the Century of the Soldier', Fulvio Testi, Poet, 1641

Helion & Company

Helion & Company Limited
Unit 8 Amherst Business Centre
Budbrooke Road
Warwick
CV34 5WE
England
Tel. 01926 499 619
Email: info@helion.co.uk
Website: www.helion.co.uk
Twitter: @helionbooks
Visit our blog http://blog.helion.co.uk/

Published by Helion & Company 2022
Designed and typeset by Serena Jones
Cover designed by Paul Hewitt, Battlefield Design (www.battlefield-design.co.uk)

Text © Michael Fredholm von Essen 2022
Colour artwork by Tomasz Nowojewski @ Helion & Company 2022
Pen and ink artwork by Sergey Shamenkov © Helion & Company 2022
Maps drawn by George Anderson © Helion & Company 2022

ISBN 978-1-915070-30-2

British Library Cataloguing-in-Publication Data.
A catalogue record for this book is available from the British Library.

For details of other military history titles published by Helion & Company
Limited, contact the above address, or visit our website: http://www.helion.co.uk

We always welcome receiving book proposals from prospective authors.

Contents

Introduction

The present book, volume two of a total of three, continues the description and analysis of the wars of the Swedish Deluge, that is, the devastating conflicts between Sweden, the Polish-Lithuanian Commonwealth, Brandenburg-Prussia, Muscovy, Transylvania, Cossack Ukraine, the Tatar Khanate of the Crimea, Denmark-Norway, the Netherlands, and the Emperor of the Holy Roman Empire during the reign of Swedish King Charles X Gustavus. By invading the Polish-Lithuanian Commonwealth, King Charles saw an opportunity to put an end to the Polish King's claim to the Swedish throne and to gain additional territories which would enable him to control the customs duties of the Baltic Sea maritime trade. Whilst the first volume described the armies and tactics of the belligerent powers during the Deluge, this second volume focuses on the campaigns and battles that took place during the first half of the 1655–1660 Swedish–Commonwealth war, which provoked the political and military collapse of the Commonwealth. Since this conflict cannot be disentangled from the simultaneous wars between the Commonwealth and Muscovy, from 1654 to 1667, and between Sweden and Muscovy, from 1656 to 1661, the latter wars will be described as well for the same time period. All these conflicts took place simultaneously and on the same terrain, which stretched from Arctic Scandinavia to the shore of the Black Sea. Since the common denominator was Swedish King Charles, the book will focus on the Swedish wars. Events which took place farther afield will be covered in somewhat less detail.

As noted in Volume 1, some of the belligerent powers at the time of the war followed different calendars. The Gregorian calendar, named after the sixteenth-century Pope Gregory XIII who introduced it, had been developed as a correction to an observed error in the old Julian calendar. The visible result of the correction was that the date was advanced 10 days, that is, 4 October 1582 was followed by 15 October 1582. The Holy Roman Empire changed calendar on this date, as did most Catholic nations. However, many Protestant countries initially objected to adopting a Catholic innovation. The Duchy of Prussia was the first Protestant nation to adopt the Gregorian calendar. However, neither Brandenburg nor Denmark adopted the new calendar until 1700, while Sweden delayed yet longer. Muscovy's successor Russia delayed further still, until 1918. Most of the belligerents in the war accordingly used the Julian calendar, which for this reason differed from the one used in Catholic nations and at present. Old Style (O.S.) and New

Style (N.S.) are terms commonly used with dates to indicate that the calendar convention used at the time described is different from that in use at present. Unless noted otherwise, the dates given here will be N.S.

Similarly to Volume 1, the linguistic, ethnic, and regional diversity in Eastern Europe does not allow for a single, fully consistent system for the spelling of seventeenth-century names. Major parts of the region were in the seventeenth century dominated by speakers of non-Slavic languages, including Lithuanian, Tatar, and German. The written forms of, say, modern-day Polish, Belarusian, Ukrainian, and Russian have diverged from one another, and at present some take the choice of one over the other as acceptance of modern-day claims of territory or cultural 'ownership'. No such suggestion is implied in this work. Instead, I have, whenever possible, used the traditional English versions of names (which commonly were based on Russian name-forms), or when it seems appropriate, the German name-forms typically employed in contemporary works of history. For obvious reasons, German geographical names were particularly common in Prussia but also in north-western Poland.

For a full chronology as well as biographical data on all commanders mentioned in the text, please refer to the appropriate sections within the front matters of Volume 1.

1

The Outbreak of War

With the Treaty of Pereyaslav in January 1654, Bogdan Khmel'nitskiy, Hetman of the Ukrainian cossacks, acknowledged Tsar Alexis of Muscovy as his suzerain. This act immediately led to a state of war between the Commonwealth, which wished to reclaim its Ukrainian territories, and Muscovy, which under the terms of the Treaty took Cossack Ukraine under its wings. This conflict, which eventually became known as the Thirteen Years' War (1654–1667), ignited the wars of the Deluge. The combat operations during the Deluge began not with Swedish King Charles but with the rivalry between the Commonwealth and Muscovy over the Ukraine.

Following Khmel'nitskiy's defection to Muscovy, King John Casimir already in the spring of 1654 dispatched two Commonwealth armies into the Ukraine against him. The Lithuanian Army, under Field Hetman Janusz Radziwiłł, went on the offensive towards the south from Gomel' through Starodub, aiming for Kiev, the ancient capital of Ruthenia. However, it reached no closer to Kiev than Borodenets, about 30 km away. At the same time, the Crown Army under Field Hetman Stanisław 'Rewera' Potocki (1589–1667) advanced from the west, aiming for the Ukrainian towns of Uman' and Belotserkov'. However, Khmel'nitskiy's cossacks pushed Potocki's army back to Kamenets-Podol'skiy in western Ukraine. The Kiev region remained under Khmel'nitskiy's control. Kiev itself was garrisoned by an estimated 2,000 Muscovites under first Prince Fyodor Kurakin (d. 1656) and then Prince Fyodor Volkonskiy (d. 1665).[1] Although the Kiev fortifications were in poor repair, Khmel'nitskiy and his men accordingly saw no immediate cause for concern, and when, as we will see, Tsar Alexis invaded Lithuania, the pressure on Cossack Ukraine decreased further.

Tsar Alexis had not been so rash as to sign the Treaty of Pereyaslav without preparing for offensive war. Beginning in late February, he issued orders for a campaign aimed not at Cossack Ukraine – but the Lithuanian heartland. Tsar Alexis divided his available forces on the Lithuanian border into three separate armies: a northern one under Vasiliy P. Sheremetyev (d. 1659) from Novgorod

---

1 Brian L. Davies, *Warfare, State and Society on the Black Sea Steppe, 1500–1774* (Abingdon, Oxon: Routledge, 2007), p.118.

and Pskov (Table 1), a main army from Moscow under his own command, assisted by Princes Yakov Cherkasskiy (d. 1666), Nikita Odoyevskiy (c. 1605–1689), and Ivan Khovanskiy (d. 1682) (Table 2), and a southern army under Prince Aleksey Trubetskoy (1600–1680) from Bryansk and Sevsk (Table 3).

Despite the detailed information available in the service records, uncertainties remain with regard to army sizes, since the records essentially offer the *maximum* strength available for mobilisation at the time. In short, Tsar Alexis's main field army had a mobilisation potential of 45,664 men. Likewise, the Bryansk field army had a mobilisation potential of 18,952 men. But the questions of how many men actually set out, and how many of them remained in the field army when combat operations began, cannot easily be resolved from the remaining records. Most historians have based their assessment on the records but then revised the figures slightly downwards. The most thorough discussion suggests a total of some 40,000 for the Moscow Army and some 17,700 for the Bryansk Army.[2] The Novgorod Army is, for similar reasons, assessed as having contained at most some 13,000 men.[3]

The same difficulties remain with strength of the Lithuanian defenders. Service records of a type similar to those in Muscovy exist also for the Lithuanian Komput army (Table 4).

Tsar Alexis planned the campaign carefully. First, to save time he already in early March 1654 sent his heavy siege artillery from Moscow to Vyaz'ma, close to the Lithuanian border, ahead of the main army. The forested borderlands of eastern Lithuania and western Muscovy were not as densely inhabited, or developed, as western Europe, but they had been settled for centuries. Even so, the road network was less extensive than further to the west, which hampered logistics. The chief population centres were walled towns, often located on the major rivers which provided the primary communication routes. In comparison to western Europe, towns were few and widely separated. Most had stone walls, but the majority were obsolete in the face of modern siege methods. Smolensk, on the Commonwealth border, was an exception, since it was well-fortified and more up to date with regard to defences. The town was a key communications hub and accordingly the primary objective of the Muscovite invasion force. Tsar Alexis was well aware that the late arrival of the siege artillery had been a major factor in dooming the previous attempt to retake Smolensk, in the Smolensk War of 1632–1634, but this time the artillery was already on its way. Likewise, the Tsar established a supply depot for the Novgorod Army at Velikiye Luki. Then, in late May 1654, the main army under the Tsar himself and Prince Yakov Cherkasskiy, with a planned strength of some 40,000, marched out.[4] Its first and primary objective was Smolensk. The Tsar's army was dispatched in several contingents to facilitate logistics. The

---

2   I.B. Babulin, *Smolenskiy pokhod i bitva pri Shepelevichakh 1654 goda* (Moscow: Russkiye Vityazi, 2018), pp.41–7.

3   Aleksey A. Novosel'skiy, 'Ocherk voyennykh deystviy boyarina Vasiliya Petrovicha Sheremeteva v 1654 gody na Novgorodskom fronte', L.G. Dubinskaya (ed.). *Issledovaniya po istorii epokhi feodalizma* (Moscow: Nauka, 1994), pp.117–35, on pp.118–19.

4   Babulin, *Smolenskiy pokhod*, p.39. The figure 41,400 men is often given as the strength of the main army. However, this figure derives from a misreading of a source. *Ibid.*, p.41.

Tsar himself accompanied the great division, which marched out three days after the departure of the vanguard.

Further to the north, Tsar Alexis ordered the Novgorod Army, some 13,000 men under Vasiliy P. Sheremetyev, to gain control of the River Dvina (Düna) and take Polotsk and Vitebsk. Sheremetyev's primary task was to safeguard the Smolensk operation from any threats from the north-west, including from Swedish Livonia. The Novgorod Army was made up of several contingents which marched along different routes. Units of this army were the first to cross the border into Lithuania, moving into enemy territory already in late May 1654 on its way to Nevel'.

To the south, Tsar Alexis dispatched the Bryansk Army, some 17,700 men under Prince Aleksey Trubetskoy, to take Roslavl', Mstislavl', and Borisov.[5] Trubetskoy was a former administrator and diplomat with military experience who had achieved high rank under Tsar Alexis.[6] Trubetskoy's chief task was to safeguard the Smolensk operation from any hostile action deriving from the south-west. Trubetskoy easily took Roslavl'. Mstislavl' resisted for several days but soon fell, after which the town was pillaged and much of the population massacred.

Crown Field Hetman Stanisław 'Rewera' Potocki. He was promoted to Grand Hetman in 1654.

Meanwhile, Bogdan Khmel'nitskiy did his part in the Muscovite invasion by dispatching a cossack army of reportedly 20,000 men under Ivan Zolotarenko (d. 1655) to join the Tsar's men.[7] Zolotarenko's army, which consisted of the Nezhin and Chernigov regiments, invaded Lithuania from Kiev in the south. To stiffen the cossacks, Tsar Alexis dispatched a corps of some 4,000 Muscovites (246 old-style cavalry, 3,950 dragoons from the Komaritsk district around Sevsk, and a few cossacks) from Ryl'sk under Andrey Buturlin (d. 1676) to join forces with Zolotarenko.[8]

Finally, Tsar Alexis also made sure that the 12,000 men of the Belgorod Division, under Vasiliy B. Sheremetyev (1622–1682), remained available for campaign service. The Belgorod Division, deployed to guard Muscovy's southern border, must be on full alert, since Tsar Alexis knew that the Crimean Khanate, which he knew was hostile to the Treaty of Pereyaslav, easily might attack from this direction, which the Crimeans had done so many times in the past. The Belgorod Division also functioned as a strategic

---

5   *Ibid.*, 39.

6   In 1672, Tsar Alexis named Trubetskoy the godfather of his son, the future Tsar Peter the Great.

7   The numbers reported for cossack armies almost invariably appear too high to be credible, since they, like the Commonwealth Komput armies and the Muscovite service lists, are based on the total mobilisation potential available within the participating regiments. The actual number of men raised for a specific campaign were presumably significantly lower.

8   Aleksandr V. Malov, *Russko-pol'skayavoyna 1654–1667* (Moscow: Zeughaus, 2006), pp.15–16; Davies, *Warfare, State and Society*, 118; Babulin, *Smolenskiy pokhod*, p.40.

Lithuanian Field Hetman Janusz Radziwiłł, c. 1652 or 1654. He was promoted to Grand Hetman in 1654. (Daniel Schultz)

reserve in case Khmel'nitskiy needed additional support in the Ukraine.[9]

It was obvious to all – both in the Commonwealth and Sweden – that Tsar Alexis had sent the bulk of his forces into Lithuania, not Cossack Ukraine, and that he intended to conquer at least Smolensk and perhaps other territories, too. Moreover, it was an invasion, not a raid. In response, the parliament in June, as we have seen, agreed to fund a Lithuanian Army of 18,000 and a Crown Army of 35,000 soldier units.[10]

However, these were promises only. As noted in Table 4, Janusz Radziwiłł's field army acquired a nominal strength of at most 11,151.[11] In reality, his army was even weaker. Estimates range from as little as perhaps 4,000 soldiers, supplemented by a noble levy of some 2,000,[12] to 9,500 to 10,000 men.[13] Perhaps 8,000 is a realistic estimate. The conditions of war made it impossible to raise more men. As a result, the estimated 8,000 men under Radziwiłł in early summer found themselves facing three Muscovite armies as well as Zolotarenko's cossacks, in total possibly more than 80,000 men.[14] These were not enviable odds, even though, as we have seen, there were other armed men in Lithuania, including the garrison of Smolensk.

Unfortunately for the Commonwealth, Smolensk was in a bad state. The fortifications damaged in 1632–1633 had not yet been repaired, and nobody had taken the time to fill in the Muscovite siege trenches dug at the same time. The garrison of Smolensk consisted of barely 3,500 men, although it was based on two modern regiments of German infantry, under Wilhelm Korff and Nicholas von Tiesenhausen, respectively, backed by a few hundred haiduk infantry and the burgher militia.[15]

---

9   Malov, *Russko-pol'skayavoyna*, 16; Babulin, *Smolenskiy pokhod*, p.39.

10 Jan Wimmer, 'Armé och finansväsen i Polen under kriget med Sverige 1655–1660', Arne Stade and Jan Wimmer (eds), *Polens krig med Sverige 1655–1660: Krigshistoriska studier* (Stockholm: Kungl. Militärhögskolan, *Carl X Gustaf-studier 5*, 1973: pp.41–101), p.53.

11 There exist, in fact, several archival documents with slightly different figures. However, all give roughly similar strengths. Wimmer, *ibid.*, pp.53, 90 n.55.

12 Robert I. Frost, *The Northern Wars: War, State and Society in North-eastern Europe, 1558–1721* (Harlow, Essex: Pearson Education, 2000), p.165.

13 Michał Paradowski, *The Lithuanian Army 1653–1667* (Daniel Schorr's *Northern Wars* website (now defunct), 2008), p.1.

14 Jan Wimmer, *Wojsko polskie w drugiej połowie XVII wieku* (Warsaw: Wojskowy Instytut Historyczny, Ministerstwo Obrony Narodowej, 1965), pp.82–3.

15 Frost, *The Northern Wars*, pp.165–6; Babulin, *Smolenskiy pokhod*, p.87.

At least Radziwiłł's Lithuanian Army enjoyed freedom of movement. While he could not prevent Tsar Alexis from laying siege to Smolensk in early July, the Tsar did not want to risk storming the city while Radziwiłł's Lithuanian Army remained undefeated not far away.

For this reason, Tsar Alexis ordered his deputy Cherkasskiy further westwards with a strong detachment, with orders to take Orsha and engage and defeat Radziwiłł's Lithuanians. Cherkasskiy belonged to a well-known Kabardian princely family from the Caucasus. Known as Uruskan Murza before his conversion to Christianity, he was an able man whom the Tsar had learnt to trust. In mid August, Cherkasskiy and Radziwiłł encountered each other on opposite sides of the river at Shklov. The result was a confused action which took place during a solar eclipse. The battle was inconclusive, with each side claiming victory and each side remaining on its side of the river. Contemporary sources offer irreconcilable information not only on the outcome of the battle but also on the respective strength and casualties of the two armies. The Lithuanians seem to have been outnumbered, yet appear to have given the Muscovites a bloody nose. It was a contest between old and new styles of fighting. The Lithuanian dragoons, enlisted, equipped, and trained by Germans in the Continental manner, played a decisive role, not only overpowering the Muscovite old-style cavalry with flanking fire but also preventing a Muscovite flank march.[16]

However, the success was short-lived. Days later, Radziwiłł, having received reinforcements but still outnumbered (having no more than some 8,000 men as compared to Trubetskoy's almost 18,000 men),suffered a decisive defeat at Shepelevichi against Trubetskoy's Bryansk Army.[17] The Muscovites crossed the River Oslivka at three locations, including in the Lithuanian flank, and overwhelmed Radziwiłł's men. The defeat neutralised the Lithuanian Army for the duration of the campaign season. Having lost both his

Above: Prince Yakov Cherkasskiy.

Below: Vasiliy Borisovich Sheremetyev, Commander of the Belgorod Division.

---

16 Babulin, *Smolenskiy pokhod*, pp.102–19.
17 Igor' B. Babulin, 'Vazhneyshiye pobedy Possii v russko-pol'skoy voyne 1654–1667 gg.: Otvet retsenzentu', *Istoriya voyennogo dela: issledovaniya I istochniki* 9 (2017), pp.375–397, on p.389. Available from the website, <www.milhist.info/2017/12/30/babylin_6>.

The banner of Aleksey Trubetskoy's Great Division, Bryansk Army, 1654.

artillery and supply train, Radziwiłł abandoned Smolensk and retreated to Minsk, pursued by units from the Bryansk Army under Yuriy Dolgorukov.

Smolensk held out for a long time, but it could not last. Having repulsed several assaults, on 3 October Filip Kazimierz Obuchowicz (Lithuanian: Filipas Kazimieras Obuchovičius), the voivode of Smolensk, surrendered to Tsar Alexis.[18]

Meanwhile, the Novgorod Army under Vasiliy P. Sheremetyev had taken Polotsk already in late June. This enabled Sheremetyev to send significant units further to the east, to take Vitebsk. Outnumbered and soon out of supplies, the Vitebsk garrison nonetheless held out until early December.

Further to the south, Zolotarenko's cossacks and Andrey Buturlin had successfully advanced towards the north, taking Gomel', Chechersk, and Novyy Bykhov in the process, but Staryy Bykhov withstood them.

By autumn, Muscovy controlled the rivers Dvina (Düna) and Berezina. Tsar Alexis had taken both Smolensk and Kiev, as well as a host of smaller towns. Muscovy also controlled the River Dnieper from Dorogobuzh to Mogilyov. By the end of the year, most of the Muscovite army returned home for demobilisation. So did Tsar Alexis. For him, the year had been a great success. Many Lithuanian nobles in the conquered territories had sworn fealty to the Tsar. The Commonwealth's strong pro-Catholic policy had alienated many of other faiths. As a result, some swore fealty to Tsar Alexis because of their shared Orthodox faith. Others swore fealty merely as a means to

---

18 Babulin, *Smolenskiy pokhod*, pp.81–91, pp.152–64; Andrzej Haratym, *Smoleńsk 1654* (Warsaw: Mówiąwieki, 2020), pp.55–83. The latter also contains transcriptions of several archive documents.

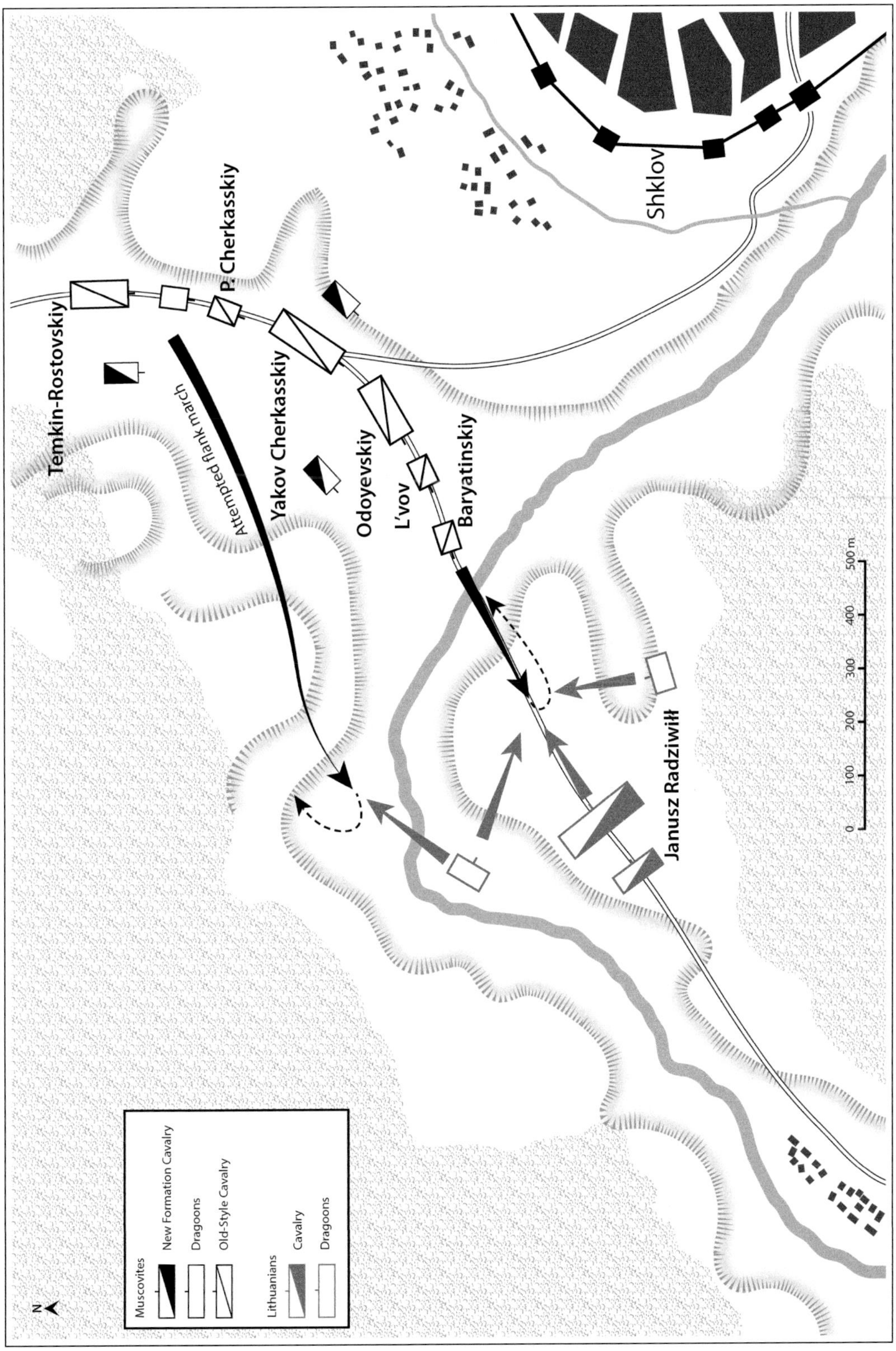

The Battle of Shklov, 12 August 1654.

Shklov

Temkin-Rostovskiy

P. Cherkasskiy

Yakov Cherkasskiy

Attempted flank march

Odoyevskiy

L'vov

Baryatinskiy

Janusz Radziwiłł

N

Muscovites
New Formation Cavalry
Dragoons
Old-Style Cavalry

Lithuanians
Cavalry
Dragoons

0 100 200 300 400 500 m

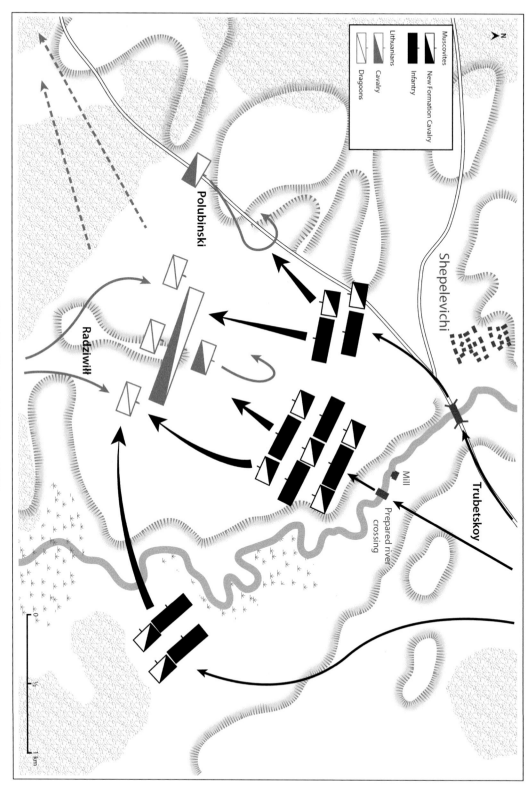

The Battle of Shepelevichi, 24 August 1654

Legend:
- Muscovites
- New Formation Cavalry
- Lithuanians
- Infantry
- Cavalry
- Dragoons

Polubinski

Radziwiłł

Shepelevichi

Trubetskoy

Mill

Prepared river crossing

N

0 ½ 1 km

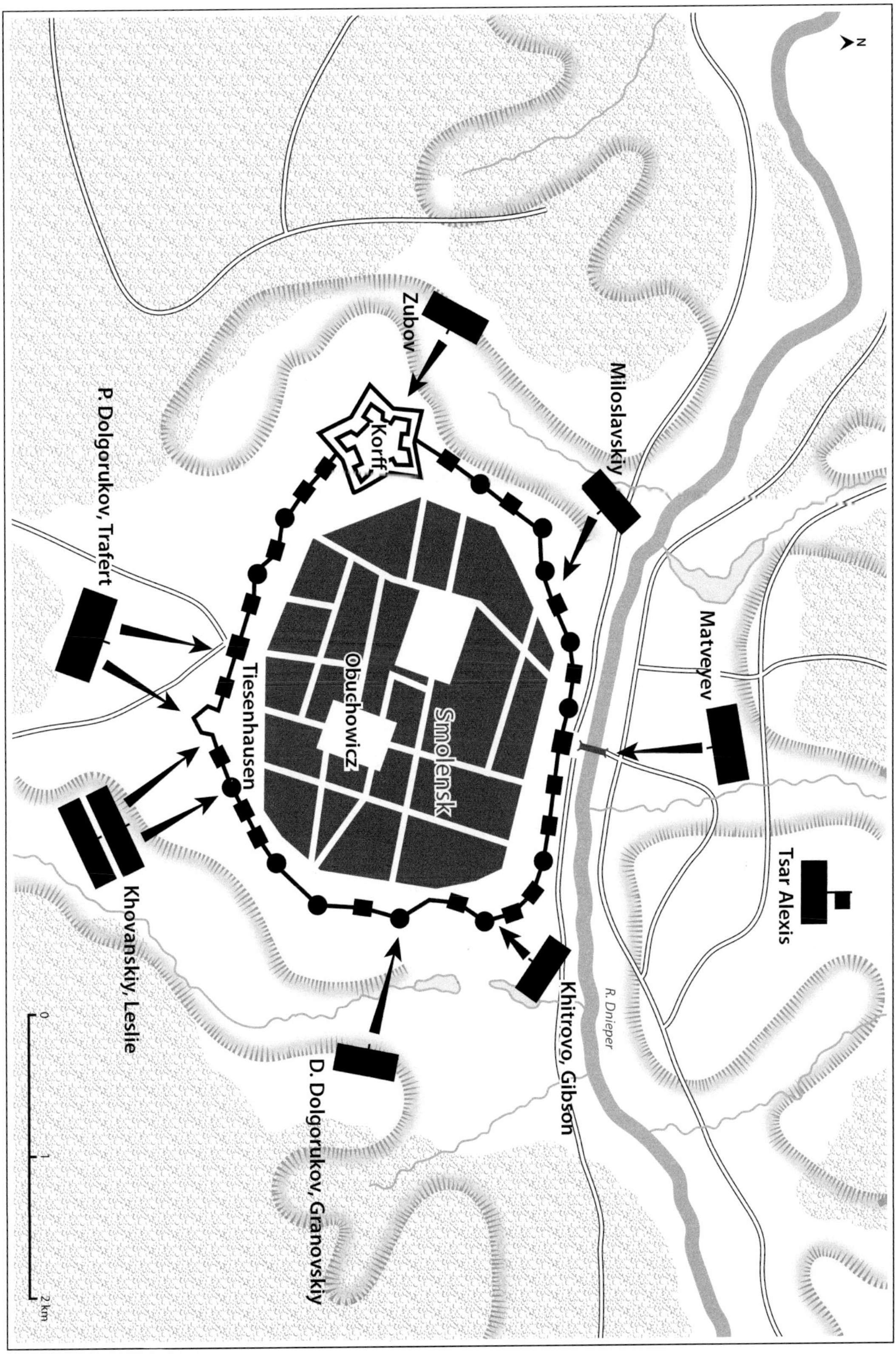

The Assault on Smolensk, 26 August 1654

Zubov

Mioslavskiy

Korff

P. Dolgorukov, Trafert

Tiesenhausen

Obuchowicz

Smolensk

Matveyev

Tsar Alexis

Khovanskiy, Leslie

Khitrovo, Gibson

R. Dnieper

D. Dolgorukov, Granovskiy

0

1

2 km

15

retain their estates. An Orthodox noble, Konstanty Pokłoński (Ruthenian: Konstantin Yurievich Poklonskiy), even raised a regiment (*pułk*) of reportedly 6,000 (or perhaps more likely 4,000) cossack-style cavalry on behalf of the Tsar.[19] While many Orthodox voluntarily joined the Muscovites, others had no choice, including those peasants and craftsmen who were abducted to provide much-needed additional labour in Muscovy's sparsely inhabited borderlands. If not already of the Orthodox faith, the abductees were customarily baptised as Orthodox, sometimes against their will. The baptism automatically made them Muscovite subjects, and they could then be relocated or even sold as serfs as needed. If previously married, the Muscovite view was that the baptism dissolved the previous marriage, so that the abductee could be married off to an Orthodox partner. This was a pattern repeated from earlier wars, and one that also would repeat itself elsewhere in the borderlands, from the Ukraine in the south to Karelia in the north. The only bad news for the Tsar was that the plague had broken out in the area of operations. The plague would remain a serious problem in Lithuania, ravaging the country into 1656 and beyond. The plague also affected Muscovy in a bad way, and would eventually ravage Swedish Livonia as well.

But this was not yet known in Stockholm. What was known, was that Muscovite military might easily had gained control of major parts of Lithuania and that the Novgorod Army was advancing in the direction of Swedish Livonia. This potential threat worried the Swedish Council of the Realm, which, as we have seen, in late December agreed to prepare for war. Beyond Sweden's existing conflict with the Commonwealth, there was also a perceived need to pre-empt what increasingly looked like a Muscovite land grab in progress.

Was the Swedish Council of the Realm correct in assuming that the Tsar's real objective was the Baltic shore? This is often taken for granted, in the light of later developments. The key exhibit of evidence for this view is the fact that although Tsar Alexis had entered the war in support of Cossack Ukraine, his operational focus lay on Lithuania, not the Ukraine. This suggests that the Tsar indeed regarded the west as more important to Muscovy's long-term development than the south. However, his primary concern was to regain the important town of Smolensk, which Muscovy had won from Lithuania in 1514, lost to the Commonwealth in 1611, and fought to regain in the Smolensk War of 1632–1634. It has been argued that the conquests of Polotsk and Vitebsk in reality was a means to protect the Muscovite flank against any sudden attack from the direction of Swedish Livonia, and such a precaution seems likely.[20] However, Smolensk in particular, but also Polotsk and Vitebsk, were vital to Muscovite interests. Smolensk was on the main road between Moscow and Warsaw. But even more importantly, Smolensk blocked the river route between the Baltic and the Black Seas. Together, the two rivers Dvina (Düna; which flowed into the Baltic Sea at Riga) and Dnieper (which by way of Kiev reached the Black Sea through Zaporozhia) since time immemorial linked the north with the south with one important exception: the corridor between Vitebsk and

---

19 Frost, *The Northern Wars*, p.185–6.
20 Babulin, *Smolenskiy pokhod*, p.39.

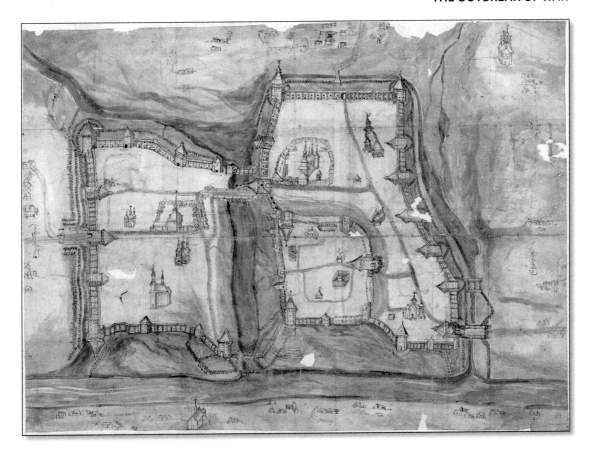

Above: Contemporary map of Vitebsk, 1664.

Below: Detail of Vitebsk, 1664.

Smolensk. The power which held the rivers and the land corridor controlled the north–south river trade as well as much of the east–west overland trade. Tsar Alexis certainly knew this, and with Kiev and Zaporozhia he was already close to acquiring control over the Dnieper.[21]

The geostrategic context of the river trade was well-known in Moscow. However, yet another international crisis was developing, which was known in Stockholm but perhaps not quite as well understood in Moscow, because Muscovy had not yet become a regular player in European diplomacy. The Holy Roman Emperor, the Netherlands, and Denmark all wanted the Tsar to go to war with Sweden, and such sentiments were expressed through diplomatic means. The reasons were geopolitical and mercantile, and they had nothing to do with buttressing Muscovy's power. In particular the Netherlands and Denmark argued that Sweden had grown too powerful for their mercantile interests. Swedish control over the entire Baltic shore, which indeed was a Swedish strategic objective, would enable Sweden to set and control customs duties. The Baltic Sea trade was the primary source of revenue for both Danzig and the Netherlands. Already involved in an unresolved conflict with England, the Dutch realised that a war between Sweden and Muscovy would prevent the Swedes from growing yet more powerful, which in turn might retain the status quo in the Baltic region. We have seen that what the Swedish Council of the Realm perceived as the chief threat at the time was indeed not Muscovy, but the machinations of Sweden's Continental rivals.

Tsar Alexis probably did perceive a strategic interest in gaining a foothold on the Baltic coast, something which Muscovy had lost when it signed the 1617 Treaty of Stolbovo with Sweden. It would be unsurprising if Tsar Alexis regarded access to the Baltic Sea his next military objective, after the capture of Smolensk. However, whether this idea motivated him already in 1654 or emerged only after the conquest of Smolensk is unknowable in light of the available evidence.

The Swedish Reaction

When news arrived about the Muscovite invasion of the Commonwealth, King Charles ordered an increased state of alert on the eastern border. Moreover, he deployed additional units to Livonia, so that the army there should be able to respond, if so was required. King Charles ordered three Finnish regiments to the eastern border: the Tavastehus Cavalry Regiment and the Björneborg Regiment of foot to Dorpat (Russian: Yur'yev; modern-day Tartu) in Livonia, and the Österbotten Regiment of foot to Narva in Ingria. The remaining regiments in Finland were ordered to prepare for deployment, too, if required. All three regiments had arrived by December 1654.

---

21 The two other main north-south routes between the Baltic and Black Seas also depended on river transport: one followed the River Vistula and then proceeded overland to Kiev, while the other began in the Gulf of Finland, from which the river route took the traveller to Lake Ladoga, Novgorod, and onwards to the Vitebsk and Smolensk area. Hence, all three communication routes ended with the Dnieper.

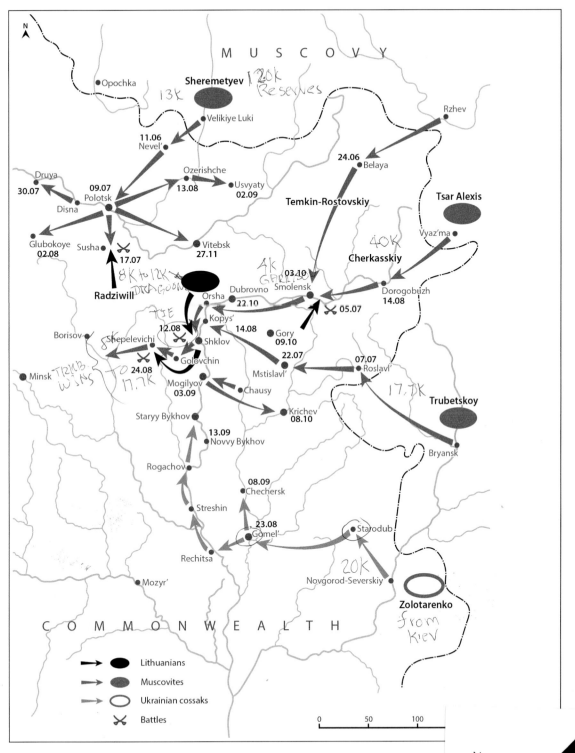

The Smolensk Campaign, 1654

In late January 1655, additional regiments were ordered immediately to proceed to Livonia, in anticipation of the Muscovite spring offensive. This time, marching orders were sent to the Åbo Cavalry Regiment and the Tavastehus Regiment of foot. To save time, the units were ordered to march across the frozen Gulf of Finland, assuming the ice cover was sufficiently strong. If this was not the case, they would march overland by way of Viborg and Nyen. In the end, the Tavastehus infantry marched across the ice, arriving in March, while the Åbo cavalry took the longer overland route, arriving in April.

By then, King Charles had ordered yet more regiments in Finland to Livonia. In early April, the Viborg Cavalry Regiment, one squadron of the Karelian Dragoon Regiment, and the Savolax Regiment of foot received their marching orders, the dragoons across the frozen Gulf of Finland and the others by the overland route. With these deployments, the already strong Swedish army in Estonia and Livonia was reinforced with 3,620 horse and 4,660 foot.[22] However, we have seen that by this time, King Charles and the Council of the Realm had already decided to go to war against the Commonwealth, in part to pre-empt the Muscovites from penetrating deeper into the country. However, Muscovy was not regarded as an urgent threat to Sweden's eastern border.

Tables

Table 1 (see p.8). The Novgorod Army, Spring 1654
Source: Novosel'skiy, 'Ocherk', pp.118–19

Note that the number of men in each unit derives from the mobilisation potential documented in 1654. Real numbers were certainly somewhat lower. The numbers do not quite add up because of difficulties in the interpretation of the data.

Novgorod Army, commanded by Prince Vasiliy P. Sheremetyev	
Old-Style Cavalry	
Prince Vasiliy P. Sheremetyev's Division	1,555
Semyon Luk'yanovich Streshnev's Division	850
Zhdan Vasil'yevich Kondyrev's Division	658
Total Old-Style Cavalry	3,063
Streltsy	
Unknown Regiment(s)	
Total Streltsy	500?
Town Cossacks	
Lutsk (?)	383
Novgorod	300

---

22 Lars Tersmeden, 'Carl X Gustafs armé 1654–1657', Arne Stade (ed.), Carl X Gustafs armé. (Stockholm: Militärhögskolan, Carl X Gustaf-studier 8, 1979: pp.163–276) pp.177–8.

Pskov	100
Ladoga	100
Total Town Cossacks	883
New Formation Infantry	
Units from Moscow, Onega, and Sumersk	
Total New Formation Infantry	8,700
Tatars	
Unit from Astrakhan'	
Total Tatars	500 (of whom 372 arrived in Pskov)
Grand Total	13,146(?)

Table 2 (see p.8). The Moscow Field Army, Spring 1654
Source: Babulin, *Smolenskiy pokhod*, pp.41, 213–16

Note that the number of men in each unit derives from the mobilisation potential documented in 1651 (or 1653 for the Astrakhan' Tatars). Real numbers were certainly somewhat lower. Names of foreign officers are sometimes listed in Russified name form, since many assumed Russian names.

Sovereign's Division (*Gosudarev polk*), commanded by Tsar Alexis	
Old-Style Cavalry	
Moscow, 32 sotni	2,971
Vladimir, 2 sotni	297
Kazan', 1 sotnya	364
Kashira, 2 sotni	403
Smolensk defectors, 4 sotni	480
Belyana, 2 sotni	198
Kolomna, 1 sotnya	152
Ryazhsk, 1 sotnya	106
Court retainers (*dvor*), 1 sotnya	*c.* 100
Astrakhan' Tatars, 2 sotni	300
Don cossacks, 2 sotni	187
Arzamas Mordvins, 1 sotnya	236

Mozhaysk and Borisovsk cossacks, 1 sotnya	179
Total Old-Style Cavalry	5,973
Moscow Streltsy	
Mikhail Zybin's Mounted Regiment	600
Semyon Poltev's Regiment	500
Ivan Baskakov's Regiment	500
Osip Kostyayev's Regiment	500
Vasiliy Filosofov's Regiment	500
Ivan Nelidov's Regiment	500
Dmitriy Zubov's Regiment	500
Artamon Matveyev's Regiment	500
Matvey Spiridonov's Regiment	300
Total Streltsy	4,400
New Formation Cavalry and Hussars	
Vasiliy Fandrotskiy's Cavalry Regiment	1,000
Khristofor Ryl'skiy's Hussar Regiment	1,000
Dragoons attached to the two above	600
Total New Formation Cavalry	2,600
New Formation Dragoons	
Jean de Grone's (or Jean de Greon's, russified as Anton Granovskiy's) Dragoon Regiment	1,000
Claudius Reinaldus de Speville's Dragoon Regiment	1,600
Total New Formation Dragoons	2,600
New Formation Infantry	
Abraham Leslie's Regiment	2,400
Alexander Gibson's Regiment	1,600
Casper Jander's Regiment	1,600
Yuriy (John?) Kitt's Regiment	1,600
Total New Formation Infantry	7,200
Total New Formation Soldiers	12,400
Grand Total	22,773
Great Division (*Bol'shoy polk*), commanded by Prince Yakov Cherkasskiy	
Old-Style Cavalry	
Prince Yakov Cherkasskiy's Regiment	

– Tula	683
– Ryazan'	1,937
– Alatyr'	650
– Kadom Tatars	319
– Arzamas Tatars	231
Total	3,820
Prince Semyon Prozorovskiy's Regiment	
– Kostroma	1359
– Kasimov Tatars	363
Total	1,722
Prince Andrey Litvinov-Mosal'skiy's Regiment	
– Galich	592
– Shatsk Tatars	101
Total	693
Fyodor Yelizarov's Regiment	
– Klin	19
– Zvenigorod	46
– Belozero district	350
Total	415
Total Old-Style Cavalry	6,650
Moscow Streltsy	
Avram Lopukhin's Regiment	500
Login Anichkov's Regiment	500
Total Streltsy	1,000
New Formation Cavalry	
Isaac van Bokhoven's Cavalry Regiment	1,000
Total New Formation Cavalry	1,000
New Formation Infantry	
Aleksey Butler's Regiment	1,600
Total New Formation Infantry	1,600
Total New Formation Soldiers	2,600
Grand Total	10,250

Vanguard Division (*Peredovoy polk*), commanded by Prince Nikita Odoyevskiy	
Old-Style Cavalry	
Prince Nikita Odoyevskiy's Regiment	
– Arzamas	663
– Nizhniy Novgorod	330
– Vyaz'ma	160
– Dorogobuzh	46
– Alatyr' Tatars	722
Total	1,921
Prince Fyodor Khvorostinin's Regiment	
– Suzdal'	289
– Sviyazhsk	117
– Yur'yev	195
– Lukh	57
– Gorokhovets	16
– Kasimov Tatars	147
Total	821
Prince Dmitriy L'vov's Regiment	
– Kashin	229
– Bezhetskiy Verkh	130
– Uglich	154
– Romanov	125
– Dmitrov	70
– Mozhaysk	89
– Romanov newly baptised and Tatars	111
Total	908
Total Old-Style Cavalry	3,650
Moscow Streltsy	
Stepan Kokovinskiy's Regiment	500
Total Streltsy	500
New Formation Cavalry	
Philipius Albertus van Bokhoven's Cavalry Regiment	1,000
Total New Formation Cavalry	1,000

New Formation Infantry	
Franz Trafert's Regiment	1,600
Total New Formation Infantry	1,600
Total New Formation Soldiers	2,600
Grand Total	6,750
Rearguard Division (*Storozhevoy polk*), commanded by Prince Mikhail Temkin-Rostovskiy	
Old-Style Cavalry	
Prince Mikhail Temkin-Rostovskiy's Regiment	
– Rzhev	266
– Ruza	42
– Tver'	78
– Torzhok	112
– Staritsa	36
– Rostov	131
– Pereyaslavl'	152
– Yaroslavl' newly baptised and Tatars	106
– Cheboksary	56
– Koz'modem'yansk	40
– Tsivilensk	28
– Tsarevokokshaysk	23
– Astrakhan' Tatars	200
Total	1,270
Vasiliy Streshnev's Regiment	
– Meshchora	385
– Poshekhon'ye	131
– Volok	18
– Kurmysh and Kurmysh Tatars	145
Total	679
Ivan Olfer'yev's Regiment	
Vologda	663
Belozersk	90
Yaransk	12
Sviyazhsk Tatars	277
Total	1,042
Total Old-Style Cavalry	2,991

Moscow Streltsy	
Ivan Azar'yev's Regiment	500
Total Streltsy	500
New Formation Cavalry	
Vasiliy Krechetnikov's Cavalry Regiment	800
Total New Formation Cavalry	800
New Formation Infantry	
Arist Famendin's Regiment	1,600
Total New Formation Infantry	1,600
Total New Formation Soldiers	2,400
Grand Total	5,891
Great Artillery Train (*Bol'shoy naryad*), commanded by Fyodor Borisovich Dolmatov-Karpov	
40 cannons (six from Muscovy and 34 from the Netherlands)	
Army Grand Total	45,664

Table 3 (see p.8). The Bryansk Army, Spring 1654
Source: Babulin, *Smolenskiy pokhod*, pp.216–17

Note that the number of men in each unit derives from the mobilisation potential documented in 1651. Real numbers were certainly somewhat lower. Incidentally, significant numbers of Ruthenian defectors from the Commonwealth served in this army, which illustrates the widespread discontent with the Commonwealth leadership in most Ruthenian-speaking and Orthodox regions.

Bryansk Army, Commanded by Prince Aleksey Trubetskoy	
Old-Style Cavalry	
Prince Aleksey Trubetskoy's Regiment	
– Yaroslavl'	630
– Kozel'sk	67
– Likhvin	60
– Vorotynsk	20
– Tarusa	103
– Vereya	16
– Borovsk	52

– Ruza	42
– Temnikov Tatars	720
Total	1,710
Prince Grigoriy Kurakin's Regiment	
– Kaluga	145
– Meshchovsk	116
– Serpeysk	49
– Medyn'	50
– Aleksin	76
– Serpukhov	16
– Yaroslavets Malyy	48
– Odoyev	277
– Odoyev cossacks	35
Total	812
Prince Yuriy Dolgorukov's Regiment	
– Karachev	170
– Bryansk	144
– Pochep (Smolensk Province)	46
– Starodub (Smolensk Province)	58
– Defectors from Roslavl' (Smolensk Province) in Bryansk	85
– Putivl', including defectors from Chernigov (Ukraine) in Putivl'	477
– Putivl' cossacks	157
Total	1,137
Prince Semyon Pozharskiy's Regiment	
– Ryl'sk	312
– Defectors from Chernigov (Ukraine) in Ryl'sk	36
– Novgorod Severskiy (Ukraine)	161
– Ryl'sk cossacks	99
Total	608
Semyon Izmaylov's Regiment	
– Solova	141
– Newly baptised and Ukrainians	344
Total	485
Total Old-Style Cavalry	4,752

Moscow Streltsy	
Yakov Efim'yev's Regiment	500
Leontiy Azar'yev's Regiment	500
Total Streltsy	1,000
New Formation Cavalry	
Lorentz Martot's Cavalry Regiment	1,000
Fyodor Wormser's Cavalry Regiment	1,000
Total New Formation Cavalry	2,000
New Formation Infantry	
Daniel Crawford's Regiment	1,600
Yuriy Ven's – Ivan Nirotmortsev's Regiment	1,600
Hermann van Staden's Regiment	1,600
Alexander Barclay's Regiment	1,600
Yakov Flek's Regiment	1,600
Yelisey Tsykler's Regiment	1,600
Nikolay van Staden's Regiment	1,600
Total New Formation Infantry	11,200
Total New Formation Soldiers	13,200
Army Grand Total	18,952

Table 4 (see pp.8, 10). The Lithuanian Komput Army, Summer 1654
Source: Bobiatyński, *Od Smoleńska do Wilna*, pp.233–6

Note that the strength is denominated in horses or (for infantry) portions, that is, the unit's establishment, not real, strength. Other sources give similar but not always identical figures. Real strength was probably around 10,000 men. Many names are of Ruthenian or Tatar origin, which complicates the choice of spelling (Polish, Ruthenian, Tatar, or Lithuanian?) Some names are German. In most cases, the Polish forms have been used.

Hussars	
Janusz Radziwiłł's Banner	159
Aleksander Hilary Połubiński's Banner	122
Hrehor Mirski's Banner	83
Total Hussars	364
Cossack-Style Cavalry	
Janusz Radziwiłł's Banner (*Pancerni*)	150

Jerzy Karol Hlebowicz's Banner	120
Bogusław Radziwiłł's Banner	120
Krzysztof Potocki's Banner	100
Aleksander Hilary Połubiński's Banner	120
Krzysztof(?) Potocki's Banner	100
Jerzy Niemirycz's Banner	100
Zygmunt Słuszka's Banner	100
Jerzy Chalecki's Banner	120
Jan Bychowec's Banner	120
Lew Pogirski's Banner	80
Piotr Kamiński's Banner	120
Jerzy(?) Niemirycz's Banner	64
Chryzostom Jundziłł's Banner	86
Nikodem Skinder's Banner	50
Samuel Wysocki's Banner	100
Jan Romanowski's Banner	100
Szymon Pawsza's Banner	100
Stanisław Bobrownicki's Banner	69
Konstanty Obodyński's Banner	39
Jan Mierzeński's Banner	100
Stefan Klimczycki's Banner	100
Lukasz Rossudowski's Banner	120
Jeremi Słuszka's Banner	26
Muchowiecki's Banner	20
Jerzi Dąbrowa's Banner	100
Total Cossack-style Cavalry	2,424
Tatars	
Islam Smolski's Banner	150
Jacha Murza's Banner	100
Mustafa Małachowski's Banner	100
Mikołaj (?) Baranowski's Banner	100
Czymbaj Ułan Maluszycki's Banner	100
Roman Sienkiewics's Banner	100
Abulewicz's Banner	60
Assan Lewaszewics's Banner	120
Mustafa Baranowski's Banner	130
Total Tatars	960

German Cavalry	
Janusz Radziwiłł's Cavalry Regiment (under Ernest von Sacken), 4 companies	660
Georg von Tiesenhausen's Company	120
Theodor Schwarzhoff's Company	120
Ernest Johann Korff's Company	120
Total German Cavalry	1,020
Dragoons	
Janusz Radziwiłł's Dragoon Regiment (under Hermann Ganskopf)	600
Bogusław Radziwiłł's Dragoon Regiment (under Eberhard von Puttkammer)	600
Ernest Johann Korff's Dragoon Regiment	700
Aleksander Hilary Połubiński's Dragoon Company	120
Krzysztof Potocki's Dragoon Company	200
Krzysztof Jesman's Dragoon Company	120
Ernest Nolde's Dragoon Company	100
Ernest von Sacken's Dragoon Company	100
Marcin Choromański's Dragoon Company	134
Total Dragoons	2,674
German Infantry (musketeers and pikemen)	
Janusz Radziwiłł's Regiment	1,050
Jerzy Niemirycz's Regiment (under Bogusław Przypkowski)	1,000
Samuel Andrzej Abramowicz's Company	176
Johann von Ottenhausen's Company	200
Mikołaj Giedroyc's Company	113
Hugh Montgomery's Company	100
Tobiasz Popiel's Company	150
Teofil Bolt's Company	120
Total German Infantry	2,909
Traditional Infantry (musketeers only)	
Janusz Radziwiłł's Life Company (under Samuel Juszkiewicz)	200
Jan Dmochowski's Company	100
Jerzy Karol Hlebowicz's Company (under Jerzy Grabiński)	100
Bogusław Radziwiłł's Company	100

Marcin Błędowski's Company	100
Wacław Szalewski's Company	100
Wojciech Sławkowski's Company	100
Total Traditional Infantry	800
Grand Total	11,151

2

Tsar Alexis Conquers Wilno

During the winter of 1654–1655, Radziwiłł did his best to harass the Muscovite units in their newly conquered territories. Radziwiłł also joined forces with his rival and colleague, Lithuanian Field Hetman Wincenty Gosiewski, who held an independent command. In January, they attempted to blockade Zolotarenko's cossacks in Novyy Bykhov. Then, they probed the defences of Vitebsk, again without success, and in February laid siege to Mogilyov. The siege of Mogilyov continued until May, but ultimately proved unsuccessful. The Muscovites had deployed a strong garrison in Mogilyov, under the able command of Ivan Alfer'yev. The garrison at first consisted of Ivan Nirotmortsev's new formation infantry regiment (331 men) and Avraam Lopukhin's and Login Anichkov's streltsy regiments (in total 787 men). To this was added Hermann van Staden's new formation infantry regiment (raised as 1,600 men although by this time some attrition would have taken place), probably other Muscovite units, and the burgher militia. However, the main force defending Mogilyov was the aforementioned locally raised regiment (*pułk*) of 4,000 to 6,000 cossack-style cavalry, formed on behalf of the Tsar by the Lithuanian noble Konstanty Pokłoński. These men were Ruthenians, they were unhappy with Commonwealth rule, and most felt that they defended their own native lands against Commonwealth oppressors. Although their commander, Pokłoński, again suddenly changed sides during the siege, most of his regiment remained loyal, and Mogilyov did not fall to the Lithuanians.

In late March Tsar Alexis returned to Smolensk to direct the campaign in person. His plan was to advance to Wilno, the capital of the Grand Duchy of Lithuania. But first, he wanted to take Minsk which would complete the conquest of eastern Lithuania. Tsar Alexis perhaps also hoped that it would be possible to continue the offensive towards Brest (a town presently better known as Brest-Litovsk, that is, Lithuanian Brest), in the hope of joining up with the army from the Ukraine. Meanwhile, further to the north the Pskov Army (a subdivision of the Novgorod Army) would secure the River Dvina (Düna) communications route by taking Dünaburg (modern-day Daugavpils), a town of great strategic importance but which was located close to Swedish Livonia.

In late May the Tsar left Smolensk, advancing towards Borisov with the main army. In early July, he crossed the Berezina at Borisov, advancing towards Minsk.

To his surprise, there was no sign of the Crown Army under King John Casimir, which he had expected to meet. In fact, the few Polish troops by then still in Lithuania departed to garrison Marienburg (modern-day Malbork) in Royal Prussia, which formed part of Poland.[1] Perhaps this was because John Casimir anticipated that Swedish King Charles would move against him, or perhaps the reason was that Royal Prussia had greater economic value than Lithuania, which the King in any case may have regarded as already mostly lost. Certainly, no Swedish army had yet showed any hostile intent toward the Commonwealth. Meanwhile, the Lithuanian Army was severely impaired by the rivalry between Janusz Radziwiłł, a Calvinist whose chief loyalty was to the Grand Duchy of Lithuania, and Wincenty Gosiewski, whose chief loyalty lay with the Catholic John Casimir. In short, the faultlines running through the Commonwealth again proved disastrous to the state's ability to defend itself. Radziwiłł attempted for a while to defend Minsk, but in light of the Muscovite numerical superiority, there was little he could do. Minsk fell in mid July.

Meanwhile, Tsar Alexis's Pskov Army marched to Rēzekne, under the command of the able Afanasiy Ordin-Nashchokin (1605–1680), who had orders to take Dünaburg.[2] The Pskov Army laid siege to Dünaburg in late May but failed to take the town. In the eyes of the Swedes, Ordin-Nashchokin's offensive against Dünaburg confirmed their suspicions about the Tsar's ultimate intentions. We will see that the Swedish army in Livonia soon took means to pre-empt the fall of Dünaburg.

Afanasiy Ordin-Nashchokin

In early August, Tsar Alexis decisively defeated Lithuanian Grand Hetman Janusz Radziwiłł at Wilno. The Muscovite victory was unsurprising, since Tsar Alexis fielded 35,000 men against 6,000 Lithuanians.[3] Afterwards, on 8 August, the Muscovites sacked Wilno. As often happened, the sack turned into a massacre of civilians. Moreover, fires broke out, which destroyed major parts of the city. Nonetheless, Tsar Alexis could claim to have conquered Lithuania's capital. In the previous year, he had taken Smolensk. Now he had taken Wilno. The Lithuanian Army was defeated, and Lithuania's remaining provinces seemed ripe for the taking.

1 Frost, *After the Deluge*, p.48.
2 Ordin-Nashchokin, the highly educated son of a minor noble, knew Latin and German, had a good understanding of European politics, and was in 1657 appointed minister plenipotentiary to negotiate a truce with Sweden. Advocating increased trade with Western Europe, he argued for Muscovite access to the Baltic Sea and a joint Muscovite–Commonwealth campaign against Sweden. While he failed to attain this goal, Ordin-Nashchokin successfully negotiated the 1667 Treaty of Andrusovo with the Commonwealth, after which he was appointed head of the Tsar's foreign ministry.
3 Babulin, 'Vazhneyshiye pobedy Possii', p.389.

Wilno, 1659

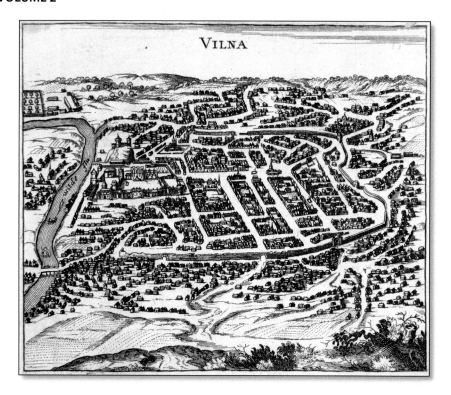

VILNA

The Crimean Tatars Help the Poles – and Themselves

As noted, neither the Lithuanian Army under then Field Hetman Janusz Radziwiłł nor the Polish Crown army under then Field Hetman Stanisław 'Rewera' Potocki made any particular progress in the Ukraine in 1654. And since then, the Lithuanian Army had been engaged in Lithuania proper and was no longer available. However, Potocki, promoted to Crown Grand Hetman, remained in the field, together with the new Crown Field Hetman, Stanisław Lanckoroński (c. 1597–1657). Moreover, Potocki in early 1655 received the support of a more formidable military than his own: a Crimean Tatar army possibly under Mehmed Khan himself and certainly with Qalgha Sultan Ghazi Geray, the Khan's deputy in military matters, in the senior command group. As noted, the primary raiding season of the Crimean Tatars began in January or early February. The Crimeans accordingly moved in along the traditional trail to the Bratslav province. Some of them, at least at first under a commander called Kammambet Mirza (more likely, Khan Mambet Mirza, or possibly Mehmed Mirza), who may have been of Noghai origin, rode off to lay siege to Uman', south of Belotserkov'. Others went raiding in the customary manner. The total strength of the Crimean army is often assessed to have been some 30,000 men.[4] Since it was commanded by the Khan or, in his absence, the Qalgha Sultan, this may be correct. Certainly, the Crimean army was stronger than Potocki's Crown Army, which made the Poles the junior

---

4   Davies, *Warfare, State and Society*, p.119.

partner in the alliance. Although we do not know for certain the number of men in Potocki's army, they were certainly no more than the Crimeans and almost certainly fewer. A figure of at most 22,000 to 23,000 has been suggested.[5]

As noted, the Crimean Khanate had a long-standing tradition of opportunistic foreign policy. Mehmed Khan did not intend to assist the Poles out of the goodness of his heart. The strategy of the Khanate was to interfere so that neither the Commonwealth nor Muscovy grew too powerful, while at the same time taking measures to contain the cossack presence in the Ukraine so that it did not constitute a threat towards the Khanate's Crimean core territories. As a result, the Khanate's objectives changed frequently. The one constant was the need to profit from raiding, in the form of plunder of goods, cattle, and most importantly captives to be sold in the slave markets.

The Muscovites had received reinforcements, too. In January, Vasiliy B. Sheremetyev's Belgorod Division (9,000 men) and Fyodor Buturlin's (d. 1673) Karpov corps joined Andrey Buturlin's already present corps at Belotserkov'. To relieve

Krzysztof Tyszkiewicz

Uman', Bogdan Khmel'nitskiy's cossack army (which primarily consisted of the Uman', Bratslav, Kal'nik, Belotserkov', and Kiev regiments[6]) and major parts of the Muscovite army moved south from Belotserkov'. Learning that the Muscovites and cossacks were approaching, Potocki, Lanckoroński, and Ghazi Geray moved their armies north to intercept them. The result was the battle of Akhmatov (modern-day Okhmativ; also known as the battle of Drozhi-polye), which was fought from 29 January to 1 February 1655.

Many details of the battle remain unclear. The Muscovite–cossack army, under Sheremetyev and Khmel'nitskiy, had established a wagon fort on open ground, without an adequate water supply. The battle lasted for several days, with repeated assaults on the wagon fort, which was defended by artillery and musket fire. On the fourth day, the Muscovite–cossack position was no longer tenable, so the defenders began to withdraw in the direction of Akhmatov, shielded by their slow-moving wagons. Since the Muscovite-cossack army retreated, the battle can be described as an inconclusive Tatar-Polish victory. However, there is little unanimity on either the number of men on each side or the casualties they suffered. The Tatar–Polish alliance was probably stronger in numbers.

The campaign had exhausted both Muscovites and Poles, which was good news for the Crimeans. Sheremetyev returned to Belotserkov', while

5   Wimmer, *Wojsko polskie*, p.83.
6   Davies, *Warfare, State and Society*, p.119.

Unit of Lithuanian hussars, 1649. (Abraham van Westervelt)

Khmel'nitskiy retreated yet further, to Tetev in the Kiev region. Potocki and Lanckoroński abandoned the offensive. Instead, they handed over responsibility to Krzysztof Tyszkiewicz (1616–1666), voivode of Chernigov. Accepting the realities on the ground, Krzysztof Tyszkiewicz allowed the Crimeans to take contributions in the form of grain and livestock from the towns and villages in Bratslav province. It soon became obvious that the Tatars interpreted this as a licence to raid for slaves, which in any case was the chief reason for their participation in the campaign. The result was disastrous. Thousands of peasants and townsmen fled from Bratslav and Podolia, which in turn made it impossible for the Crown Army to find provisions for its own sustenance. Furthermore, numerous refugees joined the cossacks, while others formed irregular bands to fight Tatars and Crown soldiers alike. Demoralised, numerous Crown soldiers deserted. By March, many of the Tatars had gathered sufficient plunder to return home. For them, it had been a very successful campaign. For their Commonwealth allies, the campaign had been a disaster. To compound the catastrophe, cossacks under Ivan Bogun (*c.* 1618–1664), one of Khmel'nitskiy's chief lieutenants, moved in as the Tatars moved out. Soon they regained control of most of Bratslav province.

3

The Swedish Invasion

While the Muscovites assumed control over major parts of Lithuania, and the Crimean Tatars did what they pleased in the Ukraine, the Swedish army invaded Poland and northern Lithuania.

King Charles and his commanders had prepared the campaign well. The Swedish plan was a two-pronged attack: the main thrust would be an invasion of the Commonwealth from Swedish Pomerania in the west while the Livonian army would invade from Swedish Livonia in the north.[1] The objective was to conquer Prussia with its wealthy ports.

In spring 1655, Field Marshal Arvid Wittenberg mustered the army in Pomerania. He had 14,350 men at his disposal, primarily enlisted soldiers from Germany (Table 5). In addition, King Charles mustered the army in Sweden, which he would accompany to Pomerania by sea from Dalarö in the southern Stockholm archipelago; he embarked 12,600 men (Table 6). In Livonia, Gustav Horn mustered 7,200 men (a force which, as will be shown, had increased to some 8,900 in October) who would be commanded by Field Marshal Gustav Adolph Lewenhaupt (1619–1656), another of Sweden's many veterans of the Thirty Years' War (Table 7). Wittenberg was ordered to attack from the west, through Eastern Pomerania (German: *Hinterpommern*), which belonged to Brandenburg. King Charles would follow in his footsteps and they would join forces in Poland. Horn was ordered to take Courland and Lithuania. The Livonian army would prevent the Muscovites from advancing further towards the Baltic Sea, where Courland and Samogitia were particularly vulnerable – and important for Sweden's future plans. Later, having personally arrived in Pomerania, King Charles ordered the Livonian army to move against specifically Wilno or Kowno (modern-day Kaunas) so as to pre-empt the Tsar. However, by then it was too late to prevent Tsar Alexis from conquering central Lithuania.

In early July, Wittenberg formally requested permission from Frederick William to march through Brandenburg on the way to Poland, in accordance

---

1   Charles, then a young general, had apparently already drawn up plans for an attack from Pomerania at the end of the Thirty Years' War, but then nothing had come of it (Peter Englund, *Ofredsår: Om den svenska stormaktstiden och en man i dess mitt* (Stockholm: Atlantis, 1993), p.483). We do not know whether he reused any part of these plans.

with Imperial regulations. Frederick William granted Wittenberg permission to march through his territory. Such a march was in accordance with Imperial regulations, and Frederick William could hardly refuse. Strictly according to regulations, Frederick William sent formal notifications to the Elector of Saxony and the Emperor that the Swedes would cross his territory. However, he also informed his formal suzerain, King John Casimir, as well as his brother-in-law, Jacob Kettler (1610–1682), the Duke of Courland and Semigallia.[2] The Swedish invasion would not be a surprise attack.

At about the same time, Field Marshal Gustav Adolph Lewenhaupt led the army of Livonia to Dünaburg in the part of Livonia still held by Lithuania. A major reason was to pre-empt the Muscovites who already had laid siege to Dünaburg once and might return for a more determined effort. Lewenhaupt hoped for a straightforward surrender, since the Lithuanians were outnumbered. However, the overall Commonwealth commander, Colonel Samuel Komorowski (d. 1659), had the town set on fire, while some Lithuanians, under Teofil Bolt, the commandant of Dünaburg, took refuge in the castle. The main force, under Komorowski, then rode away without opposing the Swedes. A siege became necessary, but the castle could not withstand the Swedish artillery fire, limited as it was, and the small garrison surrendered on the following day. The local nobility then asked for Swedish protection.

By then, Field Marshal Arvid Wittenberg mustered his army at Damm, Pomerania. He then, with the Elector's permission, marched rapidly across the Brandenburgian territory which divided Swedish Pomerania from Poland. Wittenberg crossed the border into the Commonwealth at Falkenburg. At Tempelburg (modern-day Czaplinek) in Commonwealth territory, he turned south towards the River Netze (modern-day Noteć).

The Swedes faced but little resistance from Commonwealth forces. Although the Commonwealth government had already initiated military preparations in March, it was far from enough.[3] The 1655 parliament, which opened in late May, authorised a military establishment to meet the Swedes consisting of 25,577 men (12,641 cavalry, 3,661 dragoons, and 9,275 infantry). Incidentally, the allocation shows the understanding that modern units and infantry were needed to fight a modern enemy. The army decided upon would consist of 50 percent cavalry, 14 percent dragoons, and 36 percent infantry.[4] Unfortunately, as we have seen, the authorised size of the regular army (which still had to be raised) was still slightly smaller than the Swedish invasion army under King Charles and Wittenberg alone. Parliament no doubt hoped that the Levy of the Nobility would show up in sufficient numbers to even the odds. No attention was paid to the threat from Muscovite armies in Lithuania, nor from the Swedish army of Livonia which also was posed to invade the Commonwealth. Already in April, Janusz Radziwiłł complained about the low numbers of troops allowed Lithuania by recent parliamentary decisions, and the lack of funding provided for them.

---

2   Bernhard Erdmannsdörffer, *Urkunden und Actenstücke zur Geschichte des Kurfürsten Friedrich Wilhelm von Brandenburg* 7 (Berlin: Georg Reimer, 23 vols, 1864–1930), pp.379–80.
3   Frost, *After the Deluge*, p.41.
4   Frost, *The Northern Wars*, p.245. For the actual result, see Table 8 in volume 1, p.163.

With major parts of Lithuania already under Muscovite occupation, how could the Grand Duchy find the necessary funding to pay its soldiers? In response, the Polish Senate (the upper chamber of parliament and the royal council, comprising Catholic bishops, voivodes, castellans, and government ministers) did its best to isolate Radziwiłł from the decision process. The royal chaplain, a Jesuit named Seweryn Karwat, mounted a vicious attack on all Protestant heretics. Since Janusz Radziwiłł was a Calvinist, everybody understood that the attack was aimed at him. Karwat's diatribe was so vehement that the alarmed Johann von Hoverbeck and Andreas Adersbach, two emissaries from Brandenburg, reported home that they suspected a Jesuit plot to evict all Protestants from the Commonwealth.[5] In the end, the Polish nobility refused to provide monetary support for what remained of Lithuania's army. The reason, they argued, was that Lithuania was constitutionally obliged to pay for its own defence even when under enemy occupation, and the Polish nobility saw no need to amend this fundamental constitutional principle.

It is hard to escape the conclusion that King John Casimir and the Polish nobility took little interest in Lithuania, which was considered backward and unimportant. As far as is known from preserved archive documents, John Casimir devoted all his energy to the defences of Royal Prussia. All his orders relating to the defence of the country, and their number is unexpectedly small, concerned the defences of Royal Prussia alone. John Casimir knew that although Royal Prussia not yet was under threat from Muscovy, the territory was Sweden's real objective in the war. Prussia was wealthy and its maritime trade made the territory the economic driver of the entire Commonwealth. Culturally, Prussia remained far closer to northern Germany, including Brandenburg and Swedish Pomerania, than the southern and eastern reaches of the Commonwealth which formed the major part of Lithuania. Geographically as well, Prussia was similar to northern Germany. Agricultural yields were lower than in the south, but the population lived in villages and walled towns not dissimilar to those elsewhere in Germany. Burghers were commonly German-speakers. The voivode in Marienburg, Jacob von Weiher, was ordered to occupy and hold the strongholds in Pomerelia, in particular Putzig, Marienburg, and Thorn, but also Schlochau, which was located near the border.[6] Presumably, John Casimir hoped that these well-fortified towns would be able to defend themselves until he could assemble the enlisted units and raise the Levy of the Nobility to move against the Swedish invaders. Although many archive documents may have been lost, it seems that he did not issue any orders for the defence of other parts of his country.

With such disputes being prevalent at the centre of Commonwealth government, it was unsurprising that dissension and rifts emerged in the

---

5   Andreas Adersbach to Frederick William, 10 June 1655 (O.S.), Erdmannsdörffer, *Urkunden und Actenstücke* 6, pp.698–9, on p.698.

6   Jan Wimmer, 'Polens krig med Sverige 1655–1660: Operativ översikt', Arne Stade and Jan Wimmer (eds), *Polens krig med Sverige 1655–1660: Krigshistoriska studier* (Stockholm: Kungl. Militärhögskolan, *Carl X Gustaf-studier* 5, 1973), pp.325–417, p.334.

field as well. Greater Poland (Polonia Major or Wielkopolska, centred on Posen; modern-day Poznań) was particularly unprepared. With most of the Crown Army being deployed to the Ukraine, there were no regular soldiers in Greater Poland, nor had local government undertaken any preparations for its defence. Existing fortifications had been neglected for a long time, since few expected any foreign threat to this region, located so far from Swedes, Muscovites, and Crimean Tatars alike. The situation was much the same in Lesser Poland (Polonia Minor or Małopolska, centred on Cracow), although there the major towns at least had proper garrisons.

Besides, King John Casimir had correctly gauged King Charles's intentions. It was Royal Prussia, not Greater Poland, which was the Swedish main target, with its great cities of Danzig, Marienburg, and Elbing. If these should be lost, the Commonwealth army would find it difficult to retake them, since it lacked sufficient artillery and infantry. Royal Prussia, unlike much of the rest of the Commonwealth, had modern fortifications. King John Casimir accordingly ordered some units of the Crown Army to return from the Ukraine, but to reinforce Royal Prussia, not Greater Poland.

Yet, and probably to John Casimir's great surprise, having crossed the border into the Commonwealth, Wittenberg's Swedish army suddenly turned south, moving into Greater Poland, not Royal Prussia. The primary explanation is probably the very lack of defences in Greater Poland. Thirty years earlier, Swedish King Gustavus Adolphus had invaded Prussia, learning the hard way how difficult it was to conquer. Wittenberg, who as a young man fought in this campaign, had drawn the same conclusion. He knew that in comparison to an attack on Prussia, it would be easy to take and establish a base in Greater Poland. Then, at a suitable time, they could strike north against Prussia, using the interior as a base. There may have been an ulterior motive as well. For King Charles's plan to take control of the entire Baltic coast to succeed, he must either conquer Ducal Prussia or else have something of equal value to offer Frederick William. Although no detailed plans in this regard are known, the idea to offer Frederick William Greater Poland in exchange for Ducal Prussia was mentioned in working papers produced during the King's and Erik Oxenstierna's discussions before the war.[7]

The Livonian Front

Meanwhile, the situation in Livonia and northern Lithuania remained complex. In late July, Magnus Gabriel De la Gardie (1622–1686) arrived in

---

7   C. Georg Starbäck and P.O. Bäckström, *Berättelser ur svenska historien* 6 (Stockholm: F. & G. Beijer, revised edition 1886). Modern historians have paid only limited attention to these documents, perhaps because of a preconceived supposition that King Charles acted in a purely opportunistic manner and lacked strategic insight. Additional research in this archive might be needed for assessing the King's otherwise poorly known strategic plans. Having said this, it is unlikely that Frederick William voluntarily would have agreed to swap the revenue-rich Ducal Prussia against the more agrarian Greater Poland.

Riga, where he assumed command of Livonia from the aged Gustav Horn.[8] De la Gardie was a brother-in-law of King Charles, who held him in high regard. Horn was recalled to Sweden to organise defences in case Denmark attacked (homeland defence was the formal role of the Grand Marshal of the Realm). Horn, in his sixties and the most experienced of the Swedish commanders, had been unwilling to go to war just as rapidly as King Charles had wanted. Perhaps it was merely old age, but Horn was always a careful commander who did not unnecessarily risk his men. He certainly remembered the difficulties which the Swedes had experienced during his first campaign against Muscovy, more than 40 years ago. Horn did not want to provoke an unnecessary war with Muscovy by advancing beyond Dünaburg.

Livonia, and Estonia further to the north, consisted of towns and cities characterised by the language, culture, and economy of Germany, from which the nobility and burghers had colonised the region during the Middle Ages. However, the agricultural countryside was quite different in character. The peasants were mostly serfs, their native language was not German (or for that matter, Swedish) but Estonian in the north and Latvian or Lithuanian in the south, with a significant Ruthenian population along the eastern border. The latter was Orthodox in faith and their language was a Russian dialect. Geographically and culturally, the eastern borderlands were reminiscent of the borderlands between Lithuania and Muscovy.

Magnus Gabriel De la Gardie.
(Hendrick Munnikhoven,
after David Beck)

Meanwhile, a Muscovite army was closing in from the south-east. In spring, Horn had received orders to send men to take Dünaburg before the Muscovites did so, and we have seen that days before De la Gardie arrived, Field Marshal Gustav Adolph Lewenhaupt took the town which by then had already withstood a Muscovite siege. Lewenhaupt and Magnus Gabriel De la Gardie, henceforth the overall commander, were brothers-in-law but they did not get along, which almost immediately resulted in communication problems. Following the capture of Dünaburg, the Swedes were ordered back to Kokenhusen (modern-day Koknese). Swedish orders were to deny the Muscovites access to the Baltic shore, but preferably without going to war with Muscovy.

The total Swedish military strength in the Baltic provinces, of which the bulk was in Livonia, by then consisted of 3,625 cavalry, 490 dragoons, and 10,680 infantry, in total 14,795 men.[9] A significant share of the total consisted of recent reinforcements moved in from Finland.

---

8   De la Gardie was appointed Governor-General of Livonia on 1 June 1655 (O.S.), with military responsibility for the entire north-eastern front.

9   'Kriget i östersjöprovinserna 1655–1661: Operationer och krigsansträngningar på en bikrigsskådeplats under Carl X Gustafs krig', Arne Stade (ed.), *Kriget på östfronten* (Stockholm:

De la Gardie was not averse to send additional men into the Commonwealth, with which Sweden was now again at war. So as not to risk the peace with Muscovy, De la Gardie was careful to limit operations to the coastal areas, well beyond the range of the Muscovite units further to the east. On 5 August, his younger brother Lieutenant General Jacob Casimir De la Gardie with some 1,000 cavalry moved into Pilten, a Courland bishopric under the Polish Crown.[10] Ten days later, he had secured the bishopric. Then the offensive into the Commonwealth continued. On 20 August, Lieutenant Colonel Martin Schultz with 200 cavalry left Pilten to advance into Samogitia with the aim to occupy Polangen (modern-day Palanga).[11] Although Schultz lost his way and instead took Heiligen Aa (modern-day Šventoji), he at least remained far from the Muscovite zone of influence.

Yet, De la Gardie could not afford to neglect his eastern defences, and Swedish tradition held that an active defence beyond the frontier was better than a passive one. In early September, Captain Johan von Ulenbrock with 117 Swedish dragoons from Dünaburg took Braslau (modern-day Braslav) to gain control of the Düna and shield Samogitia and Courland from Muscovite attacks.

Greater Poland and Warsaw Surrender

As we have seen, most of the Crown Army was in the Ukraine, attempting to prevent a combined Muscovite–cossack offensive. There was a Crown Army in Poland as well, which by the end of June consisted of some 15,000 men.[12] However, the major part of it was deployed in the south with King John Casimir. The only resistance to Wittenberg's Swedes was the 13,000-strong Greater Poland Levy of the Nobility. Commanded by Krzysztof Opaliński (1611–1655), voivode of Posen, and Andrzej Karol Grudziński (1611–1678), voivode of Kalisz, they assembled at Usch (modern-day Ujście) together with 1,000 łanowa levies on foot. Another 400 łanowa levies garrisoned Draheim (modern-day Stare Drawsko) on the way to Usch.[13]

Opaliński and Grudziński deployed their men in a good defensive position on the south side of the River Netze. The Swedes had to approach across marshy ground. However, the Poles had few cannons, little infantry, and too little gunpowder. Moreover, they lacked the discipline and training of the Swedish soldiers. On 24 July, Wittenberg's experienced army began to cross the river. Grudziński and the łanowa levies still put up a fight, defending the position for five hours, until they ran out of ammunition. At that time, the Swedes had seized a crossing point further downstream, which would have enabled them to outflank the Poles. Learning of this, the Levy of the Nobility,

Militärhögskolan, *Carl X Gustaf-studier* 7:1, 1979), p.185.

10   *Ibid.*, 32.
11   *Ibid.*, 34.
12   Wimmer, 'Armé och finansväsen', p.61. Wimmer also includes slightly different data for the number of soldier units the parliament agreed to.
13   Wimmer, 'Polens krig med Sverige', p.337.

Krzysztof Opaliński, as depicted on his sarcophagus.

which had not yet engaged, panicked and began to flee. The following day, Opaliński surrendered. Grudziński, seeing no hope in continuing the struggle alone with his few men, grudgingly accepted to surrender, too. With them also surrendered the provinces of Posen and Kalisz (German: Kalisch), which accepted Swedish protection in exchange for giving King Charles the loyalty and obedience due to the King of Poland. King Charles himself had not even reached the Commonwealth, yet he had already conquered Greater Poland. On the day of surrender, King Charles was in the process of disembarking his army at Wolgast in Swedish Pomerania.

Having secured the area, Wittenberg continued east to Konin, where he awaited King Charles.

Meanwhile, King Charles and the army from mainland Sweden had departed by ship from Dalarö in the southern Stockholm archipelago. The army had embarked on 40 warships, divided into three squadrons under respectively King Charles, Field Marshal and Admiral Carl Gustav Wrangel, and Admiral Åke Hansson Ulfsparre. While the soldiers embarked on the warships, horses and the artillery were carried on 16 merchantmen.[14] After a five-day sea voyage, King Charles reached Peenemünde on Rügen in Pomerania. This was the same place where Swedish King Gustavus Adolphus had landed 25 years earlier when he invaded the Empire during the Thirty Years' War. However, on this occasion the army disembarked at Wolgast on the following day. The army then assembled in Stettin and Damm. King Charles's artillery marched towards Poland ahead of the main army, protected by some horse and foot and under the command of the national

---

14 Jonas Hedberg, *Kungl. Artilleriet: Carl X Gustafs tid* (Stockholm: Militärhistoriska Förlaget, 1982 (1995 edition)), p.42.

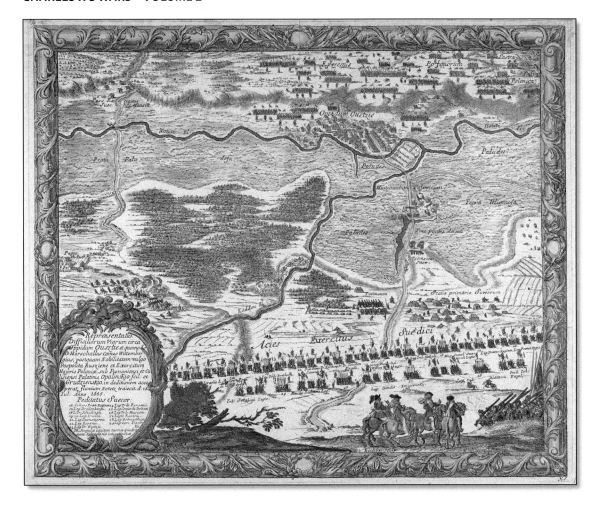

The battle of Usch, 24 July 1655. Swedes and Poles often suffered only minor casualties when they engaged in formal battle, because the Polish cavalry commonly retreated as soon as they found themselves within range of Swedish firepower. (Erik Dahlbergh)

chief of artillery (*rikstygmästare*), Gustav Otto Stenbock (1614–1685), yet another veteran of the Thirty Years' War. Stenbock had fought at Nördlingen in 1634, Wittstock in 1636, and the second battle of Breitenfeld in 1642, just to mention a few of his battles. Three days later, the King marched straight to Czarnikow, where he crossed the Netze in mid August. He continued through Kłecko and Gniezno (Gnesen) until he reached Konin, where he in late August joined forces with Wittenberg. Together, they then continued the eastward march. Strong Swedish garrisons were left in important towns, including Gniezno, Kalisz, Meseritz (Międzyrzecz), and Kosten (Kościan).

At Koło, King Charles received intelligence that King John Casimir was at Łowicz with an army of from 5,000 to 10,000 men.[15] Confident of victory, King Charles marched east to meet him. Three days later, the Swedes defeated John Casimir in a minor engagement at Sobotą. The Polish Levy of the Nobility abandoned the fight quickly, leaving a train of some 300 supply wagons to the Swedes. On the following day, another confrontation took

---

15 Torsten Holm, *Översikt över Sveriges krig under 1600-talets senare hälft* (Stockholm: Militärlitteraturföreningen 148, 1927), p.24.

Above: Polish magnates swear fealty to King Charles at Koło, 26 August 1655. The participation of members of the Drabant Guard armed with partisans gives a festive air to the event. The print does not show their uniform colours, but probably they wore pale blue coats and breeches with yellow stockings with red trim.

Below: Wrangel's blockade of Danzig. Note that the direction north on the map is at the bottom, not the top. (Drawn after sketches by Erik Dahlbergh)

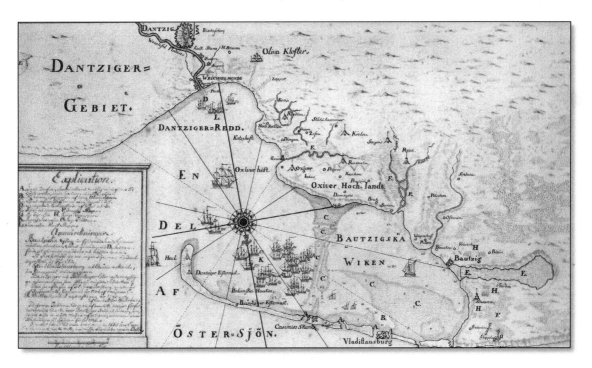

Left: Gustav Otto Stenbock. (David Klöcker Ehrenstrahl)

Right: Bengt Oxenstierna. (Anselmus van Hulle)

place at Piątek, with the Poles again abandoning the field. The Swedish army continued the march, occupying the castle of Łowicz. *LODZ*

However, now King Charles faced a dilemma. The Swedes had almost reached Warsaw, the Polish capital. Moreover, he knew that the Muscovites had taken Grodno further to the east and could be expected to continue their advance all the way to the capital, unless they were pre-empted. On the other hand, he had also learnt that John Casimir had abandoned his capital and moved south, towards Cracow. Finally, he had certainly not forgotten that the primary objective was Prussia, not the Commonwealth's interior provinces.

As a result, King Charles divided his army. On 6 September, he ordered Wittenberg towards Cracow with the main army (8,000 men), in pursuit of John Casimir. King Charles would himself lead 2,000 horse and 1,200 foot to Warsaw, to pre-empt any Muscovite attack on the Polish capital.[16] The King also knew that the Swedish fleet under Carl Gustav Wrangel was in the process of beginning a blockade of Danzig (Wrangel's fleet had already arrived, although King Charles did not yet know this, and two days later, Wrangel began to send landing parties to strategic locations on the shore). This meant that Prussia at least was contained from the sea.

On 8 September, Warsaw surrendered to King Charles without resistance. In the city, the Swedes found 125 cannons (75 of bronze, 50 of iron), 8 mortars, and plenty of supplies.[17] King Charles appointed Bengt Oxenstierna (1623–1702) Governor-General of Swedish-held Poland and thereby the civilian governor of the city.

The King then ordered Stenbock to lead an expeditionary force consisting of artillery, plenty of foot, and some horse along the Vistula to Prussia to assist Wrangel in securing its wealthy ports. If now only the laggard Magnus Gabriel De la Gardie could follow orders and move the army of Livonia overland to Prussia, as was part of the strategy already agreed upon, King Charles deemed that in due time Prussia could be persuaded to surrender as well. Henceforth, King Charles repeatedly wrote to De la Gardie, urging him to move the Livonian army to Prussia. Yet, we will see that De la Gardie was slow to set out.

At the time of the Swedish march into Warsaw, Muscovite units already stood two or three days' march to the east of Warsaw. However, learning of the Swedish move into the city, the Muscovites returned eastwards. King Charles was right; his presence in Warsaw saved the city from the Muscovites.

Lithuania Surrenders

By dividing his forces, King Charles reduced his military superiority. On the other hand, he retained freedom of manoeuvre. With a little luck, he might achieve all his objectives and not only the primary one. After all, Greater Poland and Warsaw had already surrendered to his armies. Even

---

16 Wimmer, 'Polens krig med Sverige', p.343.
17 Hedberg, *Kungl. Artilleriet: Carl X Gustafs tid*, p.51.

better news arrived from Lithuania. On 17 August, the Lithuanian Estates under Grand Hetman Janusz Radziwiłł surrendered to Sweden. By signing the articles of the Declaration of Kėdainiai, they accepted Swedish protection and King Charles as the new Grand Duke of Lithuania. Some 550 notables signed the Declaration.[18] The background was the general dissatisfaction in Lithuania with the Polish nobility's and the Senate's perceived lack of interest in their needs. While dissatisfaction had grown for years, the Muscovite invasion heightened tensions. The Lithuanian Estates felt betrayed by the Polish failure to support Lithuania against Muscovy. When the Muscovites in 1655 advanced upon Wilno with overwhelming forces, we have seen that King John Casimir ordered the Crown units to redeploy to Royal Prussia, thus depriving Janusz Radziwiłł of all Polish troops and, in effect, half his army. Then came the Polish surrender at Usch, which showed the Lithuanian Estates that not even the Poles believed in the future of the Commonwealth. Radziwiłł's personal circumstances played a role, too. Being a Calvinist, and regarding himself as the protector of the Protestant faith in Lithuania, he had grown increasingly disillusioned about Crown policies.

Lithuania was divided in its religious loyalties. Although the Grand Duchy had more Protestants and Orthodox than Poland, it also had a vocal Catholic minority. On 2 September, a part of the Lithuanian Army (reportedly some 2,000 men) disavowed its loyalty to Janusz Radziwiłł and the agreement with Sweden through the establishment of the Confederation of Virbalis (Polish: Wierzbołów). Yet, for Sweden and Radziwiłł this proved of far less importance than the present occupation of major parts of Lithuania by Muscovite armies.

Two months after the Declaration of Kėdainiai, Lithuania's surrender was formalised in a second agreement, the Union of Kėdainiai, which Lithuanian Grand Hetman Janusz Radziwiłł and the Lithuanian nobility, in total 1,172 notables, signed on 20 October. Lithuania formally revoked its previous union with Poland, again recognised King Charles as Grand Duke of Lithuania, and furthermore proclaimed a state union between Lithuania and Sweden.[19] In effect, the Polish–Lithuanian Commonwealth had been replaced by a Swedish–Lithuanian Commonwealth. From this date, Lithuania technically had three contenders for the title of Grand Duke: the already repudiated King John Casimir, Tsar Alexis (with some 2,000 mostly Orthodox signatories, more on which below), and King Charles (with some 1,100 predominantly Protestant signatories).

The surrender of the Greater Poland noble levy at Usch and the subsequent Declaration and Union of Kėdainiai, in which the Grand Duchy of Lithuania, *de jure* a self-governing subject, voluntarily broke its alliance with Poland and instead sought a union with Sweden, shocked the Polish Senate. King John

---

18 Andrej Kotljarchuk, *In the Shadows of Poland and Russia: The Grand Duchy of Lithuania and Sweden in the European Crisis of the mid-17th Century* (Södertörn University College, dissertation, 2006), pp.101–12.

19 *Ibid.*, pp.124–6. Although Janusz Radziwiłł since his surrender to Sweden is considered a traitor in Polish historiography, he remains popular in Lithuania where an army brigade bears his name and is also regarded with affection by many Belarusians. The Grand Duchy of Lithuania was a self-governing state which had the formal right to separate itself from the Polish Crown.

Casimir and the Senate frantically began to search for support abroad, offering the throne to almost any taker who would support them against the Swedes, including but not limited to Tsar Alexis and Prince George of Transylvania. While the offers seldom were genuine in the meaning of credible, they eloquently demonstrate the panic which then had got hold of the senior levels of Polish society.

The Army of Livonia

In August, following the Declaration of Kėdainiai and at the request of Lithuanian representatives, De la Gardie deployed a Swedish garrison to Birze (modern-day Biržai) in Courland. He also offered Swedish protection to Jacob Kettler, Duke of Courland, but the Duke procrastinated, arguing that the treaty of neutrality which he had signed with Sweden in 1647 remained valid. The Duke, although technically under the suzerainty of

Duke Jacob Kettler of Courland and Semigallia

the Commonwealth, did his best to preserve his autonomy. He had already managed to have King John Casimir recognise his neutrality in January 1655 and Tsar Alexis had done the same as late as in June the same year. Both John Casimir and Tsar Alexis were far away. However, with a Swedish army practically at his doorstep, Duke Jacob in the Treaty of Poswol (modern-day Pasvalys) of 20 September agreed to abandon his neutrality. He allowed the Swedish army to march through his territory, in exchange for the face-saving gesture that King Charles might recognise his neutrality later.[20] The choice of words in the Treaty made it abundantly clear that any future recognition of neutrality was solely at the discretion of King Charles.

Nonetheless, the Swedish army of Livonia did not move for almost six weeks. Although King Charles admittedly had advised De la Gardie to advance with caution so as not to trigger a war with Muscovy, there is no doubt that De la Gardie did not act as decisively as the King desired. King Charles repeatedly wrote to De la Gardie, rebuking him for not fulfilling the strategic plan, which was to pre-empt the Muscovites and advance towards Prussia. De la Gardie did not move further until 29 October, more than a week after the Union of Kėdainiai. Then, finally, De la Gardie led most of the Livonian army, some 8,900 men, across the River Neman (Polish: Niemen; Lithuanian: Nemunas) en route to Poland and Prussia (Table 8). Fewer than 6,000 soldiers, many of whom were recently enlisted, remained to safeguard the Swedish Baltic

20 Rainer Fagerlund, 'Kriget i östersjöprovinserna 1655–1661: Operationer och krigsansträngningar på en bikrigsskådeplats under Carl X Gustafs krig', Arne Stade (ed.), *Kriget på östfronten* (Stockholm: Militärhögskolan, *Carl X Gustaf-studier* 7:1, 1979), pp.51–2.

Stefan Czarniecki, 1659.
(Attributed to Brother
Matthiesen)

provinces and the conquests in Pilten and north-western Lithuania.[21]

An agreement had by then been reached between Swedes and Muscovites which fixed the border between their respective zones of interest at the Rivers Neman and Svienta (modern-day River Šventoji). With agreements in hand with both Muscovy and the Lithuanian estates, De la Gardie finally moved his army south.

The march through Lithuania was not without difficulties. De la Gardie had to maintain a careful course so as not intrude into Muscovite-held territory or Ducal Prussia. He also had to acquire provisions en route, since supplies were lacking in Livonia. The exaction of contributions along the road caused resentment, and both De la Gardie and his officers were unhappy about the violence this engendered. Discipline broke down, too. Colonel Johann Pleitner noted with sadness that 'such violence and disorder took place that in my time I have never seen the like'.[22]

The Battle of Żarnów

While the Senate in Poland panicked, other Poles kept fighting. As Wittenberg was preparing to lay siege to Opoczno which guarded the road to Cracow, Polish units in a surprise raid at Inowłódz suddenly attacked his 500-strong rearguard, commanded by Georg Forgell. The Poles, superior in numbers and commanded by Stefan Czarniecki, reportedly inflicted 200 casualties on the Swedes.[23] Czarniecki was a very experienced officer, who had learnt the ruthless methods of modern warfare in the Thirty Years' War. By employing such means, he henceforth became the most efficient of the Commonwealth's officers. While Czarniecki's victory at Inowłódz was the first Polish success in the war against Sweden and acquired some propagandistic value (some claimed that it saved King John Casimir because the scared Wittenberg no longer dared to advance further), it had little effect on the campaign. Wittenberg had fallen ill, so he had already decided to remain at Opoczno, awaiting the arrival of King Charles before he continued to Cracow. Wittenberg suffered from

21   Tersmeden, 'Carl X Gustafs armé 1654–1657', p.220.
22   Johann Pleitner to De la Gardie, 20 October 1655 (O.S.). Swedish National Archives (RA), De la Gardieska samlingen, Serie C:1, Skrivelser till Magnus Gabriel De la Gardie, E 1526.
23   Wimmer, 'Polens krig med Sverige', p.344 with n.43; Krzysztof Nawrocki, *Pod Żarnowem – w czasach szwedzkiego 'potopu': Kolejna rocznica historycznej bitwy* (website, <http://hs.xon.pl/portal_zarnow/informacje/zrodla/bitwa_pod_zarnowem.pdf>)

bad health, and we will see that on several occasions he was laid up in bed because of gout.

Soon enough, King Charles soon left Warsaw. Moving south with a force that mostly consisted of horse, he joined forces with Wittenberg at Opoczno. John Casimir was not fleeing. The attack on the Swedish rearguard had been intended to bleed the Swedes. Now, he hoped to catch Wittenberg alone. John Casimir did not know that Charles had already joined forces with Wittenberg. On the following day, John Casimir reached nearby Żarnów, where assisted by Crown Field Hetman Stanisław Lanckoroński and Prince Aleksander Koniecpolski (1620–1659), he deployed his army against the Swedes.[24]

The Polish army consisted of an estimated regular 6,000 cavalry from the Komput army, 900 dragoons, 3,000 to 4,000 noble levies, and some four to six light cannons. The Swedish army consisted of an estimated 6,000 cavalry, 400 dragoons, 4,500 infantry, and 40 cannons.[25]

Jerzy Sebastian Lubomirski.

The two sides were fairly equal in numbers (Table 9), but it soon became clear that the Swedes surpassed the Poles in discipline, experience, and firepower.

On 16 September King Charles rode out at dawn with the entire army. A preliminary Polish cavalry charge was easily beaten off, after which the Swedes advanced. Again, it was obvious that the Polish cavalry could not withstand Swedish firepower and discipline. King John Casimir and most of the Commonwealth army withdrew, leaving only some of the cavalry and the supply train to take the brunt of the Swedish attack. A heavy rain began, which enabled most of the Polish army to retreat, although they were pursued for some time by the Swedish cavalry, most notably by Israel Isacsson Ridderhielm's and Joachim Engell's regiments. It was a decisive Swedish victory. The Poles lost an estimated 1,000 men and much of their supply train. Swedish losses were very few.[26]

The Siege of Cracow

After the defeat at Żarnów, King John Casimir hoped for reinforcements from the Levy of the Nobility of Lesser Poland. This was a forlorn hope; unwilling to assist, these nobles soon returned home.[27] The King then fled into Cracow, which he reached three days after the defeat at Żarnów. It was not a dignified flight, and the outlook was no better from Cracow. A former capital, Cracow had lost much of its former population, to diminished prospects as well as

---

24 In Swedish sources, the name is usually given as Czarnowa.
25 Wimmer, 'Polens krig med Sverige', p.345.
26 *Ibid.*, p.345.
27 *Ibid.*, p.344.

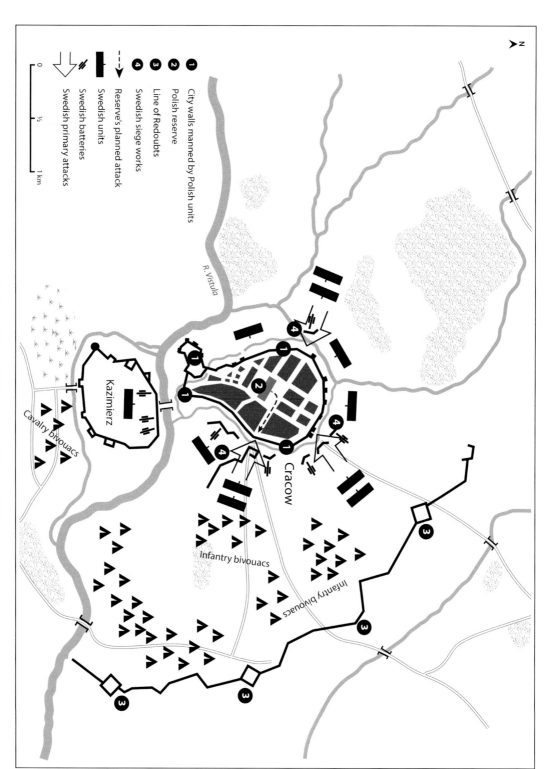

The Siege of Cracow, 26 September to 17 October 1655

Legend:
- ① City walls manned by Polish units
- ② Polish reserve
- ③ Line of Redoubts
- ④ Swedish siege works
- Reserve's planned attack
- Swedish units
- Swedish batteries
- Swedish primary attacks

Scale: 0 – ½ – 1 km

Labels on map: N, R. Vistula, Kazimierz, Cavalry bivouacs, Cracow, Infantry bivouacs

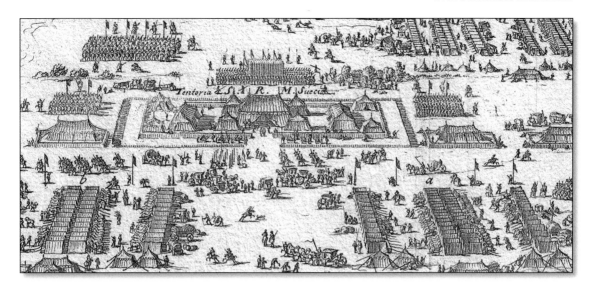

plague.[28] Now, yet more departed, because those burghers and clerics who had the means rapidly evacuated the city, moving their belongings into the Holy Roman Empire for safekeeping. John Casimir at first intended to defend the city, but he then changed his mind, in late September handing command over to Czarniecki. The King and the Crown Army then continued the flight. Upon departing Cracow, the demoralised Crown Army attempted to loot neighbouring Kazimierz – but it was again repulsed, this time by the Kazimierz burgher militia.[29]

The Swedish camp at Cracow, 1655. The great tent in the centre belongs to King Charles. (Erik Dahlbergh)

At first moving south, John Casimir soon turned west towards the safety of Silesia, which formed part of the Empire and furthermore was one of the Habsburg ancestral lands. The King entrusted the powerful magnate Jerzy Sebastian Lubomirski (1616–1667) with the crown jewels and royal archive for safekeeping. Lubomirski departed to his estate in Lubowla (modern-day Stará Ľubovňa, Slovakia) further to the south, bringing the valuables with him. Rumours about Lubomirski's departure with the crown jewels led to all sorts of rumours, because the wealthy Lubomirski had many estates, some of them near Cracow.

Meanwhile, Czarniecki did his best to defend the abandoned city. Cracow's city walls were old, but the most damaged sections were repaired before the siege. In addition, a system of modern outer fortifications had been constructed in exposed areas. Cracow also had a large supply of cannons, since it hosted one of the Commonwealth's arsenals. Moreover, Czarniecki was not short of men, having at his disposal a total force of some 4,500 men (2,200 regulars, including 175 hussars, 400 dragoons, and 1,600 infantry, in addition to 2,300 levies of various kinds) and 160 cannons of assorted

---

28 After an outbreak of plague in 1651–1652, the population had shrunk to some 13,000. Peter Englund, *Den oövervinnerlige: Om den svenska stormaktstiden och en man i dess mitt* (Stockholm: Atlantis, 2000), p.242.

29 Tadeusz Nowak, 'Carl X Gustafs Kraków-operation 1655', Arne Stade and Jan Wimmer (eds). *Polens krig med Sverige 1655–1660: Krigshistoriska studier* (Stockholm: Kungl. Militärhögskolan, *Carl X Gustaf-studier* 5, 1973), pp.157–211, on p.165.

The siege of Cracow, 1655. Protected by gabions and redoubts, the Swedish artillery bombards the city. (Erik Dahlbergh)

calibres including his quite professional field artillery: 12 light cannons under Fryderyk Getkant.[30]

The Swedish army arrived soon after King John Casimir had abandoned the city. Czarniecki burned the outlying suburbs so as to deny the Swedes their use as cover. The burning almost ended in disaster; a sudden wind spread the fire into the city itself, so that several important buildings were damaged before the fires could be put out.

Neighbouring Kazimierz, a major walled suburb on the south side of the River Vistula, surrendered to the Swedes early during the siege in an action mostly undertaken by Lieutenant Colonel Otto Wilhelm von Fersen of the Life Company of Horse. With this company and two companies of dragoons, Fersen advanced into the town to negotiate with the burghers. During the negotiations, the same Polish soldiers alternatively surrendered to Fersen and fought, except on one occasion when finding Fersen alone for negotiations, the haiduks instead beat him unconscious with their war hammers and took him prisoner. Fersen awoke in a chair, under the care of a Polish surgeon. Released by the leading burghers, Fersen then proceeded again to accept the surrender of those who had beaten him unconscious. Fersen acquired the town, but for the rest of his life he had war hammer scars in his face to remember the action.[31] A major reason for the burghers' desire to surrender was that they feared Czarniecki, who regarded Kazimierz as a strategic threat since its fortifications might aid the besiegers. Czarniecki also had a particular aversion to the town's Jewish population, whom he accused of collaborating with the invaders for reasons of profit and religion. King Charles issued a letter of protection (*salva-guardia*) to the Jews of Kazimierz on 29 September, promising them security as well as freedom of religion. For King Charles, this was standard procedure; he routinely issued security guarantees to any group in the Commonwealth which proved willing to accept his rule, and he also

30 *Ibid.*, p.164.
31 G. Bertil C:son Barkman; Sven Lundkvist; and Lars Tersmeden. *Kungl. Svea livgardes historia 3:2: 1632 (1611)–1660* (Stockholm: Stiftelsen för Svea livgardes historia, 1966), pp.243–4.

demanded that his soldiers respect the guarantees.[32] In revenge, Czarniecki sent out Cracow's students and journeymen, led by a hussar, to burn down Kazimierz. However, their enthusiasm was greater than their military skills, so the Swedes dispersed them with grenades thrown from the occupied buildings.[33] Other sallies were more successful, but nowhere did the defenders of Cracow make any significant gains.

The Battle of Wojnicz

King Charles was at Cracow when the siege began and ended, but in the meantime, he left command in Wittenberg's capable hands. The reason was that the Swedes received intelligence that the main Polish army had retreated, not with King John Casimir to Silesia, but to the area around Wojnicz further to the east. The Swedes also, no doubt, heard the rumours about the Polish crown jewels being hidden in one of Lubomirski's estates. This certainly would explain why King Charles in early October personally

Conrad Christoph von Königsmarck. (Matthäus Merian the Younger)

took Wiśnicz, one of Lubomirski's strongpoints, which surrendered without a fight. The rumours possibly also explain why Colonel Conrad Christoph von Königsmarck (1634–1673), the young son of renowned Field Marshal Hans Christoph von Königsmarck and newly appointed head of an enlisted regiment, at about the same time advanced against Tenczyn, another wealthy private estate. The defenders surrendered, but young Königsmarck had them massacred.[34] The inexperienced Königsmarck's action was severely criticised, also within the Swedish army, but seems not to have resulted in any formal charges.

King Charles also sent a detachment of cavalry (two regiments, although numbers are uncertain) under General Robert Douglas to take the town of Landskron (modern-day Lanckorona), 30 km south-west of Cracow, to intercept the fleeing John Casimir. Douglas was a Scotland-born veteran of the Thirty Years' War who had distinguished himself on numerous

---

32 The Swedish view of freedom of religion was on the surface straightforward – no such freedom was permitted – but in reality, the situation was far more complex. The Crown accepted that inhabitants in conquered territories and foreign visitors might have another faith than the state Lutheranism insisted on in the Swedish heartlands. They also accepted men of any faith into the army, as long as they attended the mandatory Lutheran services. Yet, the Crown did not wish to encourage non-Lutheran beliefs and the Church abhorred them. Jews were formally not allowed to live in Sweden but they could visit for a maximum of 14 days.

33 Nowak, 'Carl X Gustafs Kraków-operation', p.201.

34 The action is typical of what should never happen but nonetheless frequently occurs: an inexperienced young officer in charge of fresh, insufficiently trained men deployed in an unfamiliar environment causes a massacre of non-combatants.

The Siege of Cracow, 1655. (Erik Dahlbergh)

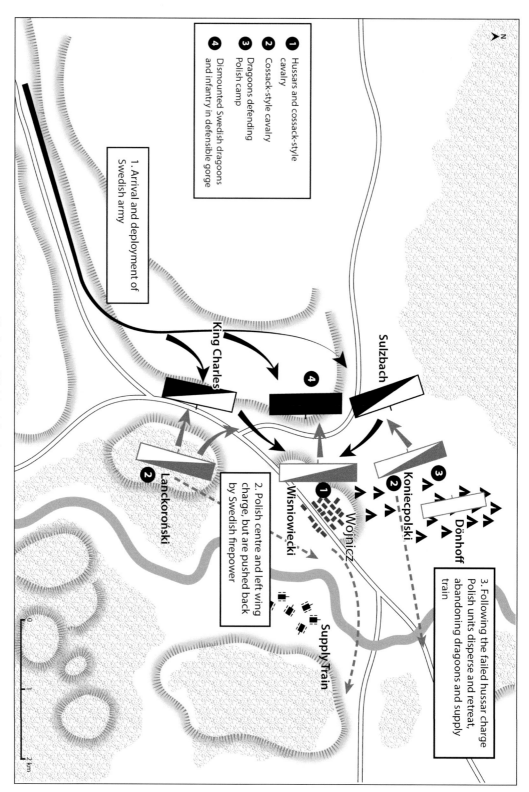

The Battle of Wojnicz, 3 October 1655

1. Hussars and cossack-style cavalry

2. Cossack-style cavalry

3. Dragoons defending Polish camp

4. Dismounted Swedish dragoons and infantry in defensible gorge

1. Arrival and deployment of Swedish army

2. Polish centre and left wing charge, but are pushed back by Swedish firepower

3. Following the failed hussar charge Polish units disperse and retreat, abandoning dragoons and supply train

King Charles

Sulzbach

Lanckoroński

Wisniowiecki

Wojnicz

Koniecpolski

Dönhoff

Supply Train

occasions, including at the battles of Lützen 1632, Wittstock 1636, and Jankow 1645. Douglas took Landskron, but he could not capture the long-since gone King John Casimir, who having abandoned the Commonwealth, found refuge in Oberglogau, Silesia (modern-day Głogówek).

Having reunited his and Douglas's forces, King Charles then set out against the Crown Army at Wojnicz. The King brought some 5,200 men, while the Crown Army, under Crown Field Hetman Stanisław Lanckoroński, counted some 6,200 (Table 10).

The intelligence available to King Charles had been correct. On 3 October, cavalry units of the Swedish and Polish army encountered each other in the early morning mist and clashed at Wojnicz. Upon learning of the Swedish advance, Lanckoroński immediately deployed his army in the traditional manner, in three cavalry wings with the hussars under young Prince Dymitri Wiśniowiecki in the centre. The old Prussian noble Heinrich Dönhoff (in Poland known as Henryk Denhoff), colonel of a dragoon regiment in the Crown Army, was left to guard the camp with his dragoons. Soon a full-scale battle developed. Things went as before. The Polish hussars, under Aleksander Koniecpolski, could not stand up to Swedish firepower. The Swedish units were more disciplined, responded faster, and employed a combined arms approach with horse and foot which the Poles could not match. As a result, the Swedes won another victory, capturing the Polish supply train, several standards, and 20 kettle-drums.[35] The Swedes pursued for a short distance, but halted at Tarnów. There major parts of the Crown Army changed sides, swearing allegiance to Swedish King Charles. Among them were Aleksander Koniecpolski and Jan Sobieski, who many years later would become King of Poland.

Heinrich Dönhoff was not among those who swore allegiance at Tarnów. With most of his dragoons, he fell into Swedish captivity when the rest of the Crown Army fled. It was not Dönhoff's first battle: in 1626–1629, he had fought in the Commonwealth army against Swedish King Gustavus Adolphus, while in 1633–1634, he had commanded a Commonwealth German cavalry regiment in the Smolensk War against Muscovy. Later, he had fought cossack rebels and Crimean Tatars.[36]

Meanwhile, King John Casimir abandoned Poland, fleeing with a few squadrons to Oppeln (modern-day Opole) in Silesia. There he went into exile,

Robert Douglas, 1651. (Jeremias Falck, after portrait by David Beck)

---

35 Nowak, 'Carl X Gustafs Kraków-operation', p.184.
36 Ryszard Dzieszyński, *Kraków 1655–1657* (Warsaw: Bellona, 2019), p.78.

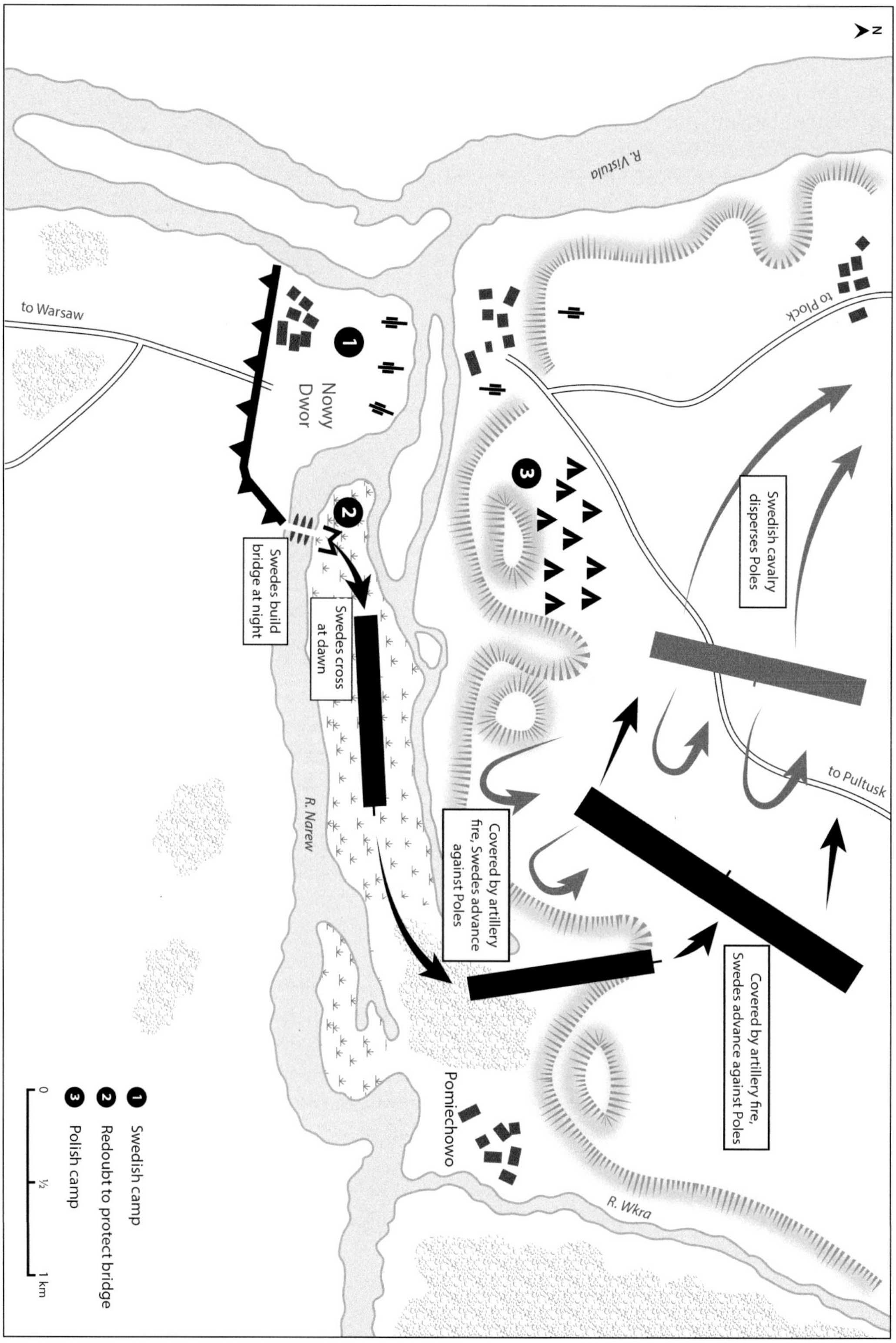

The Battle of Nowy Dwór, 30 September 1655

to Warsaw

Nowy Dwor

R. Vistula

to Plock

to Pultusk

R. Narew

R. Wkra

Pomiechowo

1 Swedes build bridge at night

2 Swedes cross at dawn

3 Covered by artillery fire, Swedes advance against Poles

Covered by artillery fire, Swedes advance against Poles

Swedish cavalry disperses Poles

N

1 Swedish camp
2 Redoubt to protect bridge
3 Polish camp

0   ½   1 km

finding shelter in one of his estates in Oberglogau, where Queen Marie Louise already awaited him.

The Battle of Nowy Dwór

Meanwhile, Gustav Otto Stenbock led the second Swedish army (some 7,000 to 8,000 men, estimated as approximately 1,500 cavalry, 6,500 infantry, and 60 cannons) in Poland north from Warsaw and into Masovia. His real objective was Prussia, so his army was optimised for siegeworks. The plan was for Stenbock to await De la Gardie's Livonian army, and then continue to take control over the Prussian shore. Unusually for a Swedish army on the Continent, most of Stenbock's army consisted of national troops.

Upon reaching Nowy Dwór, where the River Nare (Polish: Narew) joined the Vistula, the Swedes found the Levy of the Nobility of Masovia, under Jan Kazimierz Krasiński, waiting for them. Nowy Dwór was a strategically important crossing point, since the town dominated the road from Warsaw to Prussia. The Masovian army consisted of some 10,000 cavalry, 1,000 levied infantry, and some cannons.[37] Stenbock urged the noble levy to surrender. However, the Poles refused. This did not perturb Stenbock. A later eyewitness described him as 'a man of honour who would never utter a lie, but who is coldblooded and ruthless.'[38] These were the characteristics which Stenbock now displayed. Under the cover of artillery fire, Stenbock had his engineers bridge the river. The Swedish army then crossed the river, moved up on the plateau dominated by the Poles, and continued advancing. Again, Swedish firepower turned decisive. Whenever the Poles attempted to hold the Swedes, they were quickly repulsed by the Swedish regimental artillery. Finally, the Swedish horse charged. The Poles fled, losing some 300 men. They also abandoned seven cannons. Swedish losses in the battle were reportedly five men, four of whom were artillerymen killed or fatally wounded in the initial artillery exchange. On the following day, the Masovian levy surrendered to Stenbock.

Cracow Surrenders

The Swedish siege of Cracow was not long, even though it had its dramatic moments. At one point, King Charles was almost captured by a Polish cavalry patrol when he with characteristic vigour personally reconnoitred the city's surroundings. On another occasion, when King Charles wanted to survey the city walls, a Polish musketeer fired a well-aimed shot at him, missing the man but killing his horse. As usual, King Charles suffered no wound.[39] Not so Czarniecki, who on one occasion suffered a minor wound from Swedish musket fire.

Already by late September, it was obvious to Cracow's inhabitants that the city soon would surrender. As their mood fell, religious righteousness

---

37 Wimmer, 'Polens krig med Sverige', p.346.
38 Lorenzo Magalotti, *Sverige under år 1674* (Stockholm: Rediviva, 1986), p.99.
39 Nowak, 'Carl X Gustafs Kraków-operation', p.184.

coupled with a desire for profit prompted many to turn on their neighbours. Led by a Catholic canon named Ossoliński, they looted any Jewish businesses they could find. Encouraged by Ossoliński, soldiers began to desert from their posts on the walls so that they, too could join the plunderers. They also plundered those buildings which had been abandoned by their inhabitants before the siege began, among them the city's colony of Italian merchants. The homes of Cracow's colony of Scottish merchants suffered, too, but in this case because the Scots were Protestants. When his men began to desert, but only then, Czarniecki had Ossoliński thrown into jail.[40]

In mid October, Czarniecki initiated negotiations to surrender. As noted, King Charles had issued a letter of protection to the Jews of Kazimierz. The King, who wanted to extend the same protection to the inhabitants of Cracow, accordingly demanded that Czarniecki order his men to return the plunder and seal the Jewish shops to prevent further looting. The same precautions would need to be taken for other valuable property, including that of the Crown. When the capitulation act was signed on 17 October, Charles sent the commander of his Life Guard of Foot, Colonel Christoph Carl von Schlippenbach, to seal the Wawel Royal Castle and the Treasury. Schlippenbach found that the royal insignia and most of the contents of the treasury had been removed, obviously in haste.[41] This was Lubomirski's doing, with King John Casimir's blessing. Nobody had emptied the armoury, however; the Swedes found no less than 40 abandoned cannons.[42]

The capitulation act was generous to the inhabitants of Cracow, who received guarantees for their privileges, property, liberties, and faith. In many ways (although not on the crucial issue of the status of the departed John Casimir), the capitulation act signified the transfer of authority from the Polish to the Swedish king. For instance, Sweden would take custody of any Muscovite prisoners of war and in return attempt to negotiate the release of Commonwealth prisoners of war in Muscovy. So far, everything seemed to be under control. However, when Czarniecki two days after the surrender departed, disturbances broke out. Many inhabitants of Cracow, in particularly those who had lost their homes and few belongings when Czarniecki burned the suburbs, expressed their dismay and anger at the departing Polish soldiers. Things grew worse when Czarniecki, immediately before his departure, first enforced a monetary contribution from the city, then plundered all brothels and businesses owned by Protestants, and finally had his men break the Swedish seals on the Jewish shops, from which he removed all remaining valuables to his supply train. Then he marched out with his men. As a result, immediately after Czarniecki's departure a delegation of Jews approached King Charles, requesting the return of their property, which the Swedish King had promised to protect. Greatly annoyed, Charles sent cavalry after Czarniecki's men. However, the Poles formed up behind their supply wagons, trained their cannons on the Swedes, and refused to surrender the plunder.[43]

---

40   *Ibid.*, pp.178–9.
41   *Ibid.*, pp.190, 201.
42   Hedberg, *Kungl. Artilleriet: Carl X Gustafs tid*, p.51.
43   Nowak, 'Carl X Gustafs Kraków-operation', pp.193–5.

Hearing about this, Charles let Czarniecki depart. He had no intention of jeopardising the capitulation agreement.

Charles then had his own army march into Cracow. He appointed Major General Paul Würtz (1612–1676) governor of the city and provided him with a garrison of some 3,000 men.[44] Würtz, the son of a German merchant, was an experienced soldier who during the Thirty Years' War had fought in Imperial service before he joined the Swedish army. Würtz had attended a Jesuit school and was interested in literature, a taste which he shared with King Charles. After the war, they had become good friends, and Würtz had carried out several diplomatic missions. But Würtz was primarily a soldier. To impress the need for order on his men, he immediately had two gallows raised in the centre of Cracow. Sure enough, only the occasional act of theft took place after the Swedish garrison entered the city. The Swedes also enforced order among the citizens, strictly forbidding violence and looting. For the majority of the citizens, the new order was probably welcome, since discipline among Czarniecki's men was lax during the latter stages of the siege. Even so, the burghers had to hand over yet more money, because Charles, too, imposed a contribution on the city. Like Czarniecki, he had an army to support.[45]

Paul Würtz, 1668. (Lambert van den Bos, depicting Würtz in his final post, as field marshal in Dutch service)

The Crown Army Surrenders

Negotiations then began with Aleksander Koniecpolski, Voivode of Sandomierz and Grand Standard-bearer of the Crown, who had been defeated at Wojnicz but still commanded 5,174 cavalry and 211 dragoons. Within a week of Czarniecki's departure from Cracow, Koniecpolski and his men surrendered in a field outside Cracow, after which they swore allegiance to the Swedish King.[46]

Four days later, King Charles left Cracow. There were yet more Commonwealth armies which wanted to accept his protection and swear allegiance. Within a week, he had established communications with Crown Grand Hetman Stanisław Potocki. Already defeated in the south by Prince Grigoriy Romodanovskiy's Muscovites and Bogdan Khmel'nitskiy's Ukrainian cossacks, and faced with Charles's victorious Swedes approaching from the north, Potocki perceived himself caught between two fires. In early November, he informed Charles that he was ready to swear allegiance

---

44 *Ibid.*, p.197.
45 *Ibid.*, pp.195–6.
46 *Ibid.*, p.197.

The Crown army swears fealty to King Charles at Sandomierz, 13 November 1655. (Drottningholm Palace)

together with his men. Crown Field Hetman Stanisław Lanckoroński would swear together with Potocki.

On 13 November, Potocki and Lanckoroński met King Charles at Sandomierz. The two Poles were the two most senior officers of the Crown Army, and their entire armies witnessed the meeting. Charles, however, arrived with only a handful of Swedish soldiers to make a show of his confidence. Potocki and Lanckoroński then swore allegiance to him, promising that they would defend the King of Sweden with their lives and blood. With the two Poles swore all of their men (Potocki's 7,500 cavalry and 4,000 infantry and dragoons, and Lanckoroński's 5,174 cavalry and 211 dragoons). After the ceremony, the Crown Army joined the Swedish army. However, some units were deployed elsewhere at the time, so the reinforcements did not constitute the Crown Army's full strength.[47] For this reason, there is some uncertainty over how many Commonwealth soldiers actually joined the Swedish army after swearing allegiance to King Charles. It is undisputed that most of Lanckoroński's army (5,174 cavalry and 211 dragoons) entered Swedish service, and under the command of Aleksander Koniecpolski, Grand Standard-bearer of the Crown, and Jan Fryderyk Sapieha, Crown Field Scribe, they later marched with the Swedish army. It is also generally undisputed that almost all of Czarniecki's contingent in Cracow (900 infantry and dragoons) ultimately went into Swedish service. Finally, an estimated 3,000 cossack-style

---

47   Wimmer, 'Armé och finansväsen', p.71.

cavalry were enlisted for Swedish service by Commonwealth nobles. In total, the number of Commonwealth soldiers who by this time entered into Swedish service on active duty has been estimated as more than 9,000.[48]

Fate played a part in the proceedings, because when Potocki commenced negotiations for his surrender to King Charles, he was convinced that Muscovites and Ukrainians were overrunning the southern territories of the Commonwealth all the way to L'vov. In reality, the Commonwealth cause in the south was not yet lost. Potocki could not know that only two days later, Romodanovskiy and Khmel'nitskiy would learn that Mehmed Khan led a Crimean Tatar army against the Muscovites in an effort to relieve L'vov. Faced with this threat, Muscovites and Ukrainians abandoned the siege in return for a substantial monetary contribution from the L'vov burghers. So, on the very same day that Romodanovskiy began his retreat, Crown Grand Hetman Potocki agreed to swear allegiance to Sweden, and when Potocki did so, the Muscovites and Ukrainians were already on their way back home.

With all major nobles and organised military units swearing allegiance to the Swedish Crown, the provincial governors quickly followed suit. Within days, representatives of several provinces appeared in Cracow to swear allegiance to Sweden. With this act, the entirety of Poland and all of Lithuania which had not already sworn allegiance to the Tsar accepted King Charles and the Swedish Crown as their suzerain (only Prussia did not). If the Commonwealth had been a less disorganised state, the war would have been over.

Tables

Table 5 (see p.37). Wittenberg's Army, July 1655
Source: Tersmeden, 'Carl X Gustafs armé 1654–1657', p.249; Hedberg, *Kungl. Artilleriet: Carl X Gustafs tid*, pp.42, 53

Note that the Bremen field artillery company accompanied Wittenberg's army even though many historians count it together with the artillery in King Charles's army to get a total figure. The sign (E) indicates an enlisted unit.

Cavalry
Småland Cavalry Regiment
Her Royal Majesty the Queen's Life Regiment of Horse (E)
Count Palatine Philip of Sulzbach's Cavalry Regiment (E)
Duke Franz Erdmann of Saxe-Lauenburg's Cavalry Regiment (E)
Conrad Christoph von Königsmarck's Cavalry Regiment (E)
Arvid Wittenberg's Cavalry Regiment (E)
Israel Isacsson Ridderhielm's Cavalry Regiment (E)
Pontus Fredrik De la Gardie's Cavalry Regiment (E)
Christian von Pretlach's Cavalry Regiment (E)
Jacob von Yxkull's Cavalry Regiment (E)

---

48 *Ibid.*, p.70.

Hans Böddeker's Cavalry Regiment (E)
Joachim Engel's Cavalry Regiment (E)
Total: approximately 6,000
Dragoons
Count Palatine Philip of Sulzbach's Dragoon Squadron (E)
Adam von Weiher's Dragoon Squadron (E)
Total: approximately 150
Infantry
Kronoberg Regiment
Östgöta Regiment
Hälsinge Regiment
Västgöta-Dal Regiment
Västmanland Regiment
Kalmar Regiment
Värmland Regiment
Her Royal Majesty the Queen's Life Regiment of Foot, under Bengt Horn (E)
Christoph Delphicus zu Dohna's Regiment (E)
Paul Würtz's Regiment (E)
Fabian von Fersen's Regiment (E)
Georg Städing's Regiment (E)
Bernt Taube's Regiment (E)
Total: at most 8,000
Artillery
Bremen field artillery company: At least 12 24-pounders, 12-pounders, and/or 6-pounders, with 60 3-pounders
Total: 200
Grand Total: approximately 14,350

Table 6 (see p.37). King Charles's Army, August 1655
Source: Tersmeden, 'Carl X Gustafs armé 1654–1657', p.250; Hedberg, *Kungl. Artilleriet: Carl X Gustafs tid*, pp.42, 317

Note that if the artillery from Bremen, which accompanied Wittenberg's army, is taken into account, the total Swedish field artillery during the invasion of Poland consisted of at least 72 heavy cannons, 178 3-pounders, and eight mortars.

Cavalry
Garde du Corps (E)
Life Company of Horse (E)
Uppland Cavalry Regiment
Västgöta Cavalry Regiment
Östgöta Cavalry Regiment
Her Royal Majesty the Queen's Life Regiment of Horse (E)
Peder Hammarskjöld's Cavalry Regiment (E)
David Sinclair's Cavalry Regiment (E)
Jacob Johan Taube's Cavalry Regiment (E)
Total: At most 4,300

Dragoons
Karelian Dragoon Regiment (4 companies)
Total: Approximately 500

Infantry
His Royal Majesty's Life Guard (9 companies) (E)
Uppland Regiment
Skaraborg Regiment
Södermanland Regiment
Jönköping Regiment
Dalecarlia Regiment
Östgöta Regiment
Hälsinge Regiment
Västerbotten Regiment
Österbotten Regiment
Ångermanland Regiment
Total: At most 7,500

Artillery
Field artillery regiment, consisting of at least 60 heavy cannons, 118 3-pounders, and 8 mortars, as follows:
From Pomerania: At least 32 24-pounders, 12-pounders, and/or 6-pounders, with 88 3-pounders and 8 mortars, under Gustav Otto Stenbock
From Stockholm: At least 12 24-pounders, 8 12-pounders, 8 6-pounders, 30 3-pounders, with men and large amounts of ammunition and gear, under Simon Grundel Helmfelt
Total: 340
Grand Total: approximately 12,600

Table 7 (see p.37). The army of Livonia at the muster at Kokenhusen, 14 August 1655

Source: Tersmeden, 'Carl X Gustafs armé 1654–1657', p.252; Hedberg, *Kungl. Artilleriet: Carl X Gustafs tid*, p.69)

Cavalry
Åbo Cavalry Regiment
Tavastehus Cavalry Regiment
Viborg Cavalry Regiment
Total: approximately 2,600
Dragoons
Karelian Dragoon Regiment (4 companies)
Total: approximately 500
Infantry
His Royal Majesty's Life Guard (6 companies) (E)
Åbo Regiment
Björneborg Regiment
Tavastehus Regiment
Elfsborg Regiment
Savolax Regiment
Österbotten Regiment
Total: approximately 4,100
Artillery
Field artillery company of two 12-pounders, two 6-pounders, and 10 3-pounders
Grand Total: approximately 7,200

Table 8 (see p.49). De la Gardie's Livonian army which crossed the River Neman into the Commonwealth, 29 October 1655

Sources: Tersmeden, 'Carl X Gustafs armé 1654–1657', p.252; Fagerlund, 'Kriget i östersjöprovinserna', pp.228–9

Cavalry
The Retinue of Nobles in Estonia and Livonia, under Colonels Bernt Taube (Estonia) and Otto von Mengden (Livonia)
Åbo Cavalry Regiment, under Colonel Gustav Kurck
Tavastehus Cavalry Regiment, under Major General Henrik Horn

Viborg Cavalry Regiment, under Colonel Erik Kruse
Governor-General Magnus Gabriel De la Gardie's Cavalry Regiment (E)
Major General Henrik von Thurn's Cavalry Company (E)
Major General Friedrich Löwe's Cavalry Company (E)
Captain Pester's Cavalry Company (E)
Total: approximately 4,400
Dragoons
Karelian Dragoon Regiment (4 companies), under Lieutenant Colonel Albrecht von Ridder
Governor-General Magnus Gabriel De la Gardie's Dragoon Squadron (E)
Total: almost 600
Infantry
Björneborg Regiment, under Colonel Johann Pleitner
Tavastehus Regiment, under Colonel Bernt Mellin
Elfsborg Regiment, under Colonel Bengt Lilliehöök
Savolax Regiment, under Colonel Berend von Gertten
Österbotten Regiment, under Colonel Nils Bååt
Governor-General Magnus Gabriel De la Gardie's Regiment (E)
Count Jacob Casimir De la Gardie's Regiment (E)
Total: at most 4,000
Grand Total: approximately 8,900

Table 9 (see p.51). Units at the battle of Żarnów, 16 September 1655
Sources: Nowak, 'Carl X Gustafs Kraków-operation', pp.168–9; Carlbom, Tredagarsslaget, 13, which also offers the Swedish order of battle; Daniel Schorr, 'Battle of Czarnowa', Northern Wars website (now defunct).

Swedish units
Cavalry
Life Guard of Horse, also known as the Life Regiment of Horse, under Lieutenant Colonels Hans Georg Mörner af Morlanda (Drabant Guard) and Otto Wilhelm von Fersen (Life Company)
Uppland Cavalry Regiment, under Major General Johan Mauritz Wrangel
Småland Cavalry Regiment, under Lieutenant Colonel Staffan von Klingspor
Her Royal Majesty the Queen's Life Regiment of Horse, under Colonel Gustav Adam Banér (enlisted in Germany)
Frederick Landgrave of Hesse-Eschwege's Cavalry Regiment
Conrad Christoph von Königsmarck's Cavalry Regiment, also known as Königsmarck's Life Regiment of Horse (enlisted in Bremen-Verden)

Arvid Wittenberg's Cavalry Regiment (enlisted in Pomerania)
David Sinclair's Cavalry Regiment (mostly enlisted in Sweden)
Israel Isacsson Ridderhielm's Cavalry Regiment (mostly enlisted in Sweden)
Hans Böddeker's Cavalry Regiment (enlisted in Bremen)
Christian von Pretlach's Cavalry Regiment (enlisted in Bremen)
Pontus De la Gardie's Cavalry Regiment, under Georg Forgell (enlisted)
Jacob von Yxkull's Cavalry Regiment (enlisted from Swedes and Germans in Bremen and Pomerania, with one company from Livonia)
Joachim Engell's Cavalry Regiment (enlisted)
Jacob Johan Taube's Cavalry Regiment (mostly enlisted in Finland)
Dragoons
Fabian Berndes's Finnish Dragoon Regiment
Infantry
Hälsinge Regiment, under Carl Larsson Sparre
Västgöta-Dal Regiment, under Carl von Scheiding
Västmanland Regiment, under Börje Nilsson Drakenberg
Västerbotten Regiment, under Diedrich von Cappel
Kalmar Regiment, under Alexander Irwing
Värmland Regiment, under Johan von Essen af Zellie
Ångermanland Regiment, under Thomas Gärffelt
Paul Würtz's Regiment (enlisted)
Fabian von Fersen's Regiment (enlisted)
Total: 6,000 cavalry, 400 dragoons, 4,500 infantry, 40 cannons
Polish Units
6,000 regular Komput cavalry
900 dragoons
3,000 to 4,000 Levy of the Nobility from the provinces of Łęczyca, Kuyavia, Sieradz and Masovia
4 to 6 cannons

Table 10 (see p.59). Order of battle at Wojnicz, 3 October 1655
Sources: Nowak, 'Carl X Gustafs Kraków-operation', pp.180–81; Wimmer, *Polens krig med Sverige*, p.346; Daniel Schorr, 'Battle of Wojnicz', Northern Wars website, which gives the order of battle.

Swedish Units, Under King Charles
Deployment, in one line from right to left

Life Guard of Horse, also known as Burchard Müller von der Lühne's Cavalry Regiment
Småland Cavalry Regiment, under Lieutenant Colonel Staffan von Klingspor
Arvid Wittenberg's Cavalry Regiment
Dismounted dragoons (Fabian Berndes's Finnish Dragoon Regiment) and musketeers, deployed slightly ahead of the line
Jacob von Yxkull's Cavalry Regiment
Count Palatine Philip von Sulzbach's Cavalry Regiment
Hans Böddeker's Cavalry Regiment
Christian von Pretlach's Cavalry Regiment
Deployment, in reserve on the right wing
Israel Isacsson Ridderhielm's Cavalry Regiment
Grand Total: 5,200 men (4,700 cavalry together with 4 companies of dragoons and 150 infantry, in total 500 dragoons and musketeers)
Polish Units, Under Crown Field Hetman Stanisław Lanckoroński
Right wing: Aleksander Koniecpolski
Approximately 30 banners of cossack-style cavalry
In total: 2,400 cossack-style cavalry
Centre, under Dymitri Wiśniowiecki
Hetman Stanisław Lanckoroński's Hussar Banner
Władysław Myszkowski's Hussar Banner
Adam Działyński's Hussar Banner
Approximately 10 banners of cossack-style cavalry
In total: 400 hussars and 600 cossack-style cavalry
Left wing, under Stanisław Lanckoroński
Approximately 30 banners of cossack-style cavalry
In total: 2,400 cossack-style cavalry
Extreme right, in a fortified camp: Heinrich Dönhoff
Colonel Heinrich Dönhoff's Dragoon Regiment
Hetman Stanisław Lanckoroński's Dragoon Banner
Aleksander Koniecpolski's Dragoon Banner
In total: 400 dismounted dragoons
Grand Total: 6,200 men

Swedish cavalry trooper. (Illustration by Sergey Shamenkov)

Polish hussar with fur cloak (Illustration by Sergey Shamenkov)

4

Tsar Alexis as Grand Duke of Lithuania

Meanwhile, much had happened in the Ukraine. In late March, Sheremetyev and Fyodor Buturlin were recalled to Moscow. Vasiliy Buturlin (d. 1656), who in the previous year had fought in the Tsar's Smolensk campaign, and Prince Grigoriy Romodanovskiy (d. 1682) replaced them at Belotserkov'. The plan was for them to join forces with Khmel'nitskiy for a summer offensive against Podolia. And this time, Tsar Alexis had an ace up his sleeve. Moscow had ordered a force of Don cossacks, Kalmyks, and units from the Belgorod Division in southern Muscovy to advance towards the Crimea itself, so as to prevent the Khan from dispatching another army out from Perekop. Although an outbreak of plague ultimately prevented the Kalmyks and the Belgorod Division units from participating in the operation (the plague meant that logistics grew yet more difficult, at times making operations almost impossible), the Don cossack fleet successfully raided several Crimean ports. Perhaps for this reason, or perhaps because of the oppressive heat and the accompanying drought, no Crimean army set out during the summer.

In July, Vasiliy and Andrey Buturlin accordingly carried out the planned joint offensive with Khmel'nitskiy towards western Ukraine. Potocki had a small Crown Army of some 6,000 troops and 300 noble cavalry nearby, but he withdrew, choosing instead to harass the Muscovites and cossacks from the rear. In late September, Prince Grigoriy Romodanovskiy had joined the offensive. Muscovites and cossacks then laid siege to the city of L'vov (which by this time was often known under its German name Lemberg). Then, in a well-prepared, surprise night attack at Gorodok (modern-day Horodok; Polish: Gródek Jagielloński), Romodanovskiy's combined Muscovite–cossack army (some 8,000 men) defeated Potocki's Crown Army (some 5,000 men).[1] The Polish camp was protected by dense forest and several small streams, but the Muscovites and cossacks (under Grigoriy Lesnitskiy, colonel of the Mirgorod regiment) built temporary bridges, on which they swiftly advanced towards the Polish camp. Potocki's army fought well at first,

---

1 Babulin, 'Vazhneyshiye pobedy Possii', p.389.

but then panicked and fled. Being cavalry, most units escaped. Nonetheless, this signified the neutralisation of the Crown Army in the Ukraine for the duration of the campaign season. As we have seen, the disappointed Potocki, no doubt feeling that all was lost, retreated towards the west, where he and the Crown Army in early November swore allegiance to Sweden.

Yet, L'vov, ably defended by Krzysztof Grodzicki (d. 1659), the Crown General of Artillery, refused to surrender. The Muscovites wished to continue north all the way to Brest, where they hoped to join forces with Aleksey Trubetskoy's Novgorod Army. Leaving a force outside L'vov, they continued the offensive, reaching Lublin in late October. While Lublin fell to Pyotr Potyomkin (1617–1700), the Muscovites lacked the strength to advance further.[2] We will see that Trubetskoy, too, failed to reach Brest.

While the Don cossacks had kept the Crimeans busy during the summer, they had now returned home. Learning that another Crimean army had crossed the Dnieper and was advancing into Bratslav province, Romodanovskiy and Khmel'nitskiy could not know whether the Crimeans were riding against them in an effort to relieve L'vov, or planned to raid the cossack core territories. They accordingly abandoned the siege of L'vov in return for the payment of a significant monetary contribution. Although Romodanovskiy and Khmel'nitskiy could not know it at the time, months later this allowed King John Casimir upon his return from exile in Silesia to reclaim at least one still-loyal Commonwealth city (the only other unconquered city was Gdańsk, which was semi-independent anyway), where he in 1656 could swear the L'vov Oath (more on which below).

What seems to have happened was that Mehmed Khan, perhaps concerned over the apparent sudden collapse of the Commonwealth, had brought a major army across the Dnieper and joined forces with other Crimean Tatar units, apparently already in place, under Nureddin Sultan Adil Geray. Following another of the customary Tatar trails, the combined Crimean army had already reached the vicinity of Zbarazh, which suggested that it was on its way to L'vov.

Catholic L'vov had been saved by the Crimean Tatars. The Muscovites and cossacks began to retreat. To move faster, and no doubt also for supply reasons, the Muscovite–cossack army separated into several contingents and the Khan saw the chance to pick off his enemies one at a time. First, he attacked Romodanovskiy's contingent, deployed in wagon fort near Zalozhitsy, but his men were repulsed. Two days later, Mehmed Khan attacked Vasiliy Buturlin's corps as it crossed the River Ozyornaya at the settlement of Ozyornoye. Buturlin managed to beat off the attack, crossed the river, and then joined up with Khmel'nitskiy's force – but at the ultimate cost of his own life (severely wounded in the battle, he died within weeks). Mehmed Khan also attempted an attack on Andrey Buturlin's wagon fort, but this assault failed, too.

On the following day, Mehmed Khan sent an envoy to Khmel'nitskiy, offering him and his men free departure if they first handed over the

---

2   In English, the name Pyotr Potyomkin is frequently spelled Peter Potemkin but this suggests an incorrect pronunciation.

Illustrissim, Reverendissim, Dominus Bonifacius Pac Episcopus Vilnensis.

Mikołaj Stefan Pac, after he abandoned the Muscovite cause and became bishop of Wilno in 1671.

Muscovites. Either because of loyalty to his oath or because he suspected a ruse, Khmel'nitskiy refused. Perhaps thinking to offer the cossacks a chance to reconsider, the Khan then attacked, but his men only moved against Vasiliy Buturlin's section of the common camp. Whatever his motive, the attack failed to penetrate the Muscovite defences. The Tatars simply lacked the skills and equipment to take fortified places, even improvised ones such as Buturlin's camp.

Two days later, on 23 November, Mehmed Khan agreed to an armistice in return for Khmel'nitskiy's promise that he would stop any Zaporozhian raids into the Crimea. It was a face-saving agreement. The Crimean Tatars then withdrew towards the south, where he had other business to take care of in the Budjak steppe beyond the Moldavian border.

Meanwhile, Tsar Alexis had proclaimed himself Grand Duke of Lithuania, based on his conquest of the capital Wilno. Lithuania was effectively divided between Swedish and Muscovite zones of interest, even though no formal agreement on the issue existed between Sweden and Muscovy. On 8 November Tsar Alexis ordered Prince Semyon Urusov (*c.* 1610–1657) to compile an Oath Book of those Lithuanian nobles who accepted the Tsar as Grand Duke of Lithuania; eventually, 2,058 nobles and clergymen swore allegiance to the Tsar.[3] Urusov, the commander of the Novgorod Army, was of Tatar origin but his family had converted to Christianity. Soon, Lithuanian nobles began to approach the Tsar to gain (or regain) estates in exchange for their loyalty. In December 1655, the voivode of Trakai, Mikołaj Stefan Pac (*c.* 1626–1684), sent an emissary to the Tsar to promote himself as the head of a pro-Muscovite government. He wanted the Tsar to award him the title Hetman of Lithuania, with the right to summon parliaments and impose levies on the nobility. He also wanted Muscovite army units to maintain order.[4] The Tsar was too cautious to elevate such an obvious fortune-seeker, but he needed to integrate the conquered territories into his other possessions. This resulted in other tensions, when the Lithuanian tradition of noble liberties collided with the more autocratic Muscovite type of government.

But before this, tensions had arisen among those Lithuanian nobles who had sworn allegiance to the Tsar. Rivalry immediately arose over landed properties. Some of those nobles who previously had sworn allegiance to Sweden now found their properties redistributed to those who had sworn allegiance to Muscovy. Beyond landed property, the rivalry soon developed into a struggle

---

3   Kotljarchuk, *In the Shadows*, p.201.
4   *Ibid.*, pp.205–6.

Right: Paweł Jan Sapieha. (Pierre Landry)
Below: Michał Kazimierz Radziwiłł
Below right: Bogusław Radziwiłł

between Catholics and Protestants. The conflict grew particularly violent in Podlachia (Polish: Podlasie), where Prince Bogusław Radziwiłł (1620–1669; Lithuanian: Boguslavas Radvila), a Lithuanian Protestant who had sworn allegiance to Sweden, owned large properties. The Podlachian nobility had voluntarily accepted Swedish protection, even before any Swedish units reached the territory. Yet, southern Podlachia contained a vocal Catholic population, under the only non-Protestant branch of the Radziwiłł family, which strongly opposed the pro-Swedish policies of the rest of the territory. Headed by Michał Kazimierz Radziwiłł (1625–1680), the Catholic faction swung into action. From February 1656 to the end of 1657, an internal Podlachian civil war raged between proponents and opponents of Swedish rule, in which loyalties to a high degree coincided with religious faith.[5]

Meanwhile, in September Aleksey Trubetskoy and the Bryansk army, soon supported by Zolotarenko's cossacks, laid siege to Slutsk, south of Minsk. Slutsk was defended by William Patterson, in command of Prince Bogusław Radziwiłł's German infantry regiment. Moreover, by this time the Lithuanian Estates had already surrendered to Sweden in exchange for Swedish protection.[6] While Slutsk was far from the Swedish armies which by then had entered the Commonwealth and no material support could be expected, Trubetskoy cannot have failed to note that his actions easily might draw Muscovy into yet another war, this time with Sweden. The siege of Slutsk lasted almost a month, but in early October Trubetskoy and Zolotarenko abandoned the venture, returning towards Mogilyov. Slutsk remained unconquered until the end of the wars of the Deluge, one of only a few towns which could claim this dignity.

Zolotarenko had arrived in support of the Muscovites but he behaved as a conqueror, assuming that the Ruthenian parts of Lithuania henceforth would become part of the Cossack Hetmanate. As a result, numerous conflicts flared up between unruly cossacks and Lithuanian Ruthenians (including those who had sworn allegiance to the Tsar), and between the very same cossacks and Muscovites who attempted to maintain order in the Tsar's new territories. In late November Zolotarenko fell during the siege of Staryy Bykhov. Bogdan Khmel'nitskiy accordingly made his son-in-law Ivan Nechay (fl. 1655–1669) acting cossack overall commander in the Belarusian part of Lithuania. However, the tensions between cossacks and Lithuanian Ruthenians did not diminish, and violence continued. Nechay attempted to establish a cossack Belarusian Host of 19 regiments, in imitation of the registered cossack regiments of the Ukraine. Numerous Ruthenian peasants abandoned the nobles or Catholic clergy to whose lands they were tied, to join the new cossack units, after which they and their new cossack friends returned to plunder the very same estates from which they had fled. Muscovy had no troops to prevent cossack mayhem, since almost all units were engaged at the front, so the Muscovite commandants asked Ruthenian nobles to form self-defence units to police the territory. In effect, a local civil

---

5   *Ibid.*, pp.215–17.
6   *Ibid.*, p.269.

war broke out between various Ruthenian groups, pitting groups of different geographical, societal, and sectarian origins against each other in rivalry for landed properties and political influence.[7]

In early November, 4,500 men of the Novgorod Army under Princes Semyon Urusov and Yuriy Baryatinskiy (c. 1610–1685) rode out of Kowno, moving south towards Brest in the hope of joining up with the Muscovite and cossack forces in the Ukraine which, they hoped, were on their way to Brest from the south. Their intention was to consolidate Muscovite rule in Lithuania, by taking control of territory and by securing written declarations of allegiance by Lithuanian nobles. Urusov and Baryatinskiy almost reached their objective. On 27 November, they decisively defeated the Lithuanian main army of 7,800 men under Paweł Jan Sapieha at Verkhovichi near Brest.[8] Commencing battle in their wagon fort, the Muscovites moved out to attack the Lithuanians, who then withdrew. However, finding themselves too few in numbers, the Muscovites then were unable to advance further. The two Muscovite campaigns, in Lithuania and in the Ukraine, never managed to link up. Besides, after the defeat at Verkhovichi, Sapieha instead accepted the Swedish offer of protection and swore allegiance to King Charles.[9]

7   Ibid., pp.200, 239–40.
8   Babulin, 'Vazhneyshiye pobedy Possii', p.389.
9   Kotljarchuk, In the Shadows, p.218.

5

King Charles and Royal Prussia

Although Poland and much of Lithuania had surrendered, Swedish units had not yet made any real gains in Prussia, even though a substantial Swedish fleet under Carl Gustav Wrangel in September appeared off Danzig to blockade the city. The effect was minimal, since trade was simply rerouted to Pillau and other ports. As noted, Swedish troops had landed on the Prussian coast on more than one occasion, but they had failed to reach any significant objective.[1] King Charles had ordered Major General Henrik Henriksson Horn (1618–1693) to bring a force of 3,000 horse (Horn's Tavastehus Cavalry Regiment as well as some units enlisted in Germany) from Pomerania to support Wrangel's operations along the shore, and in particular for the conquest of Putzig. However, the able Jacob von Weiher, Voivode of Marienburg, prevented Horn and Wrangel from joining forces through skilful operations with his German cavalry, dragoons, and units of the Levy of the Nobility of Royal Prussia.[2]

Even so, Frederick William, Elector of Brandenburg and Duke of Prussia, grew increasingly concerned over the Swedish successes in the Commonwealth. The reason was not due to any sympathy for King John Casimir but because Frederick William, too, had plans for increasing his territory at the Commonwealth's expense. He also worried that Sweden might gain an even more powerful position in the Baltic region than the one already acquired in the Peace of Westphalia. For this reason, he had gathered some 14,000 men in Prussia.[3]

On 12 November, that is, more or less at the same time when Poles and Lithuanians lined up to swear fealty either to King Charles or Tsar Alexis, Frederick William and the nobility of Royal Prussia signed the Treaty of Rheinsberg (Rinsk), in which the Commonwealth representatives requested Brandenburgian support in the form of garrisons in Royal Prussia to defend

---

1   Finn Askgaard, *Kampen om Östersjön på Carl X Gustafs tid: Ett bidrag till nordisk sjökrigshistoria* (Stockholm: Kungl. Militärhögskolan, *Carl X Gustaf-studier* 6, 1974), pp.30–33.

2   Wimmer, 'Polens krig med Sverige', p.406, n.61. Unable to support Wrangel, Horn instead joined forces with Stenbock at Nowy Dwór.

3   Jany, *Geschichte der Königlich Preußischen Armee bis zum Jahre 1807* (Berlin: Karl Siegismund, 4 vols, 1928–1933), vol. 1, p.120.

it against the Swedes. Their decision was not unanimous. While Marienburg, Dirschau, Strasburg, Braunsberg, Graudenz, Schlochau, and Lauenburg requested Brandenburgian garrisons, the more important and self-reliant Danzig, Elbing, and Thorn chose to stand outside the treaty and trust to their own resources.

For Royal Prussia, there was cause for concern. Hitherto, King Charles had been busy in Lesser Poland. Now he turned his attention to Sweden's primary objective, Prussia. In Lesser Poland, King Charles left garrisons in Cracow, under Würtz, and the strategically important town of Sandomierz, under Douglas who also had orders to continue incorporating Potocki's units in his army as they showed up to swear fealty. King Charles appointed Wittenberg governor of southern Poland, with a field army of some 3,000 Swedes and at least 2,000 Polish cavalry.[4] The Swedish units in the south were expected to monitor developments in the Ukraine and hold the line against (but not commence hostilities with) any Muscovites and cossacks who might advance from L'vov.

King Charles himself on 19 November set out from Warsaw towards Prussia, where he now intended to concentrate his forces to achieve the conquest of the Baltic shore which he desired. King Charles brought 5,000 Swedish horse as well as Koniecpolski's 5,000-strong Crown Army. He expected to unite his forces first with those of Stenbock (possibly 6,000 men at this time), and then with De la Gardie's Livonian army (some 8,900 men, more on which below).[5]

In late November, King Charles joined forces with Stenbock and Horn at Nowy Dwór, just north-west of Warsaw. With these additions, the King's army by then can be estimated to have consisted of 17,000 to 18,000 men – a significant force even for the well-defended Prussia to deal with.[6] King Charles continued to Strasburg (modern-day Brodnica) in Royal Prussia, which surrendered. The army then marched to Thorn, which surrendered in early December. The same happened at Elbing, which was the King's next target. By then, Frederick William realised that his remaining garrisons in Royal Prussia were on the verge of being cut off from Ducal Prussia.

As if these successes were not enough, King Charles in December received strong reinforcements. First, three recently enlisted cavalry regiments of a total of 1,500 men arrived from Swedish Pomerania under Major General Erik Stenbock (1612–1659).[7] Stenbock, a brother of Gustav Otto Stenbock, was another veteran of the Thirty Years' War who among other achievements had commanded the Life Guard at the battle of Lützen 1632. Moreover, in December De la Gardie's Livonian army (some 8,900 men), too, finally joined King Charles, having marched by way of Vileny on the River Neman, Filipów, Strasburg, and Saalfeld. Until the last moment, when he advanced to Saalfeld on his way to Elbing, De la Gardie had been careful to skirt the Ducal Prussian border, to avoid antagonising either Frederick William or the

---

4   Wimmer, 'Polens krig med Sverige', p.349.
5   *Ibid.*, p.406 n.61
6   Holm, *Översikt*, p.30. His estimate seems credible although not provable.
7   Wimmer, 'Polens krig med Sverige', p.406 n.61

Muscovites, who controlled most of this part of Lithuania. At Elbing, De la Garde united the Livonian army with that of the King.

Having assembled such a powerful force, King Charles turned his attention to Ducal Prussia's capital, Königsberg, to which Frederick William and the Brandenburgian army had retreated. During the march through Prussia, the Swedish army had repeatedly encountered Brandenburgian units. However, these had retreated without seeking to engage, since Frederick William was anxious not to confront the victorious Swedes. King Charles did not at this point worry overly over any hostility from Frederick William's side. Yet, so as not to lose track of events elsewhere in Prussia, he ordered Stenbock, with part of the army, to consolidate the Swedish hold over Royal Prussia (Stenbock subsequently took Mewe, Dirschau, Stargard, and finally Marienburg, after which Weiher and his men withdrew to Putzig). Meanwhile, in late December King Charles rode to Königsberg, where he established a base in Schippenbeil, south of Frederick William's capital. King Charles explained to Frederick William in no uncertain terms that they would have to come to an agreement. Frederick William immediately commenced negotiations. In January, this resulted in the Treaty of Königsberg, which will be described below.

By the end of 1655, King Charles had conquered much of Royal Prussia as well, in addition to Poland. The only exceptions were Danzig, Marienburg, and Putzig which still held out. In spring of 1656, Marienburg and Putzig surrendered, too. By then, only Danzig remained – but this city had no intention to surrender. The strongly fortified Danzig also had the means to defend itself and, moreover, had enlisted Colonel Valentin von Winter (1608–1671), a veteran of Swedish service, as commander of the Danzig Army. In siege warfare, Danzig was second to none.

6

The Anti-Swedish Uprisings

Despite King Charles's numerous victories and the multitudes who showed up to swear fealty, not all Poles and Lithuanians had surrendered and many of those who did had no intention of keeping their pledge. Among those few notables who actually refused to swear allegiance to King Charles was the powerful magnate Jerzy Sebastian Lubomirski. Instead, he advised King John Casimir to return to fight for his throne. We will see that Lubomirski regarded himself as something of a kingmaker, so perhaps his refusal to swear was more of a reflection on his own ambition. Another key leader who refused to swear allegiance was Stefan Czarniecki. While he could not compare to Lubomirski in wealth and power, he had the necessary experience from domestic and foreign wars to wield his units into an efficient fighting force. The number who swore but had no intention of keeping their pledge was far greater, and their names will show up at the time when switching sides began to look more advantageous than staying on course.

But before desertions got started, persons of lesser stature began to take action against the Swedes. In October 1655, insurgents began to harass the Swedish forces. While the first attacks, in Greater Poland, took place already in August, these were more a reaction against the demand to provide contributions than the signs of a committed anti-Swedish uprising. The Swedish commanders still punished soldiers severely, if they took advantage of civilians. However, over time resentment grew. Soon, disgruntled Polish nobles began to mobilise bands of irregulars. In early October, some 200 to 300 irregulars under a noble, Krzysztof Żegocki, surprised the small Swedish garrison at Kosten (modern-day Kościan), near Posen. In the engagement, they killed many Swedes and also inflicted a mortal wound on Major General Frederick Landgrave of Hesse-Eschwege (1617–1655), King Charles's brother-in-law. The irregulars won a rich booty, which enabled them to finance further operations. In retaliation, Major General Johann Weyckhardt von Wrzesowitz und Neuschloss (1623–1656), a Moravian in Swedish service, six days later burned Kosten. For both sides, the war had suddenly become much uglier.

Playing the religious card, in late November 1655 King John Casimir issued a manifesto at Oppeln (modern-day Opole), calling for all Commonwealth citizens to rise against the Swedes in preparation for his return. What the

King asked for was, in effect, a Catholic war of liberation against the heretics. In April 1656, at L'vov, John Casimir went so far as to proclaim the Virgin Mary as 'Queen of the Polish Crown and other of his countries' (the L'vov Oath). At the same time, he also promised that when he was restored to power, he would reduce the burdens of the peasantry, if they now only rose against the invaders. Furthermore, John Casimir assigned all blame for the present disasters to others:

> This has occurred not through our neglect or oversight but due to the behaviour of those of you who have pursued your own private interests, either by breaking whole parliaments [through the use of *liberum veto*, the right of every Commonwealth noble to veto all parliamentary decisions], or by delaying so long over defence, in order finally to satisfy your ambitions. With regard to taxes voted

A burning Polish village. (Erik Dahlbergh)

by the parliament, some have simply not paid; others, who have paid, have been most profligate. Thus, the army remains unpaid and mutinous, refusing to obey the hetmans.[1]

John Casimir conveniently forgot to mention his own claim to the Swedish throne as part of the chain of causes and effects. Yet, his words correctly explained the realities of Commonwealth political life. The beloved liberties of the nobles constituted an attractive dream and would have functioned in a utopia. However, they did not work in war-torn seventeenth-century Europe.

The irregulars who began to strike back against Swedish targets fundamentally consisted of two types. Some were nobles, often remnants of defeated units or those who had lost their estates or simply acquired a hatred for the invaders. They fought on horseback, much in the same manner as when they served in the army. Others were peasants who had suffered persecution and losses during the widespread looting which accompanied every army, including the Polish ones. They fought on foot, with improvised weapons and farming tools together with a sprinkling of captured firearms. Not only peasants joined such bands; many also consisted of townsmen and army deserters and some bands were led by nobles or members of the clergy. The latter encouraged feelings of and preached religious war against all who did not share their faith. Most bands were small, but at times they joined in groups several hundred strong. As in all guerrilla warfare, they relied on superior knowledge of the terrain and the element of surprise to ambush and defeat small enemy forces, supply convoys, and couriers. They generally took no prisoners, and they did not hesitate to slaughter non-combatants, including women and children.

Soon Poles fought against Poles. In early December Colonel Gabriel Wojniłłowicz led a revolt in the town of Krosno, which had previously sworn allegiance to King Charles. Wojniłłowicz and his men defeated the garrison left in place by the Swedes, which was a Polish unit, Aleksander Pracki's Regiment. In many ways, this can be said to symbolise the misfortunes of the country, in which the conflict soon led to breakdowns in local allegiances as well as public order.

On 16 December, little more than a month after swearing loyalty to King Charles, Crown Grand Hetman Potocki and Crown Field Hetman Lanckoroński renounced their oaths and began to advocate an uprising. Their motives may have been personal and opportunistic rather than a response to King John Casimir's call to arms from Oppeln. Senior officers in John Casimir's employ had repeatedly demanded that he appoint Czarniecki hetman in their stead, something which greatly would weaken Potocki's and Lanckoroński's personal standing vis-à-vis their peers, if the Polish King returned and was successful.[2] On 29 December, Potocki and Lanckoroński established the anti-Swedish Confederation of Tyszowce, in which much of the Crown Army

---

1   Based on Frost, *After the Deluge*, p.138; citing the royal proclamation at Oppeln, 20 November 1655.
2   Jerzy Teodorczyk, 'Czarnieckis vinterfälttåg januari–februari 1656: Slaget vid Gołąb', Arne Stade and Jan Wimmer (eds). *Polens krig med Sverige 1655–1660: Krigshistoriska studier* (Stockholm: Kungl. Militärhögskolan, *Carl X Gustaf-studier* 5, 1973), pp.213–54, on p.214.

A Polish peasant, in the popular 'peasant and Death' motif which was particularly appropriate for the wars of the Deluge. (Cracow, late seventeenth century)

returned its loyalty to John Casimir. This event can be said to have initiated organised resistance to Swedish rule within the Commonwealth.

Nineteenth-century historians and writers were quick to describe the Polish insurgents as motivated by patriotism and national sentiments of the type common in their own time. However, it would be anachronistic to claim that these sentiments were prevalent in seventeenth-century Europe, and we should be cautious in attributing modern-day sentiments such as patriotism to the uprisings. In the same manner as in Lithuania after the Muscovite conquest, rivalry soon arose over landed properties. Some of those nobles who had sworn allegiance to King Charles now found their properties redistributed to those who claimed loyalty to King John Casimir. Personal feuds flared up between old enemies, and former or new declarations of loyalty were valid pretexts for slaughter and the redistribution of wealth. Moreover, religious issues had divided the population for centuries, and many priests regardless of faith did their utmost to stir up faith-based conflicts, whether for reasons of personal conviction or the desire for gain.

In addition, the war led to a growing feeling of 'us versus them' in which 'them', as we will see, represented all who spoke foreign languages and professed other religious beliefs, regardless of whether they were Swedish or Muscovite invaders, local rivals, or even the Commonwealth's Imperial allies. So did, for instance, most Polish peasants describe King Charles's soldiers not as 'Swedes' (*szwedzi*) but as 'Germans' (*niemcy*; 'mutes'), the old Slavic term for anybody who spoke a foreign language. Others referred to all who wore foreign-style clothes as Lutherans (*luterski*), a term which made these unfortunates eligible targets for plundering and killing. Religious righteousness coupled with personal greed was, as always, a potent brew which attracted anybody who had a grudge to settle or wanted to gain a fortune, or at least some loot, at the expense of others. Protestant congregations were particularly hard-hit, particularly so after King John Casimir's L'vov Oath, and few of them survived the Deluge. Unsurprisingly, these sentiments rapidly led to a state of general lawlessness, which even King John Casimir found counterproductive. Indeed, quite a few Polish nobles loyal to him lost their estates and families to peasant irregulars who, unable to find more Lutherans and Jews to slaughter, instead turned on any weakly guarded noble residence. Moreover, the unrest was not limited to Poland. We will see that the same development took place throughout the war-ravaged territories, from the Ukraine in the south all the way through Poland, Lithuania, Livonia, Ingria, Kexholm County, Karelia, and to some extent even in the Finnish north.

The Siege of Jasna Góra

Most symbolic, and most misunderstood, of the uprisings was the siege of Jasna Góra, a Catholic monastery near Częstochowa in western Poland. From late November to mid December 1655, units of the Swedish army laid siege to Jasna Góra. The monastery was located on the border with Silesia and less than 100 km from Oppeln where the exiled King John Casimir was in the process of writing his call to arms. Although the monastery had limited strategic value, except as a border fortress, and the siege was abandoned before it was carried to conclusion, the siege of Jasna Góra because of its proximity to the exiled King became one of those events which rapidly caught the attention of propagandists and the public alike. The siege accordingly acquired a mythology of its own that eventually gave the defenders great fame as defenders of the Catholic faith. The siege thus had strategic consequences never foreseen by those who took part in the operation.[3]

The events began to unfold on 8 November, when a Swedish unit under Major General Johann Weyckhardt von Wrzesowitz und Neuschloss showed up at the gate to the monastery. The Swedish commander was the same who in the previous month had burned Kosten in retaliation for the death of Frederick of Hesse and his men at the hands of irregulars – but this potent source of symbolism became evident only after the events. Neither Swedes nor monks had reason to expect trouble. Like so many of his countrymen, the Prior of Jasna Góra, Augustyn Kordecki (1603–1673), had already surrendered and recognised the authority of King Charles. A letter by Kordecki to this effect remains in the Swedish National Archives, in which he refers to his submission of 28 October – before the Swedes arrived at his gate. In return, he received a written guarantee (*salva-guardia*) that the monastery would not be harmed.[4] The Major General was, no doubt, a rough character, some unpleasantness may have taken place (apparently somebody fired at the Swedes who responded by burning two barns outside the complex), and the Prior did not allow him entry. However, nothing of consequence happened.

However, when Lieutenant General Burchard Müller von der Lühne (1604–1670), the commander of another corps, 10 days later arrived with

---

3   A sober analysis can compare the propaganda value of the successful defence of Jasna Góra against the Swedes with the equally successful defence in 1660 of Lyakhovichi, located between Brest and Minsk and famous as the only fortress of the Grand Duchy of Lithuania that withstood the Muscovites. On both occasions, brave defenders fought overwhelming odds and prevailed. Yet, the fame of the mixed Catholic and Orthodox defenders of Lyakhovichi (an icon of the Virgin Mary was there, too) was local only and is today mostly forgotten, while virtually every Pole still knows of the Catholic defenders of Jasna Góra, which in addition to its traditional role as a pilgrimage centre has developed into a popular sightseeing spot. King John Casimir and his court needed a rallying point for his Catholic Polish supporters, not for those of other faiths or backgrounds.

4   Kordecki to Müller von der Lühne, 21 November 1655, Swedish National Archives (RA) reference code: SE/RA/720049. See also Janusz Sikorski, *Jasna Góra 1655* (Warsaw: Bellona, 1994), pp.19–20. When Kordecki published the letter after the war, he changed the words, omitting his submission to King Charles. Theodor Westrin, 'Om Czestochowa klosters beläring af Karl X Gustafs trupper 1655', *Historisk Tidskrift* 24 (1904), pp.301–20; Filip Mazurkiewicz, 'Artykuł Theodora Westrina o oblężeniu Jasnej Góry przez wojska Karola X Gustawa w 1655 roku, opublikowany w Szwecji w 1904 roku', *Pamiętnik Literacki* 2019: 2, pp.133–154.

The siege of Jasna Góra.

orders to garrison the fortified monastery, the Prior again refused to let them in. We can only speculate on Kordecki's reasons for his refusal, since no first-hand information exists. Perhaps he simply was afraid that the soldiers would misbehave. Burchard Müller von der Lühne had served in the Swedish army since 1623. He had fought under King Gustavus Adolphus in the war against the Commonwealth as well as in numerous battles in Germany, including those of Lützen and Nördlingen. After the battle of Wojnicz, he was promoted to Lieutenant General. With orders to garrison the fortified monastery, Lühne could not take no for an answer. He had some 1,700 men at his disposal (400 Swedish horse, 600 Polish horse, 400 additional cavalry and dragoons, and 300 Swedish foot) together with an artillery unit of eight 3- and 4-pounders.[5] Moving into positions below the fortified monastery, the siege of Jasna Góra began.

The greatest treasure of the monastery was an icon of the Virgin Mary named the Black Madonna. On 7 November, after his surrender but before the first Swedes showed up, Kordecki moved the icon out of the monastery for safekeeping; it ultimately was brought to King John Casimir's court in Oberglogau in Silesia. Yet, it was soon said that the Black Madonna helped the defenders against the invaders. It certainly also helped that the Polish kings of the Vasa dynasty earlier had fortified the monastery with modern defences, including artillery (16 to 20 cannons, including several 12-pounders) and a force of 160 professional soldiers to augment the 70 monks and 20 armed noblemen on the site.[6] In short, the defenders had more cannons than the

---

5   Sikorski, *Jasna Góra*, p.27; Hedberg, *Kungl. Artilleriet: Carl X Gustafs tid*, p.72.
6   Sikorski, *Jasna Góra*, p.13.

besiegers and also more powerful ones, with greater range. The effective range was enhanced further through the monastery's elevated position.

On 10 December, the Swedes finally brought in heavy siege artillery (two 24-pounders and four other cannons) under the well-known cartographer and artillery officer Fryderyk Getkant and additional infantry. The Swedish total thus grew into 1,800 German horse, 600 Polish horse, and 1,000 foot. Getkant had belonged to the garrison in Cracow when the city surrendered and like so many other Commonwealth officers swore loyalty to King Charles and accepted him as his suzerain. As a result, the Swedes finally had the means to reduce the monastery's walls, which soon suffered severe damage.[7]

Nonetheless, the monastery's location made the siege operation difficult. And, as we have seen, the monastery had limited strategic significance for the Swedes except as a means to protect against an incursion of Imperial troops from Silesia. By this particular time, such a threat seemed remote (and remained remote until April 1657). Finally, Field Marshal Arvid Wittenberg wrote to Müller von der Lühne, ordering him to abandon the siege if the monastery had not surrendered by 27 December. On this date, following orders, the Swedes abandoned the attempt to take Jasna Góra.[8] Two days later, as we have seen, the anti-Swedish Confederation of Tyszowce, a town much further to the east between Lublin and L'vov, was formed by Crown Grand Hetman Potocki and Crown Field Hetman Lanckoroński. As a result, much of the former Crown Army returned its loyalty to King John Casimir. It remains unclear to what extent the defence of Jasna Góra actually contributed to the formation of this Confederation. In the long term, the story of the siege certainly acquired the trappings of a rallying point, but possibly not soon enough to have an immediate impact. Be that as it may, there is no doubt that the story of the defenders of Jasna Góra over time developed into a potent symbol of Polish resistance and victory in the face of foreign invaders.

---

7   *Ibid.*, 38; Hedberg, *Kungl. Artilleriet: Carl X Gustafs tid*, p.72.
8   Sikorski, *Jasna Góra*, p.50.

7

The Treaty of Königsberg

On 17 January 1656, King Charles and Frederick William agreed to the Treaty of Königsberg. Frederick William renounced King John Casimir and instead recognised King Charles as his feudal suzerain in Ducal Prussia and Ermland (modern-day Warmia) which de facto became part of Ducal Prussia. Up to this point, Ermland had been a Polish bishopric which geographically intruded into Ducal Prussia. In return for the acquisition of Ermland, Frederick William agreed to support King Charles militarily, give Sweden half of his customs revenues from the Baltic Sea trade, and abstain from maintaining a fleet in the Baltic Sea without Swedish permission. With the Treaty of Königsberg, Frederick William joined the Swedish side in the war in an alliance which would last until September 1657.

As for the agreed upon military support, Frederick William promised to supply 500 horse and 1,000 foot to the Swedish army. This contingent seems to have consisted of Georg Friedrich von Canitz's Regiment of Horse and Christian Ludwig von Kalckstein's Regiment of Foot. Some uncertainty remains about both these regiments. Canitz's Regiment of Horse was raised in 1655 as a dragoon regiment of four companies. Presumably, Frederick William hastily upgraded the unit to cavalry status before he dispatched it to the Swedish field army. Kalckstein's regiment seems to have been the one raised in 1655 as a dragoon regiment of four companies and it acquired a fifth company only in the summer of 1656. If Frederick William honoured the agreement, additional companies must have been enlisted before the contingent joined the Swedish field army, but this is unknown. There was a known shortage of horses at the time, so Frederick William may have deprived Kalckstein's regiment of its horses, and then fielded the unit as infantry. The arrangement seems to have worked well for both parties. On 20 November 1656 Sweden and Brandenburg agreed to permanently transfer both units to Swedish service.

Having resolved the issue of allegiance with Frederick William, King Charles made other necessary arrangements for the government of Poland, Prussia, and parts of Lithuania. First, he appointed his brother Duke Adolph John (1629–1689) *Generalissimus* over the Swedish armies in the Commonwealth, making him the commander-in-chief in the King's absence.[1] Then at the same time, Charles appointed his Lord High Chancellor, Erik Oxenstierna, Governor-General of Prussia. Military command over the troops in Prussia was handed to the able Gustav Otto Stenbock. As for the Baltic provinces, the King appointed Magnus Gabriel De la Gardie Governor-General not only of Livonia but also of Samogitia and the parts of Lithuania which swore allegiance to Sweden.

De la Gardie then returned to Riga. He departed from Prussia on 30 January 1656, and with him returned part of the Livonian army (30 companies of cavalry, four companies of dragoons, and 12 companies of infantry). De la Gardie's own enlisted cavalry and infantry regiments returned with him.[2] However, more than half of the Livonian army remained in Poland. These units consisted of two cavalry regiments (16 companies), one regiment and one squadron of dragoons (four companies), and five infantry regiments (30 companies), in total approximately 1,685 cavalry, 1,030 dragoons, and 2,655 infantry.[3] The regiments which remained in Poland were the Åbo Cavalry Regiment, Tavastehus Cavalry Regiment, Björneborg Regiment, Tavastehus Regiment, Elfsborg Regiment, Savolax Regiment, and Österbotten Regiment. There is some uncertainty with regard to the Karelian Dragoon Regiment, because some of its companies had already arrived in Poland with the invasion force from Pomerania. It is evident from the figures that most units were significantly understrength, and some had never reached establishment strength. Even so, it is telling that only national regiments stayed to serve in the Polish campaign. The enlisted units, which consisted of recent recruits, all returned to Livonia, which remained at peace. During the Thirty Years' War, policy dictated that enlisted regiments were put in harm's way first, so that national regiments did not suffer unnecessary casualties. This time, it is obvious that the plan was to retain experienced and properly trained units in the Commonwealth, and this meant the national regiments.

Duke Adolph John, here portrayed in the dress of a Roman officer which he wore during a carousel. (David Klöcker Ehrenstrahl)

Counterinsurgency

Opposition to King Charles was strongest in the western parts of Poland, close to the Empire, where many nobles, following the example of King John Casimir,

1   Ulrich Lange, *Karl X Gustavs bror Adolf Johan: Stormaktstidens enfant terrible* (Stockholm: Medström, 2019), pp.126, 279 n.115.

2   Fagerlund, 'Kriget i östersjöprovinserna', pp.39–40, 241.

3   Tersmeden, 'Carl X Gustafs armé 1654–1657', p.198.

Rutger von Ascheberg, based on a later portrait. No portrait of Ascheberg seems to exist from his younger days. Although some officers had begun to adopt the allonge wig at the time of the Deluge, most field officers had not, instead allowing their hair to grow long, flowing down the shoulders.

had taken refuge. Some of them remained in safety across the border but sent men to carry out raids against the Swedes in Poland. Not so Stefan Czarniecki. He now moved into the Sandomierz province with some 300 hussars, 1,900 cossack-style cavalry, and 300 freshly enlisted dragoons, in total 2,500 men, all mounted.[4] Czarniecki had received a royal order from John Casimir with which Stanisław Witowski (d. 1669), the Castellan of Sandomierz, would raise the nobility in the province. Not all were willing, but there was a strong element of coercion in the uprising. According to the call to arms issued by Witowski, every nobleman had to sign his agreement with the anti-Swedish Confederation of Tyszowce, or forfeit all property. There was even a deadline, 14 February, to persuade the faint-hearted. After signing, the noble had to show up, fully armed, at the district parliament (*sejmik*).[5] The order shocked some nobles. King Charles was not remiss in issuing letters of protection to those who surrendered. Now, however, a noble risked forfeiting his estates not to the heretic Swedes, but to his own neighbours, unless he signed up with Witowski. And, as we have seen, this was not an idle threat. Terrorised, many complied.

Neither the noble cavalry nor the peasant irregulars were really equipped to take fortified strongholds. The insurgents lacked artillery, and, in most cases, trained infantry. On the other hand, they were well positioned to wage guerrilla warfare, cut supply lines, snatch couriers, and the like. The Swedish commander in the Sandomierz region, Robert Douglas, was unable to catch the fast-moving insurgents. The Swedes accordingly attempted to fight them through a system of active defences. Important strongholds and communications points were garrisoned, and the garrisons had orders to assist one another. Through this system, the Swedes retained overall control, although convoys and couriers remained at risk. Moreover, the system necessarily resulted in a smaller field army, since units had to be retained in garrisons.

Following the successful conclusion of the Treaty of Königsberg, King Charles again marched south. He hoped to crush the Polish resistance before it grew too strong. He also planned to take the fortress Zamość, located between Lublin and L'vov, which he believed to be the location of King John Casimir (in reality, John Casimir had not yet reached L'vov) and which Charles intended to use as a base for operations in southern Poland. He sent three regiments, including Rutger von Ascheberg's Cavalry Regiment, ahead to reinforce

---

4   Teodorczyk, 'Czarnieckis vinterfälttåg', pp.220–21.
5   *Ibid.*, pp.223, 228.

Polish officer and member of the gentry, with a war hammer, long enough to be utilised as a walking stick, to signify his status. He also carries a short whip of the Mongol style, a sabre, and suspended from the belt a wheellock spanner for his pistols. (Illustration by Sergey Shamenkov)

Douglas's operations in the Sandomierz region. By the end of January, Douglas accordingly commanded a corps with an estimated strength of some 2,500 horse in what essentially had become a counterinsurgency campaign.[6]

Rutger von Ascheberg (1621–1693), a veteran from Courland who had risen from the ranks in Swedish service during the Thirty Years' War which he had entered as a common cavalryman, was more suitable for this kind of fluid warfare than the more rigid Douglas. In mid February, Ascheberg led a small Swedish contingent (some 250 men) to gain control of Radom. The Swedes camped at the manor Zakrzów. In the morning, the manor house was attacked by a significantly stronger Polish force (reportedly some 1,500 men, although in part consisting of levies with improvised weapons) under Stanisław Witowski. Ascheberg and his men repulsed repeated Polish attacks until Witowski in the evening managed to set the manor house on fire. Ascheberg and his men fought their way out through the attackers, and then moved on under the cover of darkness. The Poles were unable to stop or follow them. On the following day, Ascheberg occupied Radom Castle, the objective of his foray. However, Witowski's men had managed to capture a few Swedes during the breakout. Both sides regarded the engagement as a victory.[7]

Despite Ascheberg's support, Douglas failed to take resolute action and go on the offensive against the insurgents. Perhaps tricked by the numerous rumours of the uprising spread by Czarniecki, he failed to strike directly at Sandomierz or any other of the strongpoints controlled by Czarniecki and Witowski. Although Douglas's corps was smaller in manpower when compared to the number of men at the disposal of Czarniecki and Witowski, the Swedes were more disciplined and would probably have been able to put down the uprising, had Douglas acted more decisively – and more ruthlessly. Douglas was a steady commander, but the small war was not his forte. The Swedes still attempted to win the hearts and minds of the Polish population, but this was a battle which they were rapidly losing.

---

6   *Ibid.*, p.216.
7   *Ibid.*, pp.232–3.

8

The Battle of Gołąb

In early February, King Charles moved south with an all-cavalry army and joined Douglas at Łowicz. As noted, Charles planned to take the fortress of Zamość, located between Lublin and L'vov. On the way, however, he received news that Czarniecki was nearby with his cavalry army. Charles accordingly set out in pursuit of Czarniecki, whose forces the Swedes surprised at the village Gołąb (known to the Swedes as Golomb).

King Charles's total strength then has been estimated as 8,000 horse. In addition, the King controlled some 3,000 Polish, Lithuanian, Tatar, and Ruthenian cavalry in Swedish service, which would produce a total of approximately 11,000 cavalry.[1] However, the unit strength figures for the Swedish units are based on figures from several months previous to this time, which means that attrition must be added to the calculation. The total strength of these units may accordingly have been approximately 6,000, which produces a grand total of 9,000 cavalry. Even with this uncertainty added to the calculation, the Swedish army was certainly stronger than Czarniecki's army, which as noted consisted of little more than some 2,500 men (Table 11).

On 18 February the Swedish army crossed the frozen Vistula, after which they surprised and rapidly defeated a Commonwealth unit (one of the Szemberk banners) stationed nearby. The Swedish vanguard, under Major General Henrik Horn, pushed on, soon reaching Gołąb itself. There a battle developed, which essentially was a meeting engagement with Swedish troops arriving on the battlefield at different times. Most never engaged the enemy.

The first Swedish unit which reached Gołąb, at around 3:30 p.m., was Count Waldemar Christian of Schleswig-Holstein's Cavalry Regiment. They lined up against the Polish line of battle, under Sebastian Machowski. Neither side charged. Then yet more Swedes arrived, including some dragoons with regimental cannons. Since no dragoon unit has been identified as taking part in the battle, these were probably dragoon companies attached to the cavalry regiments. When the dragoons and regimental cannons opened fire, the Commonwealth units wavered and retreated, in the by now all-too-familiar pattern. However, this time Czarniecki intervened. He rallied the retreating

---

1   *Ibid.*, pp.230–31.

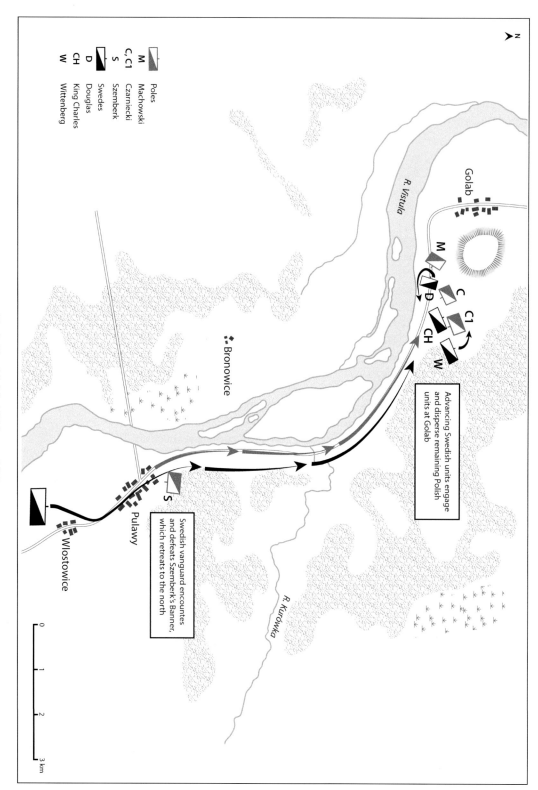

The Battle of Gołąb, 18 February 1656

	Poles
M	Machowski
C, C1	Czarniecki
S	Szemberk
D	Douglas
CH	King Charles
W	Wittenberg

Swedes

Golab

R. Vistula

M

C

C1

D

CH

W

Bronowice

Advancing Swedish units engage and disperse remaining Polish units at Gołąb

S

Pulawy

Wlostowice

Swedish vanguard encounters and defeats Szemberk's Banner, which retreats to the north

R. Kurówka

N

0 1 2 3 km

Poles, and then ordered a counter-attack, however, by then the Swedish main force had reached Gołąb and formed up in a line of battle. Additional Polish units arrived to form up, too. The result was a hard-fought encounter in which new units joined as they arrived. Meanwhile, Henrik Horn with the Tavastehus Cavalry Regiment flanked Gołąb from the north. From this vantage point, Horn advanced to block the Polish escape route to the north. Realising the danger, Czarniecki ordered a general retreat while the escape route still remained open. It was more a rout than a retreat, since Czarniecki's men were hotly pursued by Jan Sapieha's Lithuanians, several Tatar units in Swedish service, Niemirycz's men, who may have been Ruthenians, and some of the Swedish cavalry. Some 60 Poles drowned when, fleeing to the north, they crossed the River Wieprz and the ice cover broke. The battle was over at nightfall.[2]

However, battle casualties were fairly small, an estimated 150 Swedes and 100 to 200 Poles.[3] A more specific calculation has suggested that the total Polish losses were 130 dead enlisted soldiers and 17 nobles.[4] On the Swedish side, Count Waldemar Christian of Schleswig-Holstein was mortally wounded, and he died soon after the battle. The Count was a son of King Christian IV of Denmark and pretender to the Danish throne. Another notable casualty was Duke Adolph John; by a stroke of ill luck before the battle commenced, the Duke accidentally collided with a fellow cavalryman, badly injuring his right kneecap. The wound never healed properly, and he suffered with it for the rest of his life.

After the victory, King Charles continued the advance in the direction of Lublin, and beyond this town, L'vov. Czarniecki rushed on ahead of the Swedes, arriving in L'vov in early March. With the men brought by Czarniecki, King John Casimir now commanded an army of 6,000 men, divided into 75 banners, which he mustered outside L'vov. The King may have been pleased with the turnout, but the burghers of L'vov were terrified. Czarniecki's soldiers had a particularly bad reputation for taking contributions and plunder, and Czarniecki's own behaviour at his departure from Cracow was not forgotten. With the King's permission, the burghers refused to let the soldiers enter the city. This greatly annoyed Czarniecki's men, who responded by storming the city gate. The commotion developed into a full-scale mutiny, with the men refusing to follow orders. Soon, even John Casimir found himself at risk from the angry soldiers. Although Czarniecki ultimately managed to rein in his men and quell the mutiny, the burghers remained ill at ease. As a result, Czarniecki had to set up camp outside the city walls.[5]

This did not mean that John Casimir lacked supporters. At around this time, Prince Aleksander Koniecpolski and his men in northern Masovia deserted from Swedish service. By then, Koniecpolski had already sent letters to John Casimir on two occasions, asking for a pardon in return for an offer to change sides again. Koniecpolski then rode south to join John Casimir at L'vov.

---

2   *Ibid.*, pp.242–4, 246.
3   Radosław Sikora, *Fenomen Husarii* (Toruń: MADO, 2005), p.26.
4   Teodorczyk, 'Czarnieckis vinterfälttåg', p.246.
5   *Ibid.*, 247.

This did not deter King Charles. However, within days bad news followed when he reached Zamość in late February. He had been informed that the commandant, Jan Zamoyski, was ready to surrender. However, either Zamoyski never had such intentions or he had changed his mind, and his Hussar Banner had already joined Czarniecki's army. To retain mobility, the Swedes had not brought any siege artillery. Despite their engineering skills there was little they could do against Zamoyski's castle without it, and King Charles soon had to abandon the siege. A few days later he wrote that 'if I now had had a mortar with me, then next to God's help Zamość would have been mine.'[6]

Moreover, Polish irregulars in conjunction with cold and famine caused by a lack of supplies took its toll. King Charles continued south to Jarosław, which he reached in early March. His army then consisted of around 5,000 Swedish and 3,000 Commonwealth soldiers. Jarosław became the southernmost point which the Swedish army reached during the campaign. Charles hoped that Jarosław could become a strongpoint from which he could negotiate an agreement with the Ukrainian cossacks. Further to the west, Paul Würtz still held Cracow, constituting a second Swedish stronghold in the south. If the King's plan had worked out, Warsaw would have been the third. From these three strongholds, he would have been able to control Poland all the way to the Ukraine.

Tables

Table 11 (see p.95). Order of Battle at Gołąb, 18 February 1656

Sources: Teodorczyk, 'Czarnieckis vinterfälttåg', pp.230–31; Daniel A. Schorr with Radosław Sikora, 'Battle of Golombi/Golab', *Northern Wars* website, 2008.

Swedish Army	
Swedish Regiments	
Västgöta Cavalry Regiment, under Lars Cruus	
Åbo Cavalry Regiment, under Gustav Kurck	
Småland Cavalry Regiment, formally under Erik Oxenstierna but led by Lieutenant Colonel Staffan von Klingspor	
Tavastehus Cavalry Regiment, under Henrik Henriksson Horn	
Östgöta Cavalry Regiment, under Ludwig Wierich Lewenhaupt	
Arvid Wittenberg's Cavalry Regiment (enlisted in Pomerania)	
David Sinclair's Cavalry Regiment (mostly enlisted in Sweden)	
Count Waldemar Christian of Schleswig-Holstein's Cavalry Regiment (enlisted)	
Jacob von Yxkull's Cavalry Regiment (enlisted from Swedes and Germans in Bremen and Pomerania, with one company from Livonia)	

---

6   King Charles to Gustav Otto Stenbock, 29 February 1656 (O.S.); cited in Hedberg, *Kungl. Artilleriet: Carl X Gustafs tid*, p.80.

Rutger von Ascheberg's Cavalry Regiment (enlisted in Germany)	
Hans Heinrich Engell's Cavalry Regiment (enlisted)	
Note that since the battle essentially was a meeting engagement with Swedish troops arriving on the battlefield at different times, we do not know which units actually participated in the battle.	
Commonwealth Troops in Swedish Service	
Cossack-style cavalry	
Jan Fryderyk Sapieha's Banner, under Muchowiecki	118 horses
Michał Zbrożek's Banner	100 horses
Wojciech Gołyński's Banner	72 horses
Roman Zakharovskiy's Chernigov Banner	70 horses
Jerzy Wielhorski's Banner	93 horses
Mikołaj Dzieduszycki's Ruthenian Banner	90 horses
Seweryn Kaliński's Banner	150 horses
Andrzej Kuklinowski's Banner	100 horses
Jan Fryderyk Sapieha's Second Banner, under Samuel Łojowski	113 horses
Tatar Cavalry	
Mustafa Sudicz's Banner	109 horses
Halembek Morawski's Banner	118 horses
Jan Sielecki's Banner	120 horses
Adam Taraszewski's Banner	120 horses
Bohdan Murza's Banner	135 horses
Mikołaj Pohojski's Banner, under Stefan Morzkowski	100 horses
Adam Talkowski's Banner	120 horses
Jan Grzebułtowski's Wallachian Banner	51 horses
Other Commonwealth Units then with King Charles's Army	
Jan Sapieha (Castellan of Slonim)'s Regiment	
Seweryn Kaliński's Regiment, with a total of 6 banners	
Michał Zbrożek's Regiment, with a total of 6 banners	
Michał (Mikhail) Aksak's Regiment	
Jerzy Niemirycz (Yuriy Nemirich)'s Regiment	
Note that while these units belonged to the Swedish army, we do not know which of them actually participated in the battle.	

Polish Army	
The army was divided in two regiments:	
The Royal Regiment, under Stefan Czarniecki	
The Hetman's Regiment, under Sebastian Machowski	
Hussar Cavalry	
Władysław Myszkowski's Banner	220
Jan Zamoyski's Banner	150
Cossack-Style Cavalry	
A. Potocki (Castellan of Galich)'s Banner	143
Karol Potocki's Banner	93
Stanislaw Widlica Domaszewski's Banner	106
Sebastian Machowski's Banner	112
Mikołaj Potocki's Banner	150*
Samuel Rogowski's Banner	125*
Stanisław Witowski's Banner	150*
Prince Konstanty Wiśniowiecki's Banner	150
Jan Myśliszewski's Banner	90
Jacek Szemberk (Castellan of Boguslav)'s Banner	150
Michał Stanisławski's Banner	92
Samuel Hołub's Banner	70
Michał Morzkowski's Banner	78
Konstanty Soszeński's Banner	99*
Alexander Cetner's Banner	150*
Jan Karol Potocki's Banner	115
Jacek Szemberk's Wallachian Banner	99
Czarniecki's Dragoons (newly recruited)	300
Total	2,642
Units marked with * did not take part in the battle, since they were escorting recruits.	

9

The Siege of Sandomierz and the Crossing of the River San

However, even Jarosław was not safe. Within a week, Czarniecki successfully raided several Swedish outposts at Jarosław. With growing resistance and an increasing desertion rate among his Polish soldiers, King Charles realised that he had to abandon southern Poland. Soon after Czarniecki's raid, Charles marched north with the field army towards Sandomierz, following the west bank of River San. He sent Major Christer Carlsson (ennobled Lillienberg 1664; d. 1680) ahead by boat to Sandomierz, where Carlsson's engineers began to build a bridge ahead of the field army's arrival. While the artillery was transported by barge on the river, the rest of the army followed by road. The arrival of spring made many roads impassable, especially for wagons, so Charles ordered his men to burn part of the baggage train. Among many difficult marches in the Commonwealth, the passage from Jarosław towards Sandomierz was particularly unpleasant. The roads were so narrow and muddy, that among the Swedish soldiers, the march long lived in memory as the 'goose march' (Swedish: *gåsmarsch*; German: *Gänsemarsch*), because they had to march in one file only, one man after the other, and often they had to wade through shallow water and mud.

Meanwhile, Czarniecki continued to harass the marching army. On 28 March, he attempted to raid the Swedish camp at Nisko, but the venture backfired due to poor co-ordination among the Polish commanders. Repulsed, Czarniecki's men suffered significant losses. Yet, desertions continued. On the day after the failed raid, Jan Fryderyk Sapieha and most of the Commonwealth soldiers (3,000 to 4,000), who had operated as a vanguard forward of the line of march, nonetheless deserted the Swedish King.

In late March, King Charles reached the confluence of Rivers Vistula and San at Gorzyce near Sandomierz, which he knew was held by a Swedish garrison of some 100 men under Hans Cronlood (either a major or a lieutenant colonel with the Uppland Regiment). Sandomierz also functioned as a depot for gunpowder, which the field army badly needed. Finally, it was also the location where he intended to cross the Vistula. However, the King now found himself blocked on all sides except the rear by Commonwealth armies. Jerzy Sebastian Lubomirski operated north of the Vistula with a

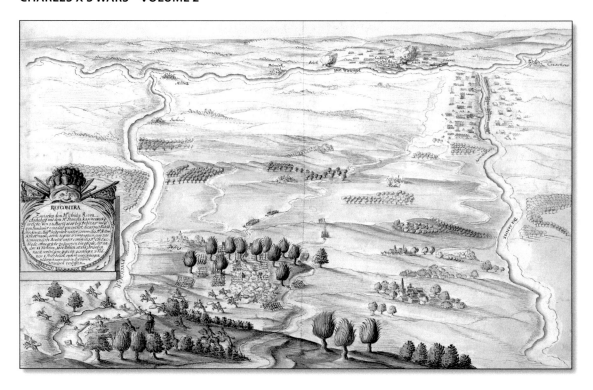

Engagement between Swedish and Polish units near the confluence of Rivers Vistula and San, 2 April 1656, depicting the strategic situation. Top: Sandomierz. Left and top: River Vistula. Right: River San. Upper right: The Swedish army has commenced an artillery barrage against the Lithuanian defences on the opposite side of the San. (Rutger von Ascheberg)

strong army, with which he intended to take Sandomierz (he had already prevented Carlsson's party from bridging the river). Czarniecki had shadowed King Charles somewhere further to the west, and he now planned to lead his army across the Vistula to join forces with Lubomirski. And to the east, on the other side of the River San, stood Grand Hetman Paweł Jan Sapieha with a Lithuanian Army. Sapieha had sworn allegiance to Charles on 5 December 1655.[1] Since then, he had changed his mind. Together, the Commonwealth armies totalled more than 20,000 men, even without counting the Levy of the Nobility, which apparently accounted for another 3,000 men, and large numbers of peasant irregulars. Lubomirski and Czarniecki commanded 12,500 Crown cavalry and almost 1,000 dragoons, while Sapieha and Aleksander Hilary Połubiński (1626–1679) led some 7,500 Lithuanians.[2] As noted, Charles's army consisted of some 5,000 men. The Commonwealth forces outnumbered him by more than four to one. Charles could have turned back, but there no more supplies remained. Instead, he relied on the one advantage that he enjoyed: Commonwealth command was divided and their forces were separated by the same rivers which hemmed in the Swedes.

As noted, Charles had planned to cross at Sandomierz, which was held by a small Swedish garrison. However, before the Swedes arrived, Lubomirski laid siege to Sandomierz. The situation was precarious. Charles accordingly ordered Lieutenant Colonel Mårten Törnskiöld and 100 musketeers to cross

1   Paweł Jan Sapieha to Magnus De la Gardie, 5 December 1655. Swedish National Archives (RA), De la Gardieska samlingen, Skrivelser till Magnus Gabriel De la Gardie, Ser. C:1. E 1543. Cited in Kotljarchuk, *In the Shadows*, p.24.
2   Wimmer, 'Armé och finansväsen', p.74; Wimmer, 'Polens krig med Sverige', p.358.

Tres Scaphæ militibus repletæ, quæ flumine adverso ad littus II tendunt, præsidiariosq; ex arce reducũt incolumes.

King Charles and his senior commanders when Törnskiöld sets out in three boats to Sandomierz, 2 April 1656. The commanders are: 1. King Charles; 2. Margrave Charles Magnus of Baden-Durlach; 3. Count Palatine Philip von Sulzbach; 4. Arvid Wittenberg; 5. Duke Charles of Mecklenburg-Schwerin; 6. Claes Tott; 7. Jacob Casimir De la Gardie; 8. Robert Douglas; 9. Henrik Horn. (Pufendorf, based on Erik Dahlbergh)

the river by boat to retrieve the supplies, then row them back to the field army.[3] Regarded by most as a suicide mission, Törnskiöld and his men set out. Under fire from Lubomirski's men, but with covering fire provided by the Swedish field army from the other side of the Vistula, Törnskiöld successfully rowed across the Vistula, retrieved the garrison and most of the supplies, and then returned across the river. Meanwhile, the commandant Cronlood, his artillery lieutenant Gabriel Anastasius, and a few men primed the remaining gunpowder supplies and grenades for delayed explosion, after which they abandoned the fortress. When the Poles entered, the fortress blew up, killing a large number of them. Cronlood and most of his men successfully escaped across the Vistula (but not Anastasius who, wounded, was captured by the Poles). In revenge for the destruction of the fortress, the Poles massacred the town's Jews.

Polish units now controlled the northern bank of the Vistula. King Charles, who had watched the entire operation from his side of the river, accordingly decided to turn to the north-east across the San, which was held by Sapieha's Lithuanians. The Swedish army had skilled engineers and pre-prepared bridging materials. On the day after the operation at Sandomierz, they began to build a bridge over the San. To hide the construction work, Charles ordered the entire army to form up on the river bank right opposite the main Lithuanian defensive line. As if this was not enough to keep Sapieha alert, he also ordered his artillery to begin pounding the Lithuanians. The effect was minor, since the Lithuanians had prepared defences, but the plan was merely to keep their heads down, not destroy them. To cause further uncertainty about his intentions, Charles sent out cavalry patrols (one

---

3   Johan Levin Carlbom, *Tre dagars slaget vid Warschau den 18, 19 och 20 juli 1656: Samt de föregående mindre fältslagen 1655 och 1656 – Ett tvåhundrafemtioårigt minne* (Stockholm: Varia, 1906), p.31.

Swedish soldiers when Sandomierz Castle explodes, 2 April 1656. (Erik Dahlbergh)

King Charles and his senior commanders when Törnskiöld sets out in three boats to
Sandomierz, 2 April 1656. (Erik Dahlbergh)

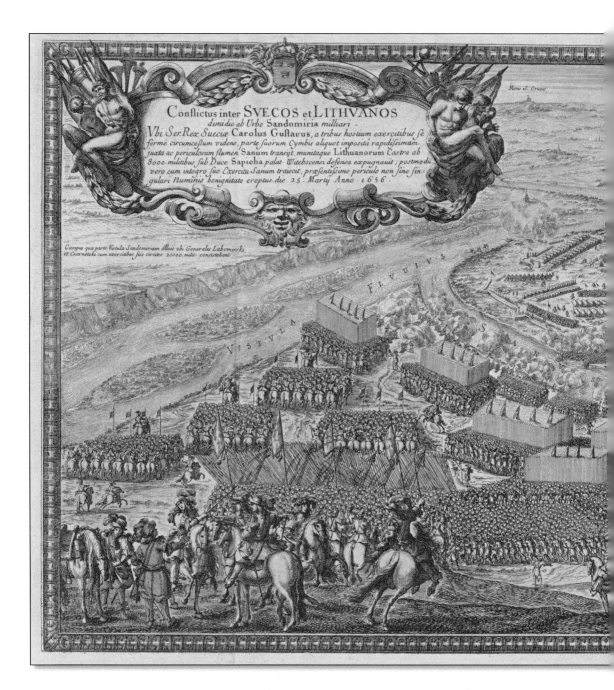

The Crossing of the San, 3–4 April 1656. (Erik Dahlbergh)

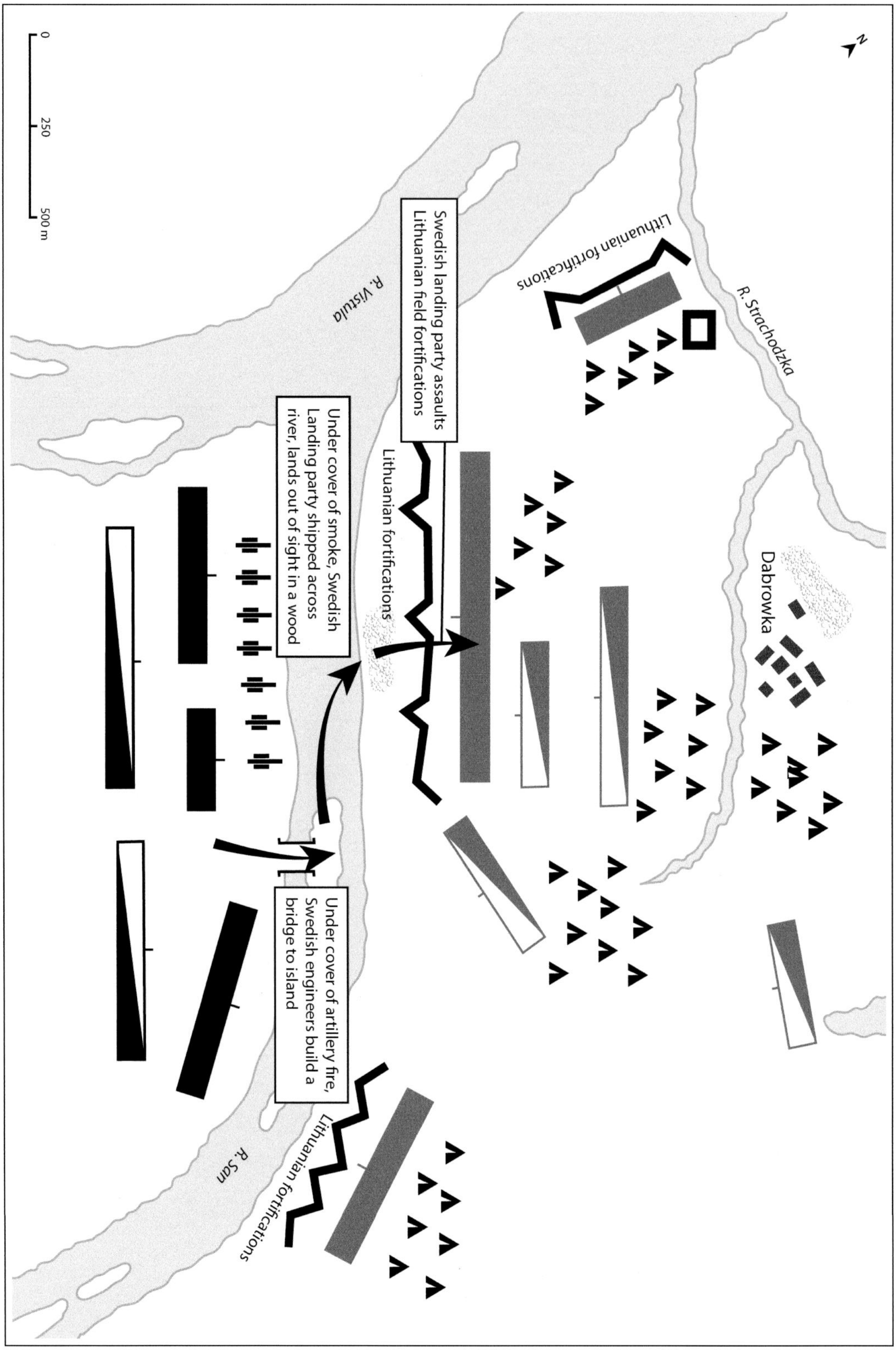
0
250
500 m
N
R. Vistula
Swedish landing party assaults
Lithuanian field fortifications
Lithuanian fortifications
R. Strachodzka
Dabrowka
Lithuanian fortifications
Under cover of smoke, Swedish
Landing party shipped across
river, lands out of sight in a wood
Under cover of artillery fire,
Swedish engineers build a
bridge to island
Lithuanian fortifications
R. San

Above (2 maps): The Crossing of the San, 3–4 April 1656

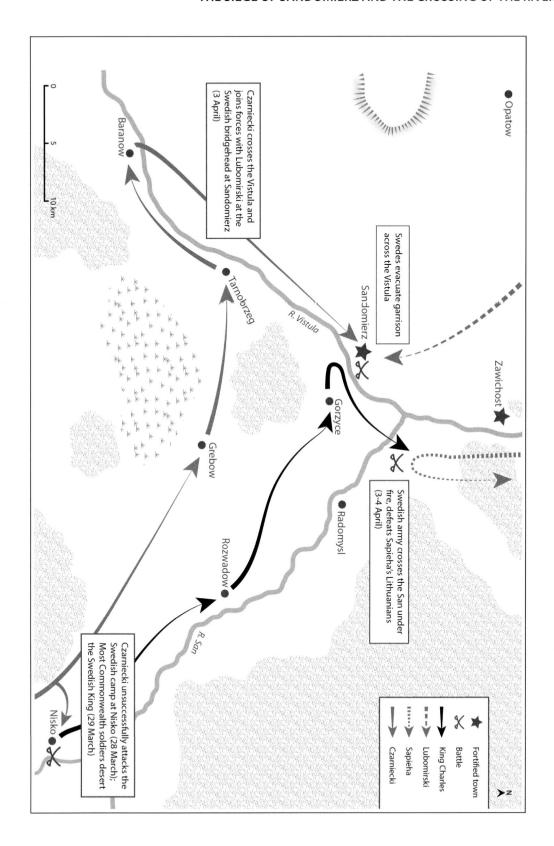

Czarniecki crosses the Vistula and joins forces with Lubomirski at the Swedish bridgehead at Sandomierz (3 April)

Swedes evacuate garrison across the Vistula

Swedish army crosses the San under fire, defeats Sapieha's Lithuanians (3-4 April)

Czarniecki unsuccessfully attacks the Swedish camp at Nisko (28 March); Most Commonwealth soldiers desert the Swedish King (29 March)

Opatow

Baranow

Tarnobrzeg

R. Vistula

Sandomierz

Zawichost

Grebow

Gorzyce

Radomysl

Rozwadow

R. San

Nisko

0
5
10km

N

Fortified town
Battle
King Charles
Lubomirski
Sapieha
Czarniecki

of which he commanded himself) to other crossing sites nearby. Meanwhile, his engineers built a bridge to a small island in the middle of the River San. Charles selected an assault force of 300 men under Colonels Gustav Cruus (1621–1665), of the Kalmar Regiment, and Diedrich von Cappel (d. 1656), of the Västerbotten Regiment.[4] During the night, the assault force crossed the bridge to the island under the cover of an artillery barrage. Unsurprisingly, Charles followed them across the bridge (a cannonball hit so close to the King that he was covered in dust and mud). The assault force (but not the King) then embarked into three barges with which they successfully crossed the remaining part of the river concealed by the darkness. They hid in a grove on the river bank.[5] In the early morning light, Cruus and Cappel emerged from their cover to attack the Lithuanian units which defended the river. The audacity of the attack panicked the Lithuanians, who fled. The rest of the Lithuanian Army then retreated, believing that the entire Swedish field army already had crossed. This allowed the Swedish engineers to finalise the bridging of the San, so that the entire army could get across.[6]

The withdrawal from the well-laid Commonwealth trap had been masterful, and the river crossings had been equally skilled, and equally audacious, as those undertaken by the Swedish army during the Thirty Years' War. Yet, in hindsight the plan to finalise the conquest of Poland by advancing to L'vov to crush King John Casimir's centre of resistance appears unrealistic. To crush the resistance in battle required resources, particularly in cavalry, since whenever defeated, the Polish cavalry immediately withdrew to fight another day. It seems likely that King Charles at the outset of the campaign intended to use his Commonwealth cavalry to prevent such an outcome by blocking the enemy's retreat. However, in light of the defections which began in the second half of February, Charles from this time onwards lacked the men for such a strategy. Moreover, to maintain speed he had not brought any siege artillery, so even had he defeated John Casimir in battle, the Polish King would still have been quite safe behind the walls of L'vov. As for the plan to dominate southern Poland from Warsaw, Cracow, and Jarosław, it was sound in principle, yet Sweden under present conditions lacked the necessary military resources to accomplish this objective as well. For sure, negotiations had been ongoing with the Ukrainian cossacks (and before that, with the Crimean Tatars), but events had already shown (and would show again) that neither would be reliable partners for Swedish policy in the south.

---

4   Diedrich von Cappel fell on 25 August 1656 at Thorn. Some modern historians mistakenly claim that it was Lars, not Gustav, Cruus who crossed the river together with Cappel, an error for the sake of dramatic impact apparently introduced by Englund, *Den oövervinnerlige*, p.379.

5   Wimmer, 'Polens krig med Sverige', p.360.

6   The crossing of the San was a complex operation, so there is some discrepancy with regard to the dates of the events. When in doubt, I have followed Wimmer, 'Polens krig med Sverige', pp.358–60. The most recent treatise is Karol Łopatecki, '"Szwedzkie napoje" czyli rzecz o wysadzeniu zamku w Sandomierzu w świetle grafiki *Gesta ad Sandomiriam* Erika Dahlbergha', W. Walczak and K. Łopatecki (eds), *Stan badań nad wielokulturowym dziedzictwem dawnej Rzeczypospolitej* 7 (Białystok, 2017), pp.151–179. Original sources include *Öfverste [Johan] Gorries von Gorgas relation* and *Erik Dahlbergs relation om svenska hufvudarmens operationerFebr. till April 1656*, Swedish National Archives (RA), Militaria 1296.

Plate A

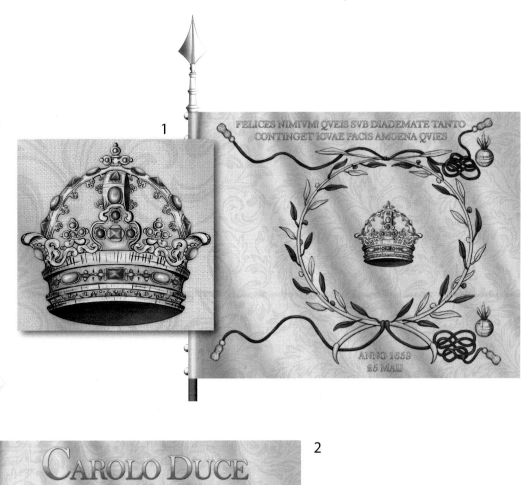

1. Sweden: Company Colour of Major General Claes Danckwardt-Lillieström's Regiment of Foot, 1647–1660 (and crown detail); 2. Sweden: Company Colour of Unidentified Regiment of Foot, 1658–1660

(Illustration by Tomasz Nowojewski © Helion & Company 2022)

See Colour Plate Commentaries for further information.

Plate B

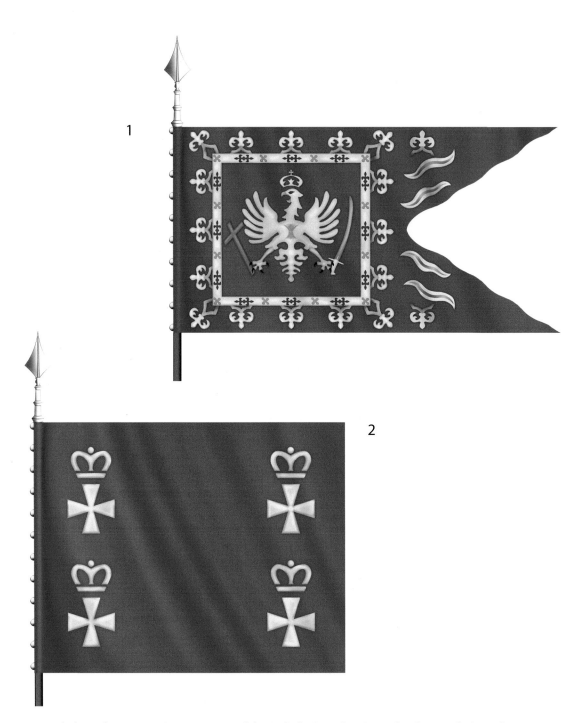

1. Polish-Lithuanian Commonwealth: Polish Cavalry Standard; 2. Polish-Lithuanian Commonwealth: Privateer Ensign of the Danzig Navy

(Illustration by Tomasz Nowojewski © Helion & Company 2022)

See Colour Plate Commentaries for further information.

Plate C

1. Brandenburg: Cornet of Georg Friedrich von Canitz's Regiment of Horse;
2. Brandenburg: Guidon of Georg Friedrich von Canitz's Dragoon Regiment

(Illustration by Tomasz Nowojewski © Helion & Company 2022)

See Colour Plate Commentaries for further information.

Plate D

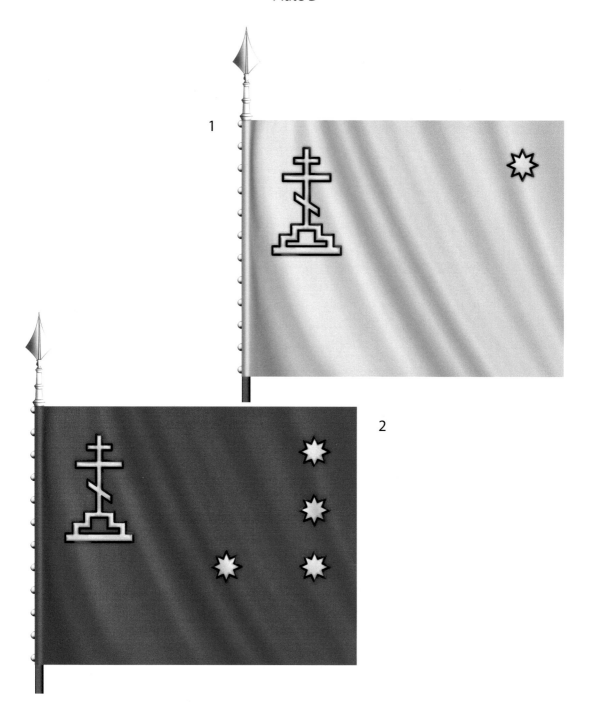

1. Muscovy: Colour of 1st Company, Jacob Leslie's New Formation Regiment of Foot (Belgorod Regiment), Belgorod Army, 1663; 2. Muscovy: Colour of 4th Company, Osip Speshnev's New Formation Regiment of Foot (Karpov Regiment), Belgorod Army, 1663

(Illustration by Tomasz Nowojewski © Helion & Company 2022)

See Colour Plate Commentaries for further information.

1. Cossack Ukraine: Bogdan Khmel'nitskiy's Personal Banner; 2. Tatar Khanate of the
Crimea: Tatar banner, possibly of Crimean origin

(Illustration by Tomasz Nowojewski © Helion & Company 2022)

See Colour Plate Commentaries for further information.

Horse of a winged hussar, again with the wings attached to the saddle in the old manner, and (although on the wrong side) a palash or possibly an armour-piercing sword, in either case with a karabela hilt. (David Klöcker Ehrenstrahl, *Certamen equestre*, 1672)

Lithuanian *pancerni*, 1645, although illustrated without lance. (Biržai Region Museum Sėla, Biržai, Lithuania)

Plate H

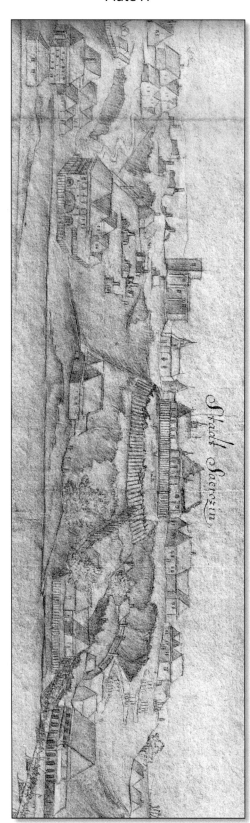

The town of Zakroczym in Masovia, March 1657. (Erik Dahlbergh)

In hindsight, it is obvious that King Charles should have halted the offensive already in late February, at Lublin or Zamość, at the latest. While an expert strategist might have realised this, we can only speculate on why King Charles pushed on. Some later observers attributed the King's decision to excessive trust in his own good fortune, while others merely condemned his lack of judgement and deficient strategic insight. However, based on surviving evidence we cannot know how Charles assessed the situation. L'vov was far away, but in Charles's lifetime, Swedish armies had successfully advanced all the way to Vienna. Distance did not in itself necessarily suggest failure. To return to Warsaw was perhaps unfeasible because no more supplies could be had along this already travelled route. Perhaps the King assessed the risk of defections to be higher if he turned back instead of pushing on. Charles was a competent but not brilliant strategist, so perhaps he simply failed to see the changed circumstances until it was too late. Be that as it may, the Swedish offensive to the south was costly, and little was achieved, except the opportunity to display audacity and superior tactics.

The Battle of Warka

Besides, the costs of the campaign were not yet fully accounted for. Having lost contact with King Charles, Czarniecki advanced a bit further to the north, where he suddenly encountered a stroke of good luck, of which he took full advantage.

Having left Jarosław, King Charles ordered his brother, Duke Adolph John, to send reinforcements from Warsaw to Sandomierz to ensure that this stronghold remained secure when the Swedish army arrived to cross the Vistula. As a result, the Duke dispatched their brother-in-law, Margrave Frederick of Baden-Durlach (1617–1677), with 2,500 cavalry and dragoons.[7] Frederick and King Charles were not only brothers-in-law-but had also been friends for a long time. Both men had served under then Major General Arvid Wittenberg in the battle of Jankow in 1645. The orders to go to Sandomierz formed part of a whole set of instructions. King Charles also ordered the Duke to send Field Marshal Carl Gustav Wrangel and Philip Florinus of Sulzbach with a corps to Lublin to pacify this area. If the Cracow–Jarosław–Zamość line could not be held, perhaps the Cracow–Sandomierz–Lublin line could.

When King Charles a few days later found himself blocked at Gorzyce and Sandomierz under siege by Lubomirski, he ordered Margrave Frederick to return to Warsaw. The Margrave, on the western side of the Vistula, accordingly turned back towards the north. However, he did not move fast enough. Not wishing to abandon the supplies which he carried, Frederick was caught by first Jerzy Sebastian Lubomirski, and then Stefan Czarniecki. The Polish armies were numerically much superior to the Swedes, with estimates

---

7   Wimmer, 'Polens krig med Sverige', p.359. Older sources often suggest that the Margrave's corps consisted of 3,000 men. This higher figure, although probably incorrect, remains occasionally cited by modern historians, including Dzieszyński, *Kraków*, p.151.

Philip Florinus of Sulzbach.
(Abraham Wuchters,
Gripsholm Castle)

ranging from 6,000 to 8,000 men.[8] The Swedes had failed to bring regimental artillery. Czarniecki and Lubomirski first defeated Frederick's rearguard on 6 April, and on the following day dispersed the rest of his corps at Warka. Most Swedes, including a number of senior officers such as the former diplomat Count Schlippenbach who participated in the battle without holding command, escaped. Although Swedish losses (reportedly only 400[9]) may have been acceptable in light of the discrepancy in numbers, this was the first battle during the conflict in which Commonwealth units defeated a Swedish corps on the field of battle. The Poles also acquired all the supplies. It was a decisive tactical victory for the Polish commanders.[10]

However, the battle of Warka also illustrates the failure of the Polish and Lithuanian armies to co-operate. Had not the Polish units drawn away from Sandomierz, they might have been able to co-ordinate their activities with Sapieha's Lithuanians in an attempt to retain King Charles in the trap between the two rivers. By chance or design, Czarniecki and Lubomirski spent their best efforts on, and employed their finest units for, chasing the Margrave's insignificant corps, when they might have done better had they instead co-ordinated their actions against King Charles. In effect, by going for the lesser threat, Czarniecki and Lubomirski spoiled their chances of neutralising the greater one – at a time when Charles and his army were almost out of gunpowder.

---

8   The number of Poles is uncertain. Dzieszyński, *Kraków*, p.151, suggests 6,000; Paweł Skoworoda, *Warka – Gniezno 1656* (Warsaw: Bellona, 2003), p.144, estimates 7,000; while Wimmer, *Polens krig med Sverige*, p.359, and Wimmer, 'Armé och finansväsen', p.74, prefer 8,000. Wimmer probably bases his estimate on Swedish sources, for example Carlbom, *Tredagarsslaget*, p.71.

9   J. Levin Carlbom, *Om Karl X Gustafs polska Krig och öfvergången till det 2:dra Sundskriget* (Gothenburg: Central tryckeriet/Oscar Ericson, 1905), p.38.

10   Peter Englund, who misses no opportunity to show King Charles in a negative light, implies that the King ordered Frederick of Baden-Durlach south as a decoy to save his own skin. Englund, *Den oövervinnerlige*, p.382. This is obviously incorrect, since King Charles sent the order before he found himself blocked. All earlier historians agree that the Margrave's mission was to reinforce Sandomierz which was a strategically significant stronghold. See, for example, Holm, *Översikt*, p.38; Wimmer, 'Polens krig med Sverige', p.358.

10

The Uprising in Samogitia

Changes were taking place in Lithuania as well. De la Gardie returned to Riga in mid February. When passing through the recently captured areas of Lithuania, he cannot have failed to notice that, like in Poland, unrest was growing there as well. In mid April, a serious anti-Swedish uprising broke out in Samogitia. The insurgents immediately received the support of several Lithuanian units. There is nothing to suggest that the uprising was spontaneous, since it was a serious undertaking and apparently well planned by the participating nobles. The cause of the uprising was debated, both then and by later historians, but seems primarily to have been the introduction of new taxes, the quartering of Swedish troops on noble estates, and the misconduct by soldiers so quartered. The religious differences between Catholics and others do not seem to have played a major role – except when the Swedish army quartered troops on Church estates. This naturally reduced the chance for Church officials to gain revenue from these properties which roused their righteous fury.[1] In short, it seems to have been the perceived threat to noble liberties inherent with the introduction of taxation, and the genuine problems associated with the lodging of soldiers, which inflamed the feelings of some members of the Commonwealth nobility and many Church officials. In May, Swedish units suppressed the uprising, burning noble estates and villages in retaliation and killing numerous insurgents. However, many of the insurgent nobles survived, seeking refuge in Muscovite-held Lithuania further to the east, from which they continued to plot. The insurgents also negotiated for military support from Muscovy and provided Muscovite officials with spurious reports claiming that Swedish units had crossed the border into Muscovy. This practice had apparently begun already in late 1655. One noble even provided the Muscovites with the *salva-guardia* (letter of protection) which a Swedish governor had given him to protect his estate from Swedish army units; however, since the estate was located near Vitebsk, which currently was held by Muscovite forces, the noble presented it as evidence that Sweden intended to attack Muscovy! Several such incidents took place, and it seems likely that they influenced Tsar Alexis in his decision

---

1   Kotljarchuk, *In the Shadows*, pp.161–5, 169.

to go to war against Sweden. Muscovite officials may even have encouraged the insurgents, since war between Muscovy and Sweden in any case was imminent. Under orders to avoid a war with Muscovy if at all possible, De la Gardie refused to allow his units to pursue the insurgents into Muscovite-held territory.[2]

De la Gardie left Lewenhaupt to eradicate opposition in Samogitia. However, the latter satisfied himself with securing the important town of Birze in Courland. By the end of May, the Swedish forces left Lithuania, except Birze. Whether the Swedes would have been able to regain control of Samogitia later is unknowable, since Muscovy then invaded Livonia (see below), which not only took priority but also demanded all available military resources. However, by then the conflict in Samogitia had developed into a civil war in which several local nobles wrote to King John Casimir, each claiming to lead the uprising. Each also denounced their rivals as traitors in order to claim their properties. John Casimir, well aware that the insurgent leaders demanded the properties of those of their rivals who had signed the Declaration of Kėdainiai and the Union of Kėdainiai, promised them what they wanted. This was strictly speaking illegal according to Commonwealth law; however, in any case the leaders of the uprising did not wait for the royal approval to plunder the estates of their rivals.[3]

Under the circumstances, the issue of Courland's neutrality, which seemingly had been resolved in Sweden's favour in the previous year, had to be renegotiated. On 30 June, representatives of Sweden and Courland signed the Treaty of Riga, according to which King Charles pawned occupied Pilten to Duke Jacob for 10 years in exchange for a monetary payment of 50,000 Reichsthalers. Charles also recognised Courland's neutrality for the time being.

---

2   *Ibid.*, pp.165–8, 171–3, 212.
3   *Ibid.*, pp.174–7.

11

The Battle of Gniezno

Having abandoned his plans for southern Poland, King Charles returned to his main objective: Prussia. He had two particularly urgent tasks to carry out there. First, he wanted to meet his Queen Hedwig Eleonora who was soon due to arrive by ship from Sweden. She had stayed behind when the King shipped out because at the time she carried their son, the future King Charles XI. Having given birth in December, it was again safe for her to travel. The baby boy remained in Stockholm for safekeeping.

King Charles also had a second task in Prussia: he needed to deal with Danzig, which still defied the Swedes. With his customary vigour, the King spent only two days in Warsaw, after which he moved on with the field army (by then, an estimated 8,000 to 9,000 men).[1] Charles left a garrison in Warsaw of 2,484 men under Wittenberg, who in any case suffered badly from gout and was unable to travel. Like its commandant, the garrison consisted of those who for one reason or another were unsuited for another campaign. For this reason, it was made up of small numbers from many regiments, in total 898 cavalry, 311 dragoons, and 1,275 infantry.[2]

Meanwhile, Lubomirski and Czarniecki, too, had moved north. Some of their men had made an attempt against Łowicz, but as in the past, they were unable to take a defended, fortified town. Lubomirski and Czarniecki then continued their advance to the north, seemingly bound for Thorn, the gateway to Prussia.

King Charles accordingly left his brother Duke Adolph John and the experienced Field Marshal Carl Gustav Wrangel with 6,000 to 7,000 soldiers, mostly horse, to deal with the two Poles, and the King brought along to Prussia the remaining 2,000 men.[3] There he picked up Queen Hedwig Eleonora at Elbing in early May, after which he joined Stenbock who was finalising the preparations for the siege of Danzig, a task for which he was eminently qualified. There was little that the King could do to overcome the well-defended city which Stenbock had not already prepared for. The siege

---

1   Holm, *Översikt*, pp.38, 40. Holm's estimate corresponds with more recent research.
2   Tersmeden, 'Carl X Gustafs armé 1654–1657', p.257.
3   Wimmer, 'Polens krig med Sverige', p.363.

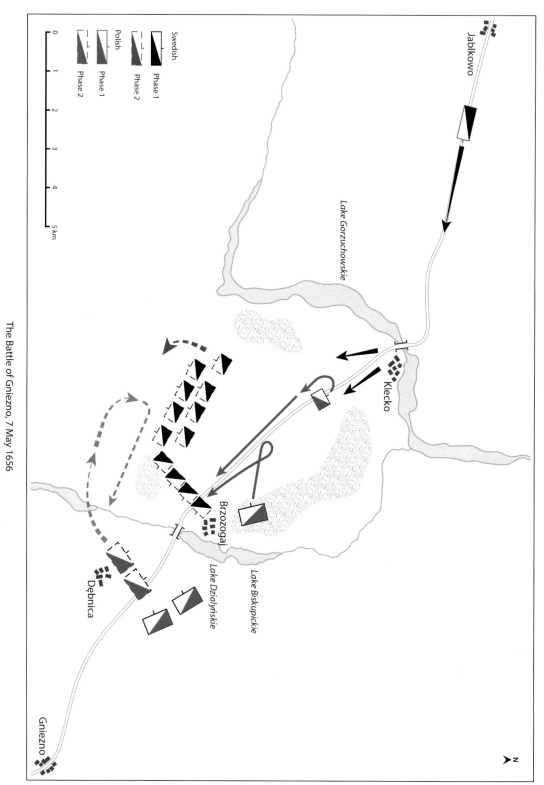

Swedish

Phase 1
Phase 2

Polish

Phase 1
Phase 2

0 1 2 3 4 5 km

The Battle of Gniezno, 7 May 1656

Jabłkowo

Lake Gorzuchowskie

Klecko

Brzozogaj

Lake Działyńskie

Lake Biskupickie

Dębnica

Gniezno

N

was not an easy task. The Swedes took a few outlying bastions but made no headway against the city itself.

To enforce a naval blockade of Danzig, a small Swedish squadron of warships under Daniel Jönsson Strussflycht had orders to blockade the city from the sea. Because of unfavourable winds, Strussflycht only reached Danzig in late May, that is, after Swedish army units already had moved into position around the city but in time to blockade it during the siege.[4] Swedish reinforcements also arrived from overseas. In early July, an enlisted Scottish regiment of infantry (William Cranstone's Regiment, with some 1,020 men) arrived in Prussia to reinforce the Swedish forces.[5]

Meanwhile, Duke Adolph John and Wrangel caught up with Lubomirski and Czarniecki at Kłecko, north of the town Gniezno (known in German as Gnesen). As we have seen, the Duke and Wrangel were accompanied by 6,000 to 7,000 men. The two Poles brought the larger army, an estimated 10,000 to 12,000 regulars and 5,000 noble levies.[6] Lubomirski and Czarniecki may have expected their superior numbers to carry the day – perhaps encouraged by the success at Warka – but they were astute enough to attempt to draw the Swedes into a trap. The Polish main force deployed behind a stream, which it did not plan to defend, while other Polish units deployed to ambush the Swedes as they approached. However, the Swedes realised what was afoot and employed their customary firepower through artillery and muskets. The Poles had begun to employ more sophisticated tactics, in effect alternating skirmishing by light cavalry with charges by armoured hussars in an attempt to break the well-ordered Swedish ranks. Yet, when faced with Swedish firepower, the Polish cavalry again was unable to make an impact, hence retreated or fled from the field. The Polish losses are disputed, but it seems that at Gniezno, a significant number of Poles fell during the Swedish pursuit. Even so, the speed of the Polish cavalry saved Lubomirski's and Czarniecki's armies. The Poles had not yet learnt to cope with disciplined Swedish artillery and musket fire.

---

4   Askgaard, *Kampen om Östersjön*, p.58.
5   Tersmeden, 'Carl X Gustafs armé 1654–1657', p.198.
6   Wimmer, 'Polens krig med Sverige', p.363; Paweł Skoworoda, *Warka – Gniezno 1656* (Warsaw: Bellona, 2003), pp.148, 221.

12

The Three-Day Battle of Warsaw

As soon as King Charles, Duke Adolph John, and Field Marshal Wrangel had moved out of Warsaw, the Commonwealth armies began to converge on the city. First to arrive, already in late April, was Grand Hetman Sapieha's Lithuanian Army which began to blockade Warsaw. In early May, Czarniecki and his army joined the Lithuanians. At the end of May, King John Casimir arrived with his forces. Finally, Lubomirski joined the others with his army. At most the Commonwealth army consisted of some 50,000 men – an impressive force by any account. Moreover, the army contained many enlisted soldiers, in total 28,500 regulars. In addition, and of far less value in a siege operation, from 18,000 to 22,000 noble levies and uncounted numbers of peasant irregulars joined the operation, too. However, the heavy artillery took time to arrive, not showing up until in late June.[1]

Warsaw was defended by the gout-ridden Arvid Wittenberg and his small Swedish garrison of leftovers from the field army. Wittenberg had reportedly defended besieged towns no less than 20 times, so he was certainly experienced. On the other hand, we have seen that he had few men at his disposal, certainly no more than 2,484. This was far from sufficient to defend a city as large as Warsaw. Wittenberg's illness hampered him, too. No longer able to walk on his own, his men often had to carry their commandant in a litter for him to exercise command from the front in the customary manner.

It took time for the Commonwealth forces to gain results. Sapieha, who arrived first, lacked artillery. A major attempt to storm Warsaw took place on 17 and 18 May, but the attack failed and fighting continued throughout June. A month later, the Polish siege artillery finally arrived and entered the action. After two days of bombardment, the Commonwealth armies were again ready to storm Warsaw. On 29 June, King John Casimir threatened that nobody would be spared, if Warsaw did not surrender. Wittenberg refused. On the following night, the Commonwealth army carried out a major attack on Warsaw, successfully penetrating the outer defensive line. Realising

---

1 Wimmer, 'Polens krig med Sverige', p.365.

that the city could no longer be defended, Wittenberg on 1 July agreed to surrender in exchange for the free departure of his men.[2] The parties also agreed that Warsaw would not be sacked, and the city's inhabitants would not be made to suffer.

Even so, some Polish units refused to acknowledge King John Casimir's ban on looting. The city's colony of Armenian merchants found themselves on the receiving end and lost all valuables. John Casimir stepped in to restore order with the help of such units that still obeyed orders. According to some, perhaps embellished, sources, the Polish King had to ask Wittenberg to assist with his remaining men. Be that as it may, the attempt to restore order did nothing to improve the savage mood in the Commonwealth army. The capitulation of Warsaw included terms that allowed the surviving Swedes to leave, under escort, to Thorn. They were not many, only 400 fit and 1,400 ill or wounded. When the Swedes began to depart, violent protests were heard from many Poles who preferred to see the Swedes dead, and in the chaos some Swedes were massacred. Unwilling to risk a full-scale mutiny, John Casimir at this point refused to honour the terms which he had agreed to and instead ordered Wittenberg and several other senior Swedish officers detained. Moreover, he refused to allow any Livonians, Courlanders, or Prussians in Swedish service to depart, since claiming them as Polish subjects he did not recognise them as Swedish soldiers. As for other foreign soldiers in Swedish service, they had to enlist in the Commonwealth army (although the capitulation agreement stated that they would be free to choose whether they wanted to depart with the Swedes or enlist in the Commonwealth army, most armies customarily enlisted captured soldiers). Soon after, Wittenberg died in captivity, likely from the illness which had already manifested itself several times since the war began, although the harsh circumstances of his imprisonment no doubt played its part.

Meanwhile, King Charles and Frederick William of Brandenburg on 25 June concluded the Treaty of Marienburg. Henceforth, Frederick William would support the Swedish army against all enemies (except Muscovy and Courland, against which the defensive alliance would not apply) with at first 2,000 horse and 2,000 foot, to be increased later according to need. In return, Frederick William would receive hereditary sovereignty over four provinces currently held by Sweden in Greater Poland (Posen, Kalisz, Łęczyca, and Sieradz[3]). Even so, Frederick William would remain a Swedish vassal in Ducal Prussia. Sweden also promised to aid Brandenburg with 6,000 men, if needed. In effect, Sweden and Brandenburg agreed to divide the Commonwealth between them.[4]

Then came the news that Warsaw had fallen, and that King John Casimir had retaken possession of his capital. King Charles and Frederick William immediately set out to rectify the situation. At this point, the Swedish–Brandenburgian army had a combined strength of around 18,000 men. The

---

2   Samuel von Pufendorf, *Sieben Bücher von denen Thaten Carl Gustavs Königs in Schweden*, vol. 3 (Nuremberg: Christoph Riegel, 1697), pp.174–5.

3   Łęczyca was known in German as Lentschitza, while Sieradz was known as Schieratz.

4   Pufendorf, *Sieben Bücher* 3, pp.171–2.

Warsaw, 1656. (Pufendorf)

Swedish army consisted of some 9,500 men (7,500 horse and 2,000 foot; Table 12). The Brandenburgers were some 8,500 (5,000 horse and 3,500 foot; Table 13).[5] The combined army also brought some 50 to 60 cannons onto the field (20 to 31 Swedish and 30 Brandenburgian cannons as well as five small Brandenburgian mortars).[6]

---

5   Carlbom, *Tre dagars slaget*, pp.118–20. Carlbom amends Pufendorf's 9,000 Swedes and 8,000 Brandenburgers without quoting archival sources. It is known that Carlbom worked with archival documents, and all subsequent Swedish historians repeat his estimates. So do most non-Swedish historians, including the Polish historians Stanisław Herbst, Jan Wimmer, and Mirosław Nagielski who all agree with Carlbom. Stanisław Herbst, 'Tredagarsslaget vid Warszawa 1656', Arne Stade and Jan Wimmer (eds), *Polens krig med Sverige 1655–1660: Krigshistoriska studier* (Stockholm: Kungl. Militärhögskolan, *Carl X Gustaf-studier* 5, 1973), pp.255–93, on p.265; Wimmer, *Polens krig med Sverige*, p.368; Mirosław Nagielski, *Warszawa 1656* (Warsaw: Bellona, 2009), p.138.

6   Carlbom, *Tre dagars slaget*, pp.96, 113.

The Commonwealth army, commanded in person by King John Casimir, was larger, although different sources give different numbers. Most Polish historians estimate that it consisted of 36,000 to 41,000 men.[7] This corresponds to the estimate by Gordon, who then served in the Polish army. He noted that John Casimir's army consisted of some 39,000 men, which he explained as 8,000 Crown regulars, 16,000 noble levies, 5,000 Lithuanians, 6,000 Tatars, and 4,000 dragoons and infantry.[8] Modern historians give slightly different figures for these categories. A Polish historian in the joint Polish–Swedish military academy project suggested 24,000 to 25,000 regulars (16,500 to 17,500 Crown and 7,500 Lithuanian soldiers, which included a total of 4,000

---

7 Herbst, 'Tredagarsslaget', p.263; Nagielski, *Warszawa*, p.130.
8 Gordon, *Tagebuch*, p.66. Gordon wrote 40,000 as the total number, but his figures add up to 39,000. Notably, Gordon's figures correspond to those employed by Pufendorf, *Sieben Bücher* 3, p.180, although Gordon's narrative differs from that of Pufendorf.

Although the Thirty Years' War was a ruthless conflict, the long duration of the struggle, its large geographical scope, and the common practice to enlist soldiers from a defeated army into the victorious one resulted in a set of common understandings of what was permissible in civilised warfare. Scholars such as the Dutch jurist Hugo Grotius (1583–1645) drew up widely read treatises on the laws of war. However, these developments so far touched Eastern Europe only to a limited extent, since most of the east was not involved in the conflict. As a result, lingering cultural practices probably affected decisions such as when the Commonwealth commanders chose not to honour the terms of surrender agreed at Warsaw. The differences in thinking are perhaps best illustrated by two paintings both from 1634 or 1635: Diego Velázquez's well-known depiction of the Dutch surrender of Breda to the Spanish and the anonymous painting of the Muscovite surrender at Smolensk to the Commonwealth. Whilst the Spanish commander Spinola shows respect and kindness to his vanquished opponents (facing page, top), the Muscovite commanders must prostrate themselves on the ground in an act of unconditional submission (facing page, bottom) which derived from Far Eastern practices brought to eastern Europe with the Mongols. The latter practice, eventually known as kowtow, is illustrated by an eleventh-century painting attributed to Li Gonglin (detail, above), depicting Tang General Guo Ziyi accepting the submission of Inner Asian Uighur chieftains.

foot), 10,000 to 13,000 noble levies, and 2,000 Tatars.[9] A more recent study suggests 25,000 regulars (16,500 to 17,000 horse, 4,500 foot portions, and 5,000 to 7,500 Lithuanians), 10,000 or more noble levies, and 2,000 Tatars.[10] A study focused on the Lithuanian Army concluded that there were between 5,000 and 6,000 of them.[11] We know some of the units of King John Casimir's army, but not all of them (Table 14).

The Tatars deserve some additional comments, since the corps from the Crimea was independent and technically did not form part of the Commonwealth army. The Crimean Khanate was not at war with Sweden. Actually, Swedish–Tatar relations were usually friendly, since both states often faced common enemies. Nonetheless, Mehmed Khan had sent a Crimean Tatar corps, commanded by Subhan Ghazi Agha, to assist King John Casimir. It is unknown if Mehmed Khan realised that this involved fighting the Swedish army. King Charles in his diplomatic correspondence chose to regard the participation of the Crimean contingent in the subsequent battle not as a declaration of war by the Khanate but as the result of Subhan Ghazi Agha exceeding his orders. A contemporary report indicated the strength of the Tatar contingent as 30,000, which is not credible, however, it was probably stronger than the 2,000 proposed by modern Polish scholars. Perhaps Gordon's assessment of 6,000 Tatars is more likely to be correct. Unfortunately, there is no other surviving contemporary documentation of the strength of the Tatar corps.

It is clear from these figures that as far as we know, the combined army of King John Casimir was at least twice the size of the combined army of King Charles and Frederick William. As for the proportions, it seems clear that Charles and Frederick William fielded more infantry than John Casimir, although the difference was not great. The Swedish–Brandenburgian army also included more field artillery than the Commonwealth army, reportedly 60 versus 18 heavy and eight regimental cannons.[12] However, it seems equally clear that John Casimir fielded far more regular cavalry than Charles and Frederick William, at least twice as many and probably yet more. Even if we discount the noble levies altogether, John Casimir enjoyed a huge advantage in trained cavalry.

However, both Swedes and Brandenburgers were better trained than their Commonwealth counterparts. Moreover, their commanders were experienced leaders who had fought in the Thirty Years' War. Quite a few of the common soldiers, both in the Swedish and Brandenburgian army, were veterans, too. Many of the Brandenburgers had previously fought under Swedish banners. Among Lithuanians who remained true to their oath to King Charles was Prince Bogusław Radziwiłł, another veteran of the Thirty Years' War who had fought in Swedish service under Carl Gustav Wrangel from 1637, followed by Dutch service from 1642 (during which time,

---

9   Herbst, 'Tredagarsslaget', p.263.
10   Nagielski, *Warszawa*, p.130, 288–91.
11   Paradowski, *Lithuanian Army*, p.6.
12   Herbst, 'Tredagarsslaget', p.264.

incidentally, Georg Friedrich von Waldeck served in his command).[13] Within the Commonwealth army, Czarniecki and a few others had fought in the same war and shared the outlook, training, and experience of these veterans, but most Commonwealth commanders had no comparable experience.

Having conquered Warsaw and restored a semblance of order among his men, King John Casimir wanted to move north, cross the River Bug, and advance on the Swedish and Brandenburgian armies before they could join forces. North of the Bug, King Charles had the same idea: to move south with the Swedish army alone, without awaiting the arrival of the Brandenburgers, so that he could defeat the Commonwealth armies one at a time. However, the water level of both the Vistula and the Bug was too great to immediately allow a safe crossing for either party. John Casimir first had to rebuild a bridge across the Vistula at Warsaw, and his men seem to have been ill-prepared for engineering work as the bridge was only ready for use on 27 July. Meanwhile, Czarniecki argued that the Commonwealth army should avoid open battle, since Swedish firepower was superior. Subhan Ghazi Agha made the same observation. However, John Casimir overruled them both. While awaiting the new bridge, the King had parts of the Crown Army ferried across the Vistula, intending to confront the Swedish army on the right (east) bank of the river. These Crown units joined up with the Lithuanian Army already on this bank. Then they dug in, following the expert advice of Imperial officers who had joined John Casimir's staff. Meanwhile, dissatisfied with the King's decision, Czarniecki moved north along the left (west) bank with the 4,000 to 5,000 men under his personal command.[14] Just like at Sandomierz previously in the year, the Commonwealth armies proved unable, or unwilling, to co-ordinate their movements. As a result, John Casimir's forces ended up widely separated from one another. The King himself with the Crown Army and Czarniecki's cavalry army deployed on the left bank of the Vistula, but at some distance from each other, while the Lithuanians and Crimean Tatars took up positions on the right bank. Their opponents were not so separated. On the very same day that King John Casimir's bridge was ready, Frederick William joined forces with King Charles at Nowy Dwór, where the Swedes erected a bridge across the River Bug.

As a result, King Charles seized the initiative. Crossing the Bug on 28 July, he marched down the right (east) bank of the Vistula, confronting the Commonwealth troops. The march took longer than anticipated because of the narrow road and hot summer weather. To compound the problem, a section of the bridge across the Bug collapsed, and while Swedish engineers were at hand to repair the damages, this resulted in additional delays before the entire army could cross. When the Swedes and Brandenburgers approached Warsaw, they first encountered the Commonwealth infantry, over 3,100 enlisted musketeers as well as two companies of national infantry, dug in across a narrow corridor of open plain beside the river, supported by the Commonwealth artillery.[15] On

---

13 Bogusław Radziwiłł was an educated man who had mastered French, German, Polish, Latin, and Ruthenian.

14 Herbst, 'Tredagarsslaget', p.268.

15 *Ibid.*, p.269.

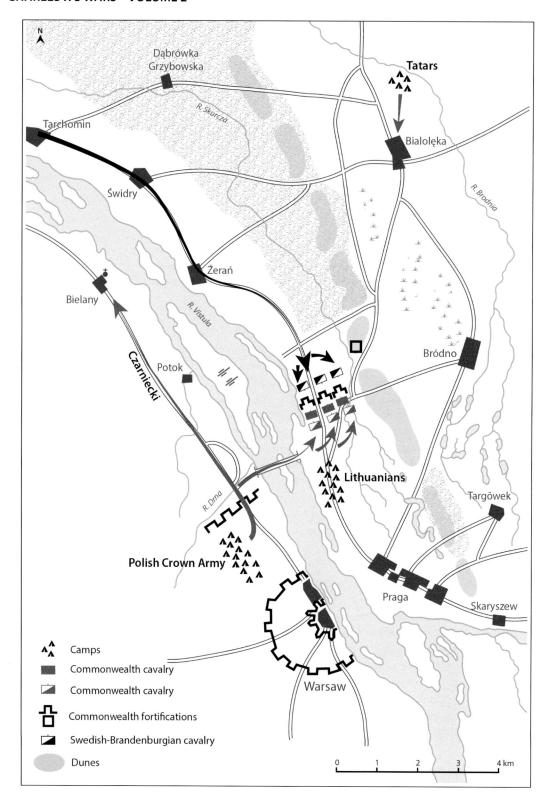

Above: The Three-Day Battle of Warsaw, 28–30 July 1656. Day 1, 28 July.

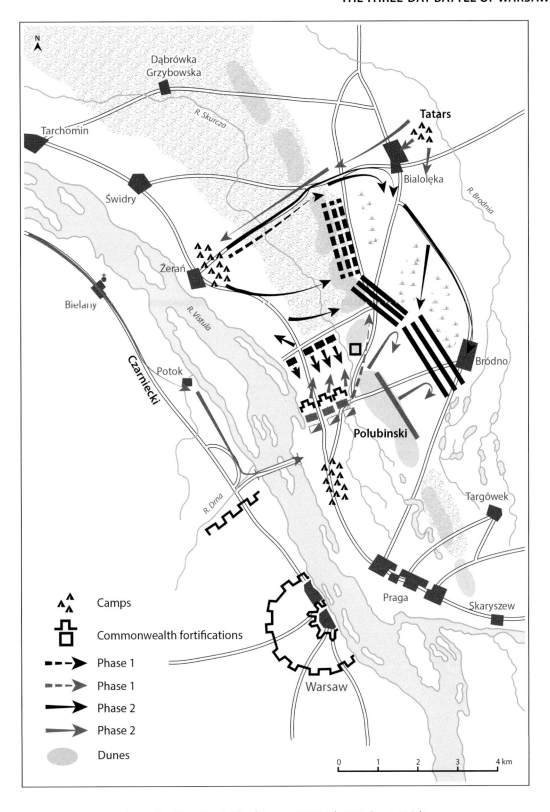

Above: The Three-Day Battle of Warsaw, 28–30 July 1656. Day 2, 29 July.

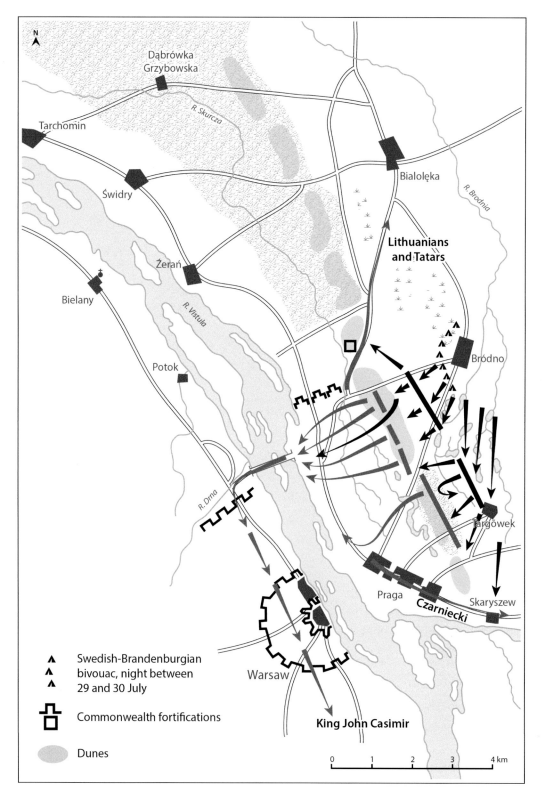

Above: The Three-Day Battle of Warsaw, 28–30 July 1656. Day 3, 30 July.

the other side of the river, Queen Marie Louise commanded her attendants to use the horses of her personal carriage to pull two cannons along the bank of the Vistula.[16] She then took personal charge of the artillery fire 'walking downe her self on foot Amazonian-lyke', in the words of Patrick Gordon.[17] While the Queen's two cannons could not influence the outcome, her initiative forms the only known case of an active redeployment of the Commonwealth artillery during the battle. While the Swedish and Brandenburgian artillery, in the manner of the Thirty Years' War, remained mobile and frequently redeployed, their Commonwealth counterparts essentially remained in fixed positions throughout the action. Perhaps this can be explained by the fact that most experienced Commonwealth artillery officers by this time remained loyal to their oath to the Swedish Crown.

Over and beyond the threat from the Commonwealth artillery, any frontal attack on the Commonwealth lines also would have to take into account the Tatar camp, which was located at Białołęka, from which the Tatars easily could fall into the rear of any attacking force.

At around 5:00 p.m. on 28 July, the three-day battle of Warsaw began with skirmishes around the Lithuanian redoubts. The sun set at 7:34 p.m., but the skirmishes continued until around midnight. The level of fighting was occasionally intense, and both sides suffered casualties from musket and artillery fire. On the Swedish side, Colonel David Sinclair suffered a fatal wound (having lost an arm in the artillery fire, he died on the following day, but not before toasting the anticipated victory with his remaining hand and asking King Charles to take care of his family).

When the fighting ended for the evening the Commonwealth commanders were confident of victory, due to their superior strength and prepared positions, while the Swedish and Brandenburgian commanders did not share the optimism of King Charles. There seemed to be an awful lot of Commonwealth soldiers ahead of them. King Charles's personal feelings at the time remain unknown, but in front of his men he downplayed their worries, saying that he expected a victory.

The battle taking place in the height of summer, the sun rose already at 3:52 a.m. on the second day. Early in the morning, King Charles set out together with Frederick William, Carl Gustav Wrangel, and the Elector's commander Otto Christoph von Sparr, with a cavalry unit for protection, to reconnoitre the enemy deployment. He realised that the Commonwealth lines were too strong to be attacked from the front. He needed to find more open terrain to deploy his units in proper order to enable full use of their firepower and manoeuvrability, all of which could be had east of the Commonwealth lines. Charles devised a bold plan. With his cavalry, he would ignore the Tatar camp in that area, instead send his army on a flank

---

16 Pierre des Noyers, *Lettres de Pierre des Noyers* (Berlin: B. Behr, 1859), p.222.

17 Waldemar Kowalski, 'Patrick Gordon in His Own Words: A Soldier, a Scot, a Catholic', *Journal of Irish and Scottish Studies* 3:2 (2010), pp.19–38, on p.22; citing Patrick Gordon's Diary, vol. I, fol. 69. For some reason most later historians, including Herbst and Nagielski, date this action to 29 July, even though the Queen's secretary Noyers is quite specific in placing the action on the first evening. Herbst, 'Tredagarsslaget', p.276; Nagielski, *Warszawa*, pp.165, 214.

Aleksander Hilary Połubiński.

march so that the eventual battle line would face the Commonwealth units not from the north but from the east. He knew that this meant that the Tatar camp then would end up in his rear, but he was willing to take the risk. The army would march and deploy in its ordinary manner, with the few infantry units in the centre. The Brandenburgers, already in the left wing, would lead the way. At around 9:00 a.m., the combined army set out. As on the previous day, King Charles led the right wing, with Duke Adolph John as his deputy. Frederick William, with Wrangel as his deputy, led the left wing. Sparr commanded the centre. In the appointment of the experienced Wrangel as Frederick William's deputy, King Charles followed Swedish practice in the Thirty Years' War, during which allied commanders were provided with Swedish deputies to ensure that overall strategic objectives and policies were adhered to. Even so, Frederick William and Wrangel got on well together and over time became close friends, a friendship which survived no less than two future wars between Brandenburg and Sweden.

Meanwhile, the Tatars attacked the Swedish rear, not only once but twice. Both attempts were repulsed, but the fighting was desperate. As usual, King Charles led from the front. On one occasion, he became separated from his men, except his personal aide, Lieutenant Colonel Bengt Trafvenfelt. Attacked by seven Tatars, the King shot two with his pistols and cut down a third whose lance got entangled in the reins of the King's horse, while Trafvenfelt shot two more and assisted Charles in chasing away the remaining two.[18]

Then Lithuanian and eventually also Polish units began to attack the marching army. The Crimean Tatars repeated their attacks from the north. However, these attacks were beaten off by superior firepower, and the Brandenburgers and Swedes then continued the flank march. The Tatars were finally driven off by Henrik Horn's Swedish cavalry. The Swedes and Brandenburgers then deployed on and in front of several sandy hills overlooking the Commonwealth army. The disciplined and rapid redeployment of the army took the defenders by surprise. By lunchtime the Commonwealth commanders had felt confident. All went well, they thought, and their commanders departed for an extended lunch break. 'The officers had all left for the banquet', in the words of one observer. However, Swedes and Brandenburgers did not stop to eat, instead moving forwards into the new positions.

---

18 Pufendorf, *Sieben Bücher* 3, p.179. Bengt Trafvenfelt (b. 1601), before he was ennobled in late 1650 (1651 N.S.) known as Trafvare,was an old, experienced soldier who had accompanied Charles as an aide ever since Charles, then a mere captain, in 1642–1645 served in the Thirty Years' War.

Above: King Charles and Bengt Trafvenfelt fighting off the Tatars. (Johann Philip Lemke; National Museum, Stockholm)

Below: Swedish or Brandenburgian cavalry fight Tatar or, less likely, Lithuanian cavalry at the battle of Warsaw. (Erik Dahlbergh)

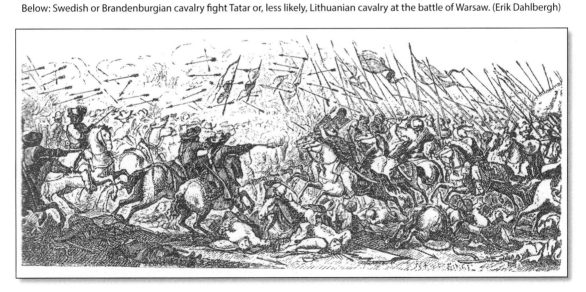

Above: Black felt hat with plume, attributed to King Charles.
Diameter 505 mm, height 190 mm. (Royal Armoury,
Stockholm; Photo: Göran Schmidt)

Below: Boots, attributed to King Charles. (Royal Armoury,
Stockholm; Photo: Göran Schmidt)

King Charles on horseback, as he customarily appeared in combat. Note that the breastplate and backplate are barely visible under his French coat.

Returning from lunch, the Commonwealth commanders discovered what was afoot and accordingly attempted, but failed, to charge the Swedes and Brandenburgers. As before, both King Charles and Frederick William led their men from the front. At around 4:00 p.m., the Lithuanian hussars (795 horses[19]) under Aleksander Hilary Połubiński, supported by several *pancerni* banners, charged the flanking units. Their target was the Swedish left wing, consisting of the Uppland and Småland Cavalry Regiments. The hussars first took casualties from the musket fire of the infantry in the Swedish–Brandenburgian centre. Then, although they broke through the first line of the Swedish cavalry and penetrated the second, they failed to reach the third line, which repulsed the hussars without any particular difficulty. Moreover, the hussars failed to inflict many casualties.

---

19 Herbst, 'Tredagarsslaget', p.278; Nagielski, *Warszawa*, pp.136, 187. The figure of 795 horses in seven banners is taken from the 1656 komput. The real figure was probably lower. First, the komput included from 10 to 15 percent 'blind' positions. Second, there was always some attrition when on campaign. Herbst, 'Tredagarsslaget', p.289 n.41, raises the possibility that only some 500 hussars participated in the charge, and that in any case the terrain allowed for no more than 300 horses in line.

Polish cossack-style light cavalryman of the national autorament, armed with wheellock carbine, pistols, and sabre.
(Illustration by Sergey Shamenkov)

The Småland Cavalry Regiment, for instance, which had already shrunk to 397 men, lost only four in the battle of Warsaw.[20] When the hussars failed to break through, the *pancerni* did not follow up the charge. Characteristically, King Charles entered the fray against the hussars, and a hussar hit him in the chest with his lance, dangerously near the throat. The hussar's name is unclear; he was apparently named Jakub Kowalewski (or Kowalowski, if a Ruthenian), or perhaps Wojciech Lipski (who apparently came from a place named Kowalewo, from which the adjective Kowalewski might derive), or possibly Odachowski (first name unknown). In any case, the King's cuirass turned the lance, and one of the King's companions then shot the hussar. The companion was either Trafvenfelt or, according to another account, Prince Bogusław Radziwiłł. Whatever the hussar's name, and regardless of who killed him, King Charles after the battle ordered a burial with full honours for his fallen enemy.[21] The confusion about the identity of the hussar derives from multiple sources giving different testimonies. In light of the intensity of the fight, it is even possible that Charles fought more than one adversary. The name Lipski, for instance, may also have derived from the incident with the Tatars, since Tatars in Commonwealth service – but not Crimean Tatars – were known as Lipka Tatars, a term which formed the adjective Lipski. Having said this, among Swedish officers at the time the story of the King's combat with the Tatars was well known. The later court artist Johann Philip Lemke, who worked with eyewitness testimonies, depicted the Tatar incident in a well-known painting.

By the evening of the second day, the mood had changed in both armies. Those Swedish and Brandenburgian commanders who earlier had doubted the audacious plan (and many had, since they knew they were outnumbered) were now confident of success. However, the Commonwealth commanders who earlier had paid more attention to their lunch banquet than their enemies had lost confidence. Some Commonwealth units deserted, and the rest, under King John Casimir, began to retreat across the River Vistula on the one bridge available.

When darkness fell, King Charles and Frederick William agreed to attack again on the following day. Despite the day's victories, the night provided little rest for the Swedish–Brandenburgian army, since Tatars made repeated approaches against their camp, attempting to catch stragglers or plunder.

On 30 July, the Swedish–Brandenburgian army attacked again around 8:00 a.m., across the open plain. It easily penetrated the remaining Commonwealth defences, and chaos broke out among the retreating Commonwealth units. The plan was to evacuate the Commonwealth supply train and infantry across the Vistula but because of poor discipline and management, parts of the supply train and infantry ended up blocking the bridge, which caused considerable confusion in the Commonwealth lines. Meanwhile, many Commonwealth units fled. In the process, they abandoned 13 cannons. The already overcrowded bridge collapsed, and both Stanisław 'Rewera' Potocki and Jan Zamoyski almost drowned in the river. Although

---

20   See, for example, Lars-Olof Larsson, *På marsch mot evigheten: Svensk stormaktstid i släkten Stålhammars spegel* (Stockholm: Prisma, 2007), p.66.

21   Nagielski, *Warszawa*, pp.198–201, 208.

hurriedly repaired so that the rest of the artillery and infantry could cross, the bridge was then burned so as to prevent the Brandenburgian cavalry from crossing. King John Casimir ordered his cavalry to delay the Swedes and Brandenburgers as long as possible, and then to retreat south. He then abandoned his capital for the second time in 12 months, retreating to the south along the Vistula. On the eastern side of the river, the Lithuanians and Tatars dispersed to the north, while Czarniecki's Polish army fled south. It took several days for John Casimir's defeated army to reassemble, on the right bank of the Vistula, south of the lower River Wieprz.

Yet, the Swedes and Brandenburgers were too few to take full advantage as the Commonwealth armies retreated. The Commonwealth's total losses in the battle remain unclear, although they were not great. Gordon noted 2,000 casualties.[22] Modern historians tend to offer similar (or even lower) figures. Cavalry losses are believed not to have exceeded 1,000 men, while known infantry losses were 600 men.[23] We can assume that losses were unremarkable for three days of fighting. However, we can also assume that not all casualties were recorded. There is, for instance, no remaining information on Tatar losses, and these tend to be ignored by historians, since the Tatars formed an independent contingent. In comparison, the Swedes and Brandenburgers lost some 1,300 men (700 according to Gordon[24]).[25] Among senior officers losses were minimal, too. As noted, Colonel Sinclair was mortally wounded on the first day of battle and died soon afterwards. Duke Adolph John was badly wounded on the second day, in the same knee as during the battle of Gołąb, for which reason he had to be sent to the Netherlands for treatment, returning only a year later.[26] Major General Christoph von Kannenberg was hit by a bullet which miraculously was stopped by the coins in his purse. The Swedes and Brandenburgers took only 18 prisoners. The small war and religiously inspired murders had caused considerable enmity, and the army was angry over the many Swedish soldiers the Poles had massacred after the surrender of Warsaw. As a result, the men were not inclined to show mercy. When Poles attempted to surrender, some Swedes merely shouted *Warschauer Accord* ('Warsaw agreement') and slaughtered them.

Warsaw again fell into Swedish hands, but King Charles did not stay for long. Soon, he again set out, leaving Major General Barthold Hartwig von Bülow in charge of the garrison. However, it was now clear that Warsaw could not be held. Already in mid August, Bülow began to move archive documents relating to taxation and land ownership out of the city. This was standard Swedish procedure in conquered capitals, since such documents were useful in administering the new territories. Bülow also moved out the captured artillery, valuable books, and other treasures, since Swedish kings considered such items more needed in Stockholm than in territories exposed to hostile powers. King Charles ordered the fortifications to be demolished,

---

22   Gordon, *Tagebuch*, p.66.
23   Herbst, 'Tredagarsslaget', p.287; Nagielski, *Warszawa*, p.241.
24   Gordon, *Tagebuch*, p.67.
25   Lars Ericson, 'Warszawa 1656', Lars Ericson et al., *Svenska slagfält* (np: Wahlström & Widstrand, 2003), pp.189–97, on pp.189, 196.
26   Lange, *Karl X Gustavs bror Adolf Johan*, pp.127–9.

so that they could not be used by an aggressor – or by the Elector, whose intentions he had good reason to distrust.

Nonetheless, in late August King Charles sent a proposal for peace negotiations to King John Casimir. He again flouted the possibility of an alliance against Muscovy, which by this time had declared war on Sweden and invaded Swedish territory. Charles demanded certain lands for his allies, chiefly Frederick William whose control of Ermland needed to be confirmed. As for Prussia, the King seems deliberately to have left the issue open until proper negotiations got underway. However, after informing the Emperor of the Swedish proposal, King John Casimir rejected it out of hand. He pointed out that a chief obstacle was that Ermland was a Catholic bishopric, and in his view, the Church's holdings were sacrosanct and could not be violated. Furthermore, John Casimir was unwilling to jeopardise his present understanding with Muscovy (the two parties had just commenced negotiations in Wilno for an armistice) – despite the fact that Tsar Alexis occupied the major part of Lithuania and had no intention of letting it go. John Casimir's rejection of negotiations with Sweden was not the result of blind piety, nor was he ignorant of the situation in Lithuania. At the time, the Polish King was engaged in canvassing support elsewhere in Europe through diplomatic means. He had already received vaguely positive messages from several European rulers, as well as significant support from the Netherlands and Denmark (more on which below). Presumably, John Casimir expected that eventually he could negotiate from a position of strength if he only waited for these deals to mature.

Tables

Table 12 (see p.120) The Swedish Army in the Battle of Warsaw, 28–30 July 1656
Sources: Carlbom, *Tredagarsslaget*; Hedberg, *Kungl. Artilleriet: Carl X Gustafs tid*, pp.93–4

Note that Her Royal Majesty the Queen's Life Regiment of Horse was enlisted in Germany separately from the unit which previously carried this name,

Cavalry
Life Guard of Horse (including the Drabant Guard), also known as the Life Regiment of Horse
Uppland Cavalry Regiment (formally under Johan Mauritz Wrangel who was imprisoned in Warsaw; commanded by Lieutenant Colonel Erik Planting)
Västgöta Cavalry Regiment (under Per Hierta since the death of regimental commander Lars Cruus)
Åbo Cavalry Regiment, also known as Fabian Berndes's Finnish Cavalry Regiment after its colonel
Småland Cavalry Regiment
Tavastehus Cavalry Regiment, also known as Henrik Henriksson Horn's Cavalry Regiment (under Lieutenant Colonel Johan Galle)
Östgöta Cavalry Regiment (formally under Ludwig Lewenhaupt who was imprisoned in Warsaw)

Duke Adolph John's Cavalry Regiment, from January 1656 also known as the Generalissimus's Cavalry Regiment (constituted from several existing companies enlisted in Germany)
Her Royal Majesty the Queen's Life Regiment of Horse, also known as Duke John George of Anhalt-Dessau's Cavalry Regiment (enlisted in Germany)
Duke Charles of Mecklenburg-Schwerin's Cavalry Regiment (enlisted in Germany), under the Duke and Dietrich von Rosen
Count Palatine Philip von Sulzbach's Cavalry Regiment (enlisted in Pomerania)
Margrave Charles Magnus of Baden-Durlach's Cavalry Regiment (enlisted in Germany)
Hans Christoph von Königsmarck's Cavalry Regiment, also known as Königsmarck's Life Regiment of Horse (enlisted in Bremen-Verden)
Carl Mauritz Lewenhaupt's Cavalry Regiment (enlisted in Germany)
Jacob Johan Taube's Cavalry Regiment (mostly enlisted in Finland)
Count Johann von Waldeck's Cavalry Regiment (enlisted in Germany)
Arvid Wittenberg's Cavalry Regiment (enlisted in Pomerania)
David Sinclair's Cavalry Regiment (mostly enlisted in Sweden)
Per Hammerskiöld's Cavalry Regiment (mostly enlisted in Sweden)
Rutger von Ascheberg's Cavalry Regiment (enlisted in Germany)
Christian von Pretlach's Cavalry Regiment (enlisted in Bremen)
Jacob von Yxkull's Cavalry Regiment (enlisted from Swedes and Germans in Bremen and Pomerania, with one company from Livonia)
Wenzel Sadowski's Cavalry Regiment (primarily Poles)
Carl Gustav Wrangel's Cavalry Regiment (enlisted in Germany)
Israel Isacsson Ridderhielm's Cavalry Regiment (mostly enlisted in Sweden)
Hans Böddeker's Cavalry Regiment (enlisted in Bremen)
Dragoons
Prince Bogusław Radziwiłł's Dragoon Regiment (enlisted in Lithuania), under Lieutenant Colonel Eberhard Puttkammer
Fabian Berndes's Finnish Dragoon Regiment (in Poland, but possibly not Warsaw)
Count Palatine Philip von Sulzbach's Dragoon Regiment, under Lieutenant Colonel Lorenz Naumann
Infantry (under Barthold Hartwig von Bülow)
Uppland Regiment, probably under Major William Nisbet
Skaraborg Regiment, under Colonel John Nairn
Södermanland Regiment, under Colonel Johan von Vietinghoff (1580–1685), a real veteran who retired later in the year
Hälsinge Regiment, under Colonel Carl Larsson Sparre
Västgöta-Dal Regiment, under Lieutenant Colonel Carl von Scheiding
Kalmar Regiment, under Colonel Gustav Cruus

Artillery
Field artillery of likely seven 12-pounders, six 6-pounders, and 18 3-pounders, under Colonel Gustav Oxenstierna

Table 13 (see p.120). The Brandenburgian Army in the Battle of Warsaw, 28–30 July 1656
Sources: Carlbom, *Tredagarsslaget*; Jany, *Urkundliche Beiträge*; Hedberg, *Kungl. Artilleriet: Carl X Gustafs tid*, p.93

Cavalry
The Elector's Life Regiment of Horse
Duke John George of Saxe-Weimar's Cavalry Regiment
Count Georg Friedrich von Waldeck's Cavalry Regiment
Christoph von Kannenberg's Cavalry Regiment
Wolf Ernst von Eller's Cavalry Regiment
Dietrich von Lesgewang's Cavalry Squadron
Georg von Schönaich's Cavalry Regiment
Christoph de Brunell's Cavalry Regiment
Dragoons
Count Georg Friedrich von Waldeck's Dragoon Regiment
Elias von Canitz's Dragoon Regiment
Christian Ludwig von Kalckstein's Dragoon Regiment
Infantry
The Elector's Life Guard of Foot
Wolrad von Waldeck's Regiment
Otto Christoph von Sparr's Regiment
Joachim Rüdiger von der Goltz's Regiment
Johann Georg von Sieberg's Regiment
Artillery
Field artillery of 30 regimental cannons

Table 14 (see p.124). Known Units of Regimental (*pułk*) Size of the Commonwealth Army in the Battle of Warsaw, 28–30 July 1656
Sources: Herbst, 'Tredagarsslaget', p.263; Paradowski, *Lithuanian Army 1653–1667*, p.6; Nagielski, *Warszawa*, pp.288–91.

Crown Army
His Royal Highness's Regiment, commanded by Stefan Czarniecki
Crown Grand Hetman Stanisław 'Rewera' Potocki's Regiment

Crown Field Hetman Stanisław Lanckoroński's Regiment
Crown Grand Marshal Jerzy Sebastian Lubomirski's Regiment (probably departed before the battle)
Aleksander Koniecpolski's Regiment
Stanisław Witowski's Regiment
Jan Fryderyk Sapieha's Regiment
Jan Zamoyski's Regiment
Aleksander Zamoyski's Regiment
Jan Sobieski's Regiment
Andrzej Potocki's Regiment
Mariusz Jaskólski's Regiment, commanded by Michał Zbrożek
Dymitri Wiśniowieckis's Regiment
Jacek Szemberk (Castellan of Boguslav)'s Regiment
Seweryn Mikołaj Kaliński's Regiment
Stefan Piaseczyński's Regiment
Jerzy Bałaban's Regiment
His Royal Highness's Dragoon Regiment, under Johann Heinrich von Alten-Bockum
His Royal Highness's Life Guard of Foot, under William Butler
Krzysztof Grodzicki's Regiment of Foot
Major General Ernst Magnus Grothusen's Regiment of Foot
Jan Zamoyski's Regiment of Foot
Possibly other dragoon or infantry units
Field artillery of at least 18 heavy and eight regimental cannons (probably significantly more but reliable data is missing)
Lithuanian Army
Lithuanian Grand Hetman Paweł Jan Sapieha's Regiment, including the Hetman's banners of Hussars and Pancerni (both of which were former units of Janusz Radziwiłł)
His Royal Highness's Lithuanian Regiment (under Lithuanian Field Scribe Aleksander Hilary Połubiński), which included His Royal Highness's Lithuanian Hussar Banner (personally led by Połubiński) and Lithuanian Grand Hetman Paweł Jan Sapieha's Hussar Banner
Prince Michał Kazimierz Radziwiłł's Regiment, including his hussar banner
Krzysztof Sapieha's Regiment
(The late) Filip Krzysztof Obuchowicz's Regiment
Several companies of dragoons and haiduk infantry
Apparently no field artillery

13

Muscovy and the Swedish North-East

The division of Lithuania into Muscovite and Swedish zones of influence had not been without incidents. In January 1656, Muscovite troops attacked Swedish units on several occasions. After formal Swedish protests, which Moscow rebuffed, the incidents ceased. It remains unclear whether the attacks were spontaneous or ordered.

Less dramatic, but more worrying, news came from Ingria. In late February, Orthodox peasants in the border region began to migrate across the border into Muscovy. There was an abundant Orthodox population in both Ingria and Kexholm County, but many of the craftsmen who lived around Estonian towns such as Narva were Orthodox, too. Some of their activities began to look suspicious to the town officials, but it was difficult to ascertain if any treachery was afoot. Then, in March, several Muscovite raids into Ingria took place. The raiders looted Protestant churches, disrupted the postal service, and intercepted and stole letters. On the Muscovite side of the border, Swedish merchants were arrested. Orthodox priests moved into Ingria to agitate against Swedish rule. False rumours grew increasingly common. In late May, following information from the Swedish embassy in Moscow, Gustav Evertsson Horn, Governor-General of Ingria and Kexholm County, ordered the arrest of the leading Orthodox merchants in Narva. The ensuing investigation revealed that they had promised to support Muscovy if war broke out.[1]

Horn's action was not premature: on 17 May 1656, Muscovy declared war on Sweden. The Swedish defences along the common border were badly, if at all, prepared. As noted, the Swedish–Muscovite common border had been quiet since the 1617 Treaty of Stolbovo, and during the Thirty Years' War Muscovy had been one of Sweden's few allies. When the war in the Commonwealth broke out, Sweden did not wish to provoke Muscovy by mobilising or reinforcing border defence forces. Even so, possibly more

---

1   Fagerlund, 'Kriget i östersjöprovinserna', pp.61–3.

Road consisting of a causeway of round logs pushed into the ground perpendicular to the direction of travel, so as to provide footing when inclement weather resulted in muddy roads, which was common. As individual logs were frequently broken or rotten to the core, loose adjacent logs rolled and shifted back and forth, and the roads were difficult and dangerous to get across, in particular for horses. Known in English as corduroy roads, this road type was common in the borderlands between Muscovy and Livonia. Roads further to the north were far worse, or non-existent. (Anthonis Goeteeris, 1619).

could have been done on the Swedish side of the border without alarming Muscovy, if local officials had been more diligent.

Because unwittingly, Sweden had provoked Muscovy in Lithuania. It was the Swedish invasion of Poland, not the Commonwealth's defences, which persuaded the Tsar to abandon further conquests in Lithuania beyond Kowno, Grodno, and Brest, where the Muscovites turned back to the east. Paradoxically and unknown to most Poles, the Swedish Deluge saved Poland from suffering the same fate as Lithuania at the hands of the Muscovites. In 1655, it seemed like all of Poland and what remained of Lithuania would fall into Swedish hands, and Tsar Alexis had no wish to fight the combined military might of the Commonwealth and Sweden. Yet, the Swedish conquests in Lithuania irked the Tsar. King Charles and Tsar Alexis could not both hold the title of Grand Duke of Lithuania. As a result, Tsar Alexis opted for war against Sweden. Despite speculation in Sweden that he wanted to reach a foothold on the Baltic shore, Tsar Alexis did not, like his predecessors, aim for Narva in Estonia, which was a primary export port for Muscovite goods. Instead, he decided to advance against Riga in Livonia, which was more important for his conquests in Lithuania.[2] Tsar Alexis also intended to engage Swedish forces in the north, as a diversion and means to apply pressure on the Swedes at the very moment when they seemed ready to consolidate their position in the Commonwealth.

Tsar Alexis's privy chancellery (*Prikaz taynykh del*), a newly established office which henceforth handled military deployments and other planning relating to national security, initially made plans for co-ordinated attacks on Sweden on 11 June (1 June O.S.) 1656. Then, for unclear reasons, the foreign ministry or, as it was then known, the ambassadors' chancellery (*Posol'skiy prikaz*), revised this plan and a new day of attack was set at 1 July (21 June O.S.) 1656.[3] We do not know if the revision took place because of a communication breakdown within the government bureaucracy (quite likely) or out of necessity, for practical reasons to do with mobilisation. In any case, Moscow planned three attacks: first, separate and somewhat restrained attacks on Ingria and Kexholm County, and then a massive main attack on Livonia's capital Riga from the south by way of Smolensk, Vitebsk, and Polotsk, in conjunction with a simultaneous attack on Dorpat in eastern Livonia.[4] It seems that Tsar Alexis intended to carry out the attacks on Kexholm County and Ingria before the main invasion of Livonia, so as to bind the Finnish units at home, thus preventing them from reinforcing the Livonian army following the outbreak of war.

It was an excellent plan, but ultimately, it did not work out quite as planned. We will see that Pyotr Potyomkin's attack on Ingria took place only two days after the appointed date according to the original schedule, but his colleague Pyotr Pushkin further to the north either had not yet finished preparations for an attack on Kexholm or, quite possibly, thought that the attack was intended to take place according to the revised schedule. Even if so, Pushkin's men were late. The attack on Kexholm only took place in mid July, on the same day when Tsar Alexis joined his main field army at Polotsk. Ultimately, the delays did not matter. Most Finnish units had already been moved to Livonia, well ahead of the war.

The Swedes had suspected hostile intentions, but they were nonetheless unprepared. Because of the war in the Commonwealth, resources had been redistributed from the north-eastern border to the south. As a result, the few Swedish strongholds in the borderlands were poorly maintained or neglected altogether. Most towns consisted only of an obsolete castle surrounded by wooden buildings, at best protected by no more than a wooden palisade. Only Viborg and Kexholm had town walls, and only Nöteborg Castle had walls in good condition. Bastions of the modern type were almost non-existent. The town of Nyen, which safeguarded land communications from the north to

2   Oleg Aleksandrovich Kurbatov, 'Rizhskiy pokhod tsarya Alekseya Mikhaylovicha 1656 g.: Problemy i perspektivy issledovaniya', Rudol'f Germanovich Pikhoya (ed.), *Problemy sotsial'noy i politicheskoy istorii Rossii: Sbornik nauchnykh statey* (Moscow: RAGS, 2009), pp.83–88.

3   S.S. Gadzyatskiy, 'Kareliya i Yuzhnoye Priladozh'ye v voyne 1656–58 gg.', *Istoricheskiye zapiski* 11, 1941 (Moscow), pp.236–81, on p.250.

4   S.S. Gadzyatskiy, 'Bor'ba russkikh lyudey Izhorskoy zemli v XVII veke protiv inozemnogo vladychestva', *Istoricheskiye zapiski* 16, 1945 (Moscow), pp.14–57, on pp.19–20.

Above, left: Watercolour painting of a peasant from Österbotten in Finland, dated to the late seventeenth century. He wears essentially the same clothes (jacket, baggy breeches, stockings, and a woollen cap) as found on the Swedish warship Vasa, lost in 1628. The faded red jacket has greenish cloth inserted in the seams, cuffs, and shoulder wings, while the cap is lined in blue. Swedish and Finnish peasants still generally wore full beards, and Muscovite peasants invariably did.

Above, right: Another watercolour painting of a peasant from Uleåborg (modern-day Oulo) in Österbotten in Finland, dated to the late seventeenth century. On the way to the market, he carries a bundle of dried pikes and a jar of butter. He wears well insulated Lapp shoes of the type which was much desired for operations during winter conditions. Many such shoes were manufactured for the Crown and distributed to the army.

the territories south of the Gulf of Finland, had no fortifications whatsoever. The town, which was surrounded by marshlands, had only received town privileges in 1642.

Moreover, while the forested borderlands between Livonia, Lithuania, and Muscovy were somewhat rough and characterised by poor roads, they were highly developed in comparison to those further to the north, in Ingria, Kexholm County, Karelia, and the lands in Finland along the eastern and northern Arctic border. The latter constituted a sparsely settled frontier region, and the Muscovite lands on the other side of the common border were no different. Towns were small and mostly built of wood. Most peasants practiced slash-and-burn agriculture which resulted in temporary swidden fields, while others lived on fishing in the rivers and lakes. The settlements of the first were temporary, while those of the latter were seasonal. Neither group cared much about on which side of the border they operated. Agriculture was barely sustainable, and even if the peasant settlements could be located, they did not have the surplus food supplies to sustain any major military operation. From a logistical viewpoint, supplies had to be brought in from elsewhere. Winters were long and harsh, but the cold season at least enabled movement along the frozen rivers or across frozen marshes. In comparison, spring caused severe flooding which might prevent military operations and logistics altogether. The forest cover was extensive, which usually prohibited the deployment of military units in the Continental manner. The dense forest made cavalry charges difficult, and at times impossible. Infantry was useful, but there are no indications that pikemen ever were used in Kexholm County during the war and probably not in Ingria or eastern Finland either. The forests also impeded cavalry movement. It was easy to close the few rough roads with timber obstacles (abatis, *zasyeka* in Russian), which consisted of barricades of felled trees and constituted a traditional feature of northern warfare, in particular against cavalry incursions. Although there were usually paths between settlements, these were commonly known only to local guides and smugglers. Except for the limited number of small, mediaeval stone castles once built at traditional marketplaces, most strongholds consisted of wooden blockhouses. Because despite attempts by both the Swedish and Muscovite governments to bring law and order through the introduction of officials and military garrisons to monitor the border and the cross-border trade, the borderlands were essentially lawless.

The oldest town, Kexholm (Finnish: Käkisalmi; Russian: Korela; modern-day Priozersk), had been established by the local Karelians before 1143 on what then was the main waterway and trade route between Novgorod and Finland. The first castle was built in 1294. Kexholm had a town wall and occupied a strategic location. Even so, it remained a wooden border town with a largely transient population which included numerous deserters and fugitives from the law from both sides of the border. The transients usually outnumbered the burghers, several hundred in number and with the exception of a few Germans and Scots mostly locals. Kexholm was the proverbial hive of scum and villainy. Swedish and Muscovite weights and measures were in simultaneous use, and both Swedish and Muscovite currency was in widespread circulation. Counterfeit coins were commonplace. On the street, the visitor would hear Swedish, Finnish, German, Russian, and perhaps other languages as well. The town officials, despite the best of intentions according to Sweden's state Lutheranism, fought a generally losing battle against violence, crime, alcoholism, and prostitution. The garrison, which was as much a part of the problem as its solution, commonly consisted of men conscripted elsewhere who had no interest in the region, except possibly its women. Archive records of court cases show that the town officials did what they could, but Kexholm was a rowdy place, and people of various backgrounds tended to drift in and out of the town as they pleased. In the north, Kexholm seems to have held a unique position as a frontier town in the wilderness on the periphery between two centralised states. The closest analogues were perhaps the Muscovite wooden frontier towns in Siberia. Presumably, the southern border towns along the Commonwealth's and Muscovy's frontier with the Muslim world faced similar problems, but less seems to be known about them.

Muscovy had sympathisers in all the Swedish border territories. While Sweden officially demanded all inhabitants to be Lutherans, the expansion of Swedish territory further to the east with the 1617 Treaty of Stolbovo brought a significant Orthodox population under Swedish rule. The treaty gave this population, henceforth Swedish subjects, the right to practice their own Orthodox faith. As a result, Orthodox priests, who in most cases came from Muscovy, operated throughout the border region. Subject to the Metropolitan of Novgorod, their religious allegiance lay in the east. Although there had been an influx of impoverished Finnish Lutheran peasants into Kexholm County in particular, they remained a minority. Moreover, the Lutheran minority represented the lower strata of peasant society, and career-minded Lutheran clergy avoided the eastern borderlands. As a result, the local Lutheran priests were of low quality. Already in 1638, there were reports that they spent most of their time in the local inns, drinking and slandering those who followed the Orthodox faith.[5] Stockholm had since 1627 attempted to find loyal and educated Orthodox priests to be sent to the Patriarch of Constantinople for nomination as Orthodox bishops. Unfortunately, no suitable priest was ever found, so the Swedish Orthodox remained linked to the Patriarch of Moscow. In Kexholm County, both merchants and leading peasants were Orthodox. Now Muscovite agitation took place among them. Many (but certainly not all[6]) Orthodox priests operated as agents of Muscovy, and they also created an agent network of Orthodox sympathisers within the border population. As a result, the Muscovites received both intelligence and volunteers as soon as they moved into Swedish territory.

---

5   Tom Gullberg and Mikko Huhtamies, *På vakt i öster*, vol. 3 (np: Schildts, 2004), p.99.
6   Among those Orthodox priests who remained loyal was Grishka Ivanov from Jama, who was captured, tortured, and imprisoned, yet remained faithful to the Swedish Crown and also, when ultimately forced to act on behalf of the Muscovites, voluntarily provided intelligence to the Swedes. Antti Kujala, 'Förrädiska ryssar och förrymda finnar: Flyttningsrörelserna från Ingermanland och Kexholms län under ryska kriget 1656–1658 och provinsens kolonisation efter kriget', *Historisk Tidskrift för Finland* 97 (2012), pp.469–98, on p.478.

At the outbreak of war, the Swedish forces in the entire north-eastern region were, at least in the eyes of King Charles, the responsibility of Magnus Gabriel De la Gardie. However, for reasons that will be explained he consistently avoided exercising command outside Livonia. As a result, the Swedish command structure in the north-east remained based on personal links.

The Swedish forces in Finland were commanded by Field Marshal Gustav Adolph Lewenhaupt, who just had returned from the war in Poland. Lewenhaupt had few men at his disposal, since most Finnish units were in Livonia or further south. Trained men – former soldiers – were available in Finland, but few had been called up.[7]

The Swedish forces in Ingria and Kexholm County were commanded by Governor-General Gustav Evertsson Horn af Marienborg (1614–1666), an experienced officer who, like Lewenhaupt, had fought in the battle of Jankow 1645. He was the nephew of the renowned Field Marshal Gustav Horn and the cousin of the aforementioned Henrik Henriksson Horn.

Gustav Adolph Lewenhaupt, 1650. (Matthäus Merian, Skokloster Castle)

Unfortunately, and again similarly to Lewenhaupt, Gustav Evertsson Horn and Magnus Gabriel De la Gardie did not get along, which hampered co-operation and ultimately led to De la Gardie de facto withdrawing from his responsibilities with regard to Ingria and Kexholm County.

For practical reasons, operations in Kexholm County became closely linked to those in Finland. Ingria experienced a similar development, but was de facto divided from a military point of view. During the war the easternmost part of Ingria, Nöteborg County, became linked to Finland and Kexholm County. However, the three western parts of Ingria, Ivangorod, Jama (Russian: Yama or, later, Yamburg; modern-day Kingisepp), and Kaporie (Russian: Kopor'ye) Counties, instead became linked to operations in Estonia and Livonia, again for practical rather than administrative reasons.

In comparison to the other territories, Estonia remained comparatively safe during the war, sheltered as it was behind Ingria and Livonia. Some Muscovite incursions took place, but not at all to the degree further to the east. The Swedish forces in Estonia were commanded by Governor-General Bengt Horn af Åminne (1623–1678), the former commander of the Queen's Life Regiment of Foot.

Most Swedish units in the region were deployed in Livonia, which was also the territory most at risk. As noted, the Swedish forces in Livonia

---

7   Jussi T. Lappalainen, 'Finland och Carl X Gustafs ryska krig: Försvaret av den östra rikshalvan 1656-1658', Arne Stade (ed.), *Kriget på östfronten* (Stockholm: Militärhögskolan, *Carl X Gustaf-studier* 7:2, 1979), p.15.

Gustav Evertsson Horn.
(Skokloster Castle)

were commanded by Governor-General Magnus Gabriel De la Gardie, the King's brother-in-law. Technically, his command also included Estonia and Ingria, but he left operations in these territories to their respective Governor-Generals. King Charles seemed to have regarded De la Gardie as overall commander in Finland as well, but De la Gardie was even more reluctant to involve himself there. His reluctance to assume command probably derived from personal reasons. Although he was the descendant of a family of warlike commanders who had achieved great success on the eastern front, De la Gardie himself was more of a diplomat than a soldier, and he was unsure of his ability to uphold senior command. De la Gardie was not inept as a commander; he just preferred to pass military tasks to professionals. When relations with Muscovy were deteriorating but before the outbreak of war, De la Gardie wrote to Per Brahe, the Lord High Justiciar, that he feared that 'my late dear father's and grandfather's renown acquired against this enemy now in my person might wither and turn into nothing'.[8] In Livonia, he was during the Muscovite war supported by the able and experienced Major General Simon Grundel Helmfelt (1617–1677), who had fought in Denmark under Torstensson from 1643 to 1644 and at Jankow in 1645. In 1646, Helmfelt become Quartermaster-General under Wrangel, and from 1649 he served as head of all Swedish artillery. Helmfelt was an expert fortification officer and engineer, but he had also commanded infantry in Torstensson's renowned Old Blue Regiment during the Thirty Years' War. Promoted to major general in 1655, Helmfelt arrived in Riga in early July 1656. De la Gardie was probably relieved when he got Helmfelt by his side. Nonetheless, De la Gardie had already, on his own initiative, commenced work on existing and new fortifications. Planning had begun in April, and because of the climate, it was not really feasible to commence construction work before May.

In addition, De la Gardie at an early stage attempted to block the River Düna by sinking obsolete river craft loaded with rocks in strategic locations. He also had three river vessels of the *struts* type rebuilt as floating cannon blockhouses.[9] The *struts* was a flat-bottomed single-masted coaster which, unlike the ubiquitous *lodja*, was decked. It was similar to the Dutch boyer (*boeier*), and in the 1650s the term boyer was commonly used in Sweden as well. The *lodja*, a term of Slavic origin, was an open rowing boat which also might carry a mast or two. The *lodja* was often some 12 m long and 4 m wide, with eight pairs of oars, but larger vessels were built, too. These were the two

8   Magnus Gabriel De la Gardie to Per Brahe, cited in Björn Asker, *Karl X Gustav* (Lund: Historiska Media, 2010), p.241.
9   Fagerlund, 'Kriget i östersjöprovinserna', pp.70–71, 231.

most common vessels used by the Swedish inshore navy on the eastern side of the Baltic Sea.[10] De la Gardie, who experienced co-operation problems with many other subordinates, by all accounts trusted Helmfelt in military affairs, and the Major General certainly had the military experience which De la Gardie lacked.

The redeployment of a major share of the army of Livonia to the Commonwealth had left the Baltic provinces dangerously exposed. By this time, the Livonian field army consisted of 2,200 cavalry and 400 dragoons, in addition to some 500 cavalry in western Ingria. Of course, yet more men were distributed in garrisons throughout Livonia, Estonia, and western Ingria. According to plans made before the war, the Baltic provinces would be defended by garrisons of 6,700 men in times of peace (5,350 in Livonia, 150 in Estonia, and 1,200 in western Ingria). In case of war, reinforcements would raise the strength to 9,850 men (7,650 in Livonia, 300 in Estonia, and 1,900 in western Ingria). However, by the summer of 1656 the Baltic provinces had only approximately 6,933 men on garrison duty. The Livonian garrisons consisted of some 5,090 men. Estonia had no more than 142 men, all of whom constituted the garrison of the capital Reval (modern-day Tallinn). Western Ingria had received reinforcements from Finland, but the total garrison strength there was still only 1,701 men – more than the peacetime complement but less than what had been planned for. Riga was supposed to have a garrison of 3,000 men but reached only 2,310. Not all garrisons consisted of professionals; in smaller towns many were recently enlisted or mere levied peasants.[11]

Simon Grundel Helmfelt

With such small numbers of men at his disposal, it was obvious that De la Gardie had to focus on his defences. In Livonia, these were Riga with Cobron's Bastion, Dünamünde, Kokenhusen, Dünaburg, Marienburg (on the road to Pskov), Dorpat (west of Lake Peipus and on the crossroads between Estonia, Livonia, and Pskov), Pernau (modern-day Pärnu), and several smaller towns such as Fellin (modern-day Viljandi), Wolmar (modern-day Valmiera), and so on. Garrisons were small. The key communications hub Dorpat had a garrison of only 450 men, while the exposed Kokenhusen had 350.[12]

In Estonia, the key town was Reval, as we have seen with a garrison of no more than 142 men.

Ingria was better defended, with Narva and Ivangorod, on opposing sides of the River Narova (modern-day Narva), particularly strongly fortified. Narva was the commercial centre, with modern defences and a garrison of

---

10   Michael Fredholm von Essen, *The Lion from the North 2: The Swedish Army during the Thirty Years War, 1632–1648* (Warwick: Helion, 2020), pp.207–9.

11   Fagerlund, 'Kriget i östersjöprovinserna', pp.77, 224.

12   *Ibid.*, p.224.

Ivangorod. (Photo: Ad
Meskens)

1,102 men. Ivangorod had been established in 1492, as a stronghold to guard Muscovy's then newly claimed access point to the Baltic Sea. Conquered by Swedish units in 1612, Ivangorod was formally ceded to Sweden with the rest of Ingria in the 1617 Treaty of Stolbovo. The town had a garrison of 466 men.[13] On the surface, Ivangorod looked the more impressive fortress. However, the mediaeval castle was old-fashioned and unprepared for modern siege methods. It also had a major Orthodox population.

In comparison, Wask-Narva (or Vasknarva, on the Lake Peipus), Jama, and Kaporie were small towns with poor defences and garrisons of respectively 18, 44, and 71 men.[14] Moreover, Ingria did not have much of a field army. In June the Governor-General of Ingria, Gustav Evertsson Horn, only had two recently enlisted companies of horse (in total 170 men), most of whom lacked weapons and gear. In early July, Horn received some reinforcements and also managed to equip his cavalry. This produced a field expeditionary force of 200 cavalry and 40 mounted infantrymen. However, the soldiers were inexperienced and we will see that when they set out against the Muscovites, they did not fare well but soon returned to Narva.[15]

Further to the north were Nyen, Nöteborg, Kexholm, and finally Viborg in Finland. Nyen was essentially undefended. Nöteborg had a garrison of 19 men, while Kexholm had no more than 100. In addition to regular soldiers, the population in both Nöteborg and Kexholm included men who for one reason or another had trained in the use of arms and were willing to use them. Viborg had a garrison of only 34 soldiers but the town was also

13   *Ibid.*, p.224.
14   *Ibid.*, p.224.
15   *Ibid.*, p.93.

the home of several units of the field army. Moreover, during the autumn Lewenhaupt increased the garrison to about 500 men.[16]

King Charles had instructed De la Gardie to employ the fortifications in southern Livonia as a defensive line. In addition, he should maintain a small field army with which to harass any invading enemy forces. However, De la Gardie instead withdrew the units of the field army into the fortified towns. While this decision may have been necessary in light of the small size of the existing garrisons, it for obvious reasons reduced the Swedish strategy to a purely static defence – not at all what King Charles had in mind. We will see that De la Gardie's subordinates elsewhere in the region did not agree with his strategy and in fact carried out several offensive operations, although with limited numbers, against the invader.

Nonetheless, the Swedish strategy in the north-east was defensive in character. This was consistent with the King's wishes. The objective was not to defeat Muscovy, nor to take Muscovite territory, but to defend Finland and the Baltic provinces until a peace treaty became possible. The Swedish focus was elsewhere, at first on the Commonwealth and, later as we will see, on Denmark. King Charles knew that he could not win any of his war objectives through the struggle in the north-east, but he certainly could lose the war as a whole there.

Sweden had a well-developed intelligence system in Muscovy, with bases in Narva, Marienburg, Neuhausen, and Dünaburg. To some extent, Dorpat functioned as a listening post, too, because of peasants there with relatives on the other side of the border. In particular Narva and Marienburg regularly received intelligence from Muscovy, in the case of Narva primarily through merchants who traded there but in Marienburg apparently from a variety of sources. Amazingly, intelligence continued to flow in through Marienburg throughout the war, even after its occupation by Muscovite forces. Already in June 1656, intelligence on the planned Muscovite offensive from Pskov reached Marienburg. De la Gardie found it hard to believe that the Muscovites were approaching. Even when the Muscovite offensive into Ingria had been confirmed (through Narva on 24 June), De la Gardie hesitated. He ordered the Livonian units to stand down, since he could not be certain that the attacks in Ingria were authorised by the Tsar. Perhaps, he argued, the attacks were the result only of local initiatives? Nonetheless, De la Gardie ordered the civil officials in Dorpat, which was particularly exposed, to relocate to Reval.[17]

Muscovite Resources and Objectives in Ingria and Kexholm County

In late 1655 or early 1656, the Muscovite commanders in the border region received new orders on how to handle Orthodox migrants from Sweden. Previously, the policy had been to restrict the influx of Orthodox migrants

---

16 Lappalainen, 'Finland', pp.43, 55, 73.
17 Fagerlund, 'Kriget i östersjöprovinserna', pp.59–61.

DIE FESTVNG GAM

Jama, 1630s. (Adam Olearius)

from Swedish territory. However, from this point onwards they embarked upon a policy of actively inviting Orthodox peasants from Sweden. This was primarily handled through the Orthodox priests who operated on Swedish territory. The number of Orthodox migrants accordingly increased markedly, and in spring many brought their cattle with them to Muscovy.

In early 1656 some of the Orthodox migrants returned to Sweden to carry out raids. They were of diverse background and fighting potential. Some were essentially bandits. Others, including some 100 freebooters from Jama eventually under the self-appointed Ataman Osip Sol'skiy organised themselves as 'free cossacks'. Swedish reports claimed that the raiders were led by Muscovite officers, which may be true in some cases. However, since the purpose of the raids was personal enrichment, it is equally possible that other raids were private initiatives.[18] Conflict was brewing not only between Orthodox and Lutherans. Patriarch Nikon of Moscow (1605–1681) in 1652 initiated and in 1654 expanded a programme to reform the Orthodox Church. Unsurprisingly, not all believers agreed with the liturgical and ritual practices henceforth imposed on them, most obviously the new manner of making the sign of the cross. Many of those who disagreed, henceforth known as Old Believers, withdrew to remote Karelia, which was already the home of other old practices, some of pagan origin. Since those Old Believers

18   Lappalainen, 'Finland', pp.19–20.

who migrated were typically those who were most insistent on the old ways and thereby least tolerant of other faiths, confrontation between different faith groups often turned violent. Some of the cruelties that took place during the war were certainly the result of religious extremism.

We have seen that the Muscovite plan was to begin the war with two simultaneous but separate offensives around Lake Ladoga, one directed at eastern Ingria and the other at Kexholm County. Both resources allocated and objectives aimed for were limited. Pyotr Pushkin (d. 1684), based in Olonets, would lead an offensive north of Lake Ladoga against Kexholm County and ultimately, perhaps, Finland. In late May, Pushkin had received reinforcements in the form of at least 170 Novgorod streltsy and some old-style cavalry under Boris Chelishchev (d. 1663). Problems immediately arose between Pushkin and Chelishchev, who apparently was an unusually violent and headstrong individual and perhaps best can be described as the subordinate from hell. Chelishchev immediately demanded full use of Pushkin's resources, bribed some of the latter's soldiers to join him, and finally took off on personal escapades which not only divided Pushkin's army but also alerted the enemy.[19] Chelishchev's activities delayed Pushkin's offensive. Besides, even with the reinforcements brought by the wilful Chelishchev, Pushkin is unlikely to have had more than 1,500 men and some light regimental artillery to work with, and this corresponds to the intelligence known to the Swedes at Kexholm.[20]

Meanwhile, Pushkin's colleague, the able voivode Pyotr Potyomkin (1617–1700) in Lava further to the south, had no such problems with his subordinates. Following the schedule in the initial set of orders, Potyomkin embarked upon an offensive south of Lake Ladoga against Ingria and the Gulf of Finland. It is difficult to ascertain the total strength of Potyomkin's corps, but it is unlikely to have exceeded 2,000 or even 1,500 men. Potyomkin personally led some 1,000 men, including, according to some accounts, 570 Don cossacks.[21] A major share of the cossacks seemed to have manned his inshore fleet, a task in which the Don cossacks excelled. For land operations, Potyomkin had only some 600 streltsy, new formation soldiers, and cossacks, as well as some light artillery. Potyomkin had two subordinate commanders, his relative Sila Potyomkin and Ivan Poltev. Sila Potyomkin operated in southern Kexholm County with a few hundred men, while Poltev moved against Kaporie in Ingria with 250 new formation soldiers and cossacks.[22] Together, they effectively cut the communications route between Finland and the southern Baltic territories. The inshore fleet employed by Potyomkin seems to have assembled in Novgorod and apparently constituted the primary reinforcement he received for the operation. Swedish intelligence described the fleet as consisting of up to 350 *lodja*-type vessels.[23]

---

19   Gadzyatskiy, 'Kareliya', pp.249–54.
20   Lappalainen, 'Finland', pp.39–40.
21   *Ibid.*, p/21.
22   Gadzyatskiy, 'Kareliya', pp.264–6.
23   Lappalainen, 'Finland', p.22.

This means that at most, Muscovy controlled some 3,500 soldiers in the Lake Ladoga region, divided between Pushkin and Potyomkin. Further north, the only regular Muscovite garrison was located in Kola, on the Barents Sea. Although we will see that the Kola garrison was mobilised for the war, it was located too far away to co-ordinate operations with the Muscovites at Lake Ladoga. Both Pushkin and Potyomkin were subordinated Prince Ivan Golitsyn (d. 1685), the commander of the Novgorod Army, who was responsible for the region. Neither Pushkin nor Potyomkin was in overall command at Lake Ladoga. With their immediate superior based in Novgorod, more than 200 km away, it was unsurprising that some co-ordination problems would occur, of the type evidenced by Chelishchev. Nonetheless, Pushkin and Potyomkin supported each other in operations, to the extent that is was possible. Besides, they had only limited objectives. Lacking men and siege artillery, it seems unlikely that Moscow expected them actually to conquer any major towns. There is nothing to suggest that Tsar Alexis at this time had any territorial ambitions in the region, and even if he had, there is no reason to believe that such ambitions reached beyond Kexholm County, the Karelian Isthmus, and possibly Ingria, all of which had been lost in 1617. Instead, Pushkin's and Potyomkin's primary objectives were, no doubt, to cut off Finland from the Baltic provinces and tie up the Finnish regiments so that they could not be used to reinforce Livonia.

The Swedish Response

As soon as King Charles received news about the Muscovite declaration of war, he immediately wrote to Stockholm as well as to De la Gardie. The King had already instructed the Admiralty to appoint Gustav Wrangel 'or some other good officer' commander of a fleet to be sent into the Gulf of Finland so as to protect against Muscovite naval attacks.[24] He now ordered De la Gardie to defend the Livonian and Estonian port-towns of Riga, Pernau, Reval, and Narva, but also Viborg, Nyen, Kexholm, and Nyslott along the Finnish border. In short, the King wanted the port-towns on the Baltic shore, vitally important for the Swedish economy, to be defended at all costs, but he also wanted a defensive line to be established around the Finnish heartland.[25] If necessary, western Ingria could temporarily be abandoned, since this territory was difficult to hold for either side in the war. De la Gardie was formally in overall command of the entire north-eastern front, even though he was reluctant to shoulder this responsibility. De la Gardie promptly dispatched Field Marshal Lewenhaupt to take charge of the Finnish front. He also appointed Major General Anders Koskull (1594–1676) governor of Viborg and Nyslott, which meant that he also assumed command of the garrison in and defences of Viborg. Koskull was a veteran of the early years of the Thirty Years' War, but by

---

24 Askgaard, *Kampen om Östersjön*, p.515 n.142; citing a letter from 6 June.

25 Lappalainen, 'Finland', p.24; citing letters from King Charles to De la Gardie from Marienburg (30 June 1656) and Nowy Dwór (5 July 1656). In this case, it is unclear whether the letters were dated O.S. or N.S., since both dating systems were used within the chancellery.

this time, age had taken its toll. In addition, De la Gardie returned the Viborg Cavalry Regiment, under Erik Kruse (1617–1655), to Viborg, which was the first redeployment of a Finnish regiment to Finland during the ongoing war. Kruse's regiment arrived in mid July. Promoted to Major General, Kruse was appointed Lewenhaupt's deputy. Notably, De la Gardie had already taken these precautions in June, before the King's orders arrived. In addition, soldiers were raised in Finland. Following an old procedure of raising cavalry, the Retinue of Nobles in Finland was expanded in size, resulting in a new unit known as the Reinforcement of Nobles in Finland (*Adelns fördubbling i Finland*). There was no shortage of experienced officers. The Finnish regiments in Livonia had suffered from losses and attrition to the extent that most regiments consisted of only six companies. De la Garde accordingly returned the supernumerary officers to Finland.[26]

The Swedish Council of the Realm in Stockholm reacted promptly to the invasion, too, and like De la Gardie, already before the King's orders arrived from Prussia. First, the Council ordered the provision of military supplies to be shipped to Finland by the Finnish sailors already in Stockholm. Second, the Council ordered the provision of a squadron of six ships to Finland, under Vice-Admiral Gustav Wrangel (who as we have seen coincidentally also was the King's choice). There was a shortage of sailing crews for the expedition, since the main fleet was being equipped at the same time. The main fleet was intended to safeguard the Baltic Sea lines of communications against possible Dutch and Danish incursions, which was a far greater threat than any Muscovite maritime activities in the Gulf of Finland. Even so, the Council found a neat solution. It decided that Wrangel's squadron would depart with skeleton crews. When the squadron reached Finland, Wrangel could reinforce his crews from the Finnish sailors sent ahead manning the supply ships.[27]

Meanwhile, Gustav Evertsson Horn, Governor-General of Ingria and Kexholm County, took charge of intelligence collection from Muscovy. Already by late March 1656, Horn had voiced suspicions about the preparations for war then ongoing in Muscovy.[28] In Livonia, intelligence reports about Muscovite preparations had reached De la Gardie at about the same time, or perhaps even earlier in March. Further north in Finland, in Kajaneborg (the castle of Kajana, modern-day Kajaani), information about the planned invasion arrived only in late June, no doubt because of the longer distances and accordingly longer travel times, but it came from Muscovite border officials in Kem, a trading town on the White Sea. The Kem officials wanted to negotiate a local border truce. Since both Muscovites and Swedes in this region depended on the cross-border trade, it was customary in times of war to negotiate a local truce regardless of decisions taken in Stockholm and Moscow (and one was agreed this time, too).[29]

---

26 Lappalainen, 'Finland', pp.25, 62, 68.

27 Askgaard, *Kampen om Östersjön*, pp.74–5; Lappalainen, 'Finland', pp.26, 80.

28 Lappalainen, 'Finland', p.27. On a captured spy, a certain Trofim Zubkov who worked for a Swedish border post, see *ibid.*, pp.39–40.

29 Lappalainen, 'Finland', pp.28–9.

Gustav Evertsson Horn had already in April devised a plan for how the army in Finland, in case of war with Muscovy, could go on the offensive. He suggested the establishment of a fleet in Lake Ladoga to prevent Muscovite maritime activities there and to sever the communications route between Olonets and the Muscovite towns in the south and east such as Novgorod and Tikhvin. Under such conditions, the fleet and army could go on the offensive towards Lake Onega further to the east, to sever the communications route between the White Sea in the north, which was the chief source of salt to Muscovy, and the Muscovite heartland (the chief salt producer was the wealthy, fortified Solovetsk Monastery, located on an island in the White Sea and a centre for Old Believers).[30] The plan was ambitious and might have caused major difficulties to Muscovy, but the problem was, Sweden did not yet have a fleet in Lake Ladoga when war broke out.

Horn also made arrangements to purchase 1,000 muskets in Narva, which he ordered delivered to Nyen. However, when the ship arrived at Nyen in mid June, Nyen was already abandoned, so the muskets were sent to Viborg instead. In addition, Horn issued orders to raise levies, but these orders seem to have come too late. In any case, there were no weapons available, nor regular soldiers to train the levies. As for Kexholm County, Horn sent reinforcements to the garrison and building materials to fortify the walls.[31] Kexholm's commandant, Olof Bengtsson (1608–1679; later ennobled Granatenburg), was a veteran of the early years of Sweden's participation in the Thirty Years' War who had served as commandant at remote Kexholm for more than 20 years. He now armed 130 burghers and 75 servants of nobles. In early July, 25 artillerymen and 222 infantry including officers arrived from Viborg. As a result, the total defensive force reached more than 400 men.[32]

In Viborg with surroundings, at least 820 peasant levies were raised and armed. Some additional peasant levies (of unknown number) who arrived mounted were promptly 'converted' into dragoons. Elsewhere, peasant levies assembled, too, effectively raising themselves. However, in most cases the officials sent them home, instead preferring to rely on conscription to get recruits for the regular army. In Viborg itself, many students temporarily joined the army as a provisional burgher militia. By providing the students with large quantities of food and alcohol, 13 of them were persuaded to enlist as regular army officers. The Viborg commanders also spent efforts repairing the town walls, which had not been maintained for decades. This was sorely needed. As late as in early August, Field Marshal Lewenhaupt, who was not known for flights of fancy, complained that the town walls were in such poor shape that 'people and cattle freely could walk across' them.[33]

Another problem was shortages in ammunition and equipment. The most urgent deficit was slow-match for the army's matchlock muskets. Despite great improvements since the early years of the Thirty Years' War, Sweden still lacked the required manufacturing capacity with regard to slow-match, so often faced

30   *Ibid.*, p.29.
31   *Ibid.*, pp.32–3.
32   *Ibid.*, p.48.
33   *Ibid.*, pp.46–8.

Top Nöteborg, seventeenth-century print; centre and above, Nöteborg from the sea (photo: Veikia) and air. (Author's collection)

shortages. Because of the urgent situation in Finland the Crown began to levy locally produced tows, that is, coarse, broken fibre removed during the processing of flax, which old, retired soldiers then spun into makeshift slow-match. Another shortage was that of bandoliers. Many newly raised soldiers received makeshift shoulder bags to hold ammunition and gunpowder instead of bandoliers, which were simply unavailable.[34]

The Invasion of Ingria

In June, Pyotr Potyomkin's Muscovite corps crossed the border to Ingria almost according to schedule. The Muscovites quickly dispersed the small border guard, 50 men under Captain Arvid Orre from the East Nyland Regiment who despite being infantry had been provided with horses for transportation and for the time being accordingly served as dragoons. Potyomkin's men captured Orre and some of his soldiers, while the other survivors fled to nearby Nöteborg.[35] The Orthodox population immediately swore fealty to the Tsar. On the following day, Potyomkin's army proceeded to Nöteborg.[36] This was a mediaeval castle built on an island at the exit of the River Neva into Lake Ladoga, some 45 km east of modern-day St Petersburg. Known as Fortress Hazelnut (Russian: *orekhov*, alternatively *oreshek*; Swedish: *Nöteborg*), the fortified island commanded a strategic location which dominated shipping along the Neva.[37] Potyomkin dispatched several inshore vessels to assist in the attack on Nöteborg.

Potyomkin did not stop there, however. Instead, on the following day he advanced overland further westwards, to the town of Nyen (named after the River Neva; Muscovites called the town's small fortress Kantsy and the location forms part of modern-day St Petersburg).

The population of Nyen rapidly panicked when the news of the invasion arrived, just ahead of Potyomkin's corps. The town had no walls, and many of the Lutheran burghers had already moved themselves or at least their belongings to Viborg. Now the few who remained rapidly skipped town. The lower strata of society were left behind, but they consoled themselves with the abundant beer and wine supplies abandoned by the burghers, most of which apparently was immediately consumed, before the arrival of the Muscovites. Potyomkin's men were only met by a few drunken soldiers. One man, waving a sword but dressed solely in a nightgown, single-handedly charged towards the Muscovites but instead of attacking merely continued running past them. The Muscovite soldiers let him pass through their ranks unharmed, since the man was obviously intoxicated. Fortunately for Potyomkin, the merchants of

---

34 *Ibid.*, p/69.

35 Orre was sent to Novgorod but was eventually released; he returned to active duty during the war and was in 1658 made commander of the Finnish Retinue of Nobles.

36 Lappalainen, 'Finland', p.37.

37 Swedish units conquered Nöteborg in 1612, and Muscovy formally ceded the castle to Sweden in the 1617 Treaty of Stolbovo. Ultimately, Tsar Peter the Great renamed the fortress Schlüsselburg (modern-day Shlissel'burg), German for Key Castle, since he regarded it as the key to Ingria.

Nyen had also abandoned the town's grain supplies. Potyomkin and his men moved into Nyen, from which they distributed the surplus grain supplies among the local Orthodox peasants. Potyomkin also found the town's eight abandoned cannons, which he used to reinforce his own small artillery train (he had no siege artillery). His main reason to take Nyen was not plunder. Several sources agree that Potyomkin awaited a shipment of ammunition from the German town of Lübeck, which was due to arrive in late June. Some Swedish observers suggested that the ship may also have brought foreign officers for the Tsar's new formation regiments.[38] This is unknown, but certainly many foreign officers travelled to Muscovy to enlist there.

Meanwhile, Potyomkin's men laid siege to Nöteborg. The garrison of Nöteborg consisted of 18 officers and 87 soldiers under Major Frans Grave. The castle had 15 cannons and some artillerymen under Lieutenant Bengt Anderson. As soon as the Muscovites arrived, Grave had the outlying buildings burned, so as to deny them to the enemy. He did not immediately burn the Orthodox church; however, the Muscovites used it for cover, so on the fifth day of the siege, Grave sent a party of men in two boats who burned the building (the now empty site still remained useful to the Muscovites, who later deployed the captured artillery from Nyen there). Potyomkin had left only a few hundred men to continue the siege, while the remaining Muscovites were dispatched in detachments to secure the countryside. By all accounts, Potyomkin treated both the Lutheran and Orthodox peasant communities well. Some Lutheran peasants joined the Muscovite cause, many probably out of fear but others because the Muscovite commanders promised tax exemptions for anybody who joined them.

The problem for Potyomkin was that Nöteborg dominated the sailing route in the River Neva. He wanted to move his inshore craft to the Gulf of Finland, and if Nöteborg refused to surrender, he would have to devise some other means. The Neva was impossible for large ships and difficult even for small vessels, in particular when moving upstream from the Gulf of Finland to Ladoga, since only a narrow channel in the middle of the river was navigable and the water flowed very fast. The river bed consisted of sand, which changed over time because of the current, making it yet more difficult. Moreover, and this affected voyages in both directions, parts of the river consisted of rapids. Fortunately, it was not unheard of in this part of the world to drag river craft overland. In early July, Potyomkin's men succeeded in dragging 20 river craft overland a distance of 2.5 km to a location beyond Nöteborg's range of fire where they could rejoin the Neva and continue by water to Nyen.[39] However limited, Potyomkin finally had maritime assets in the easternmost part of the Gulf of Finland. Over time, he brought yet more river craft into the Gulf, building a force which ultimately may have reached 50 vessels.

Despite his limited manpower, Potyomkin and his two subordinates, Sila Potyomkin and Ivan Poltev, now dominated eastern Ingria and the Karelian

---

38 Lappalainen, 'Finland', pp.38–9; Hedberg, *Kungl. Artilleriet: Carl X Gustafs tid*, p.104.
39 Lappalainen, 'Finland', pp.43–4; Hedberg, *Kungl. Artilleriet: Carl X Gustafs tid*, p.104.

Isthmus, that is, the territory between the Gulf of Finland and Lake Ladoga to the north of the River Neva. He also dominated the eastern shore of the Gulf of Finland. Potyomkin could not take Nöteborg, which refused to surrender, but on the other hand, he had found the means to negate this stronghold's importance. The entire campaign had taken only a month, and Potyomkin's rapid movements had, incorrectly, convinced most Swedish defenders that he greatly outnumbered them.

The Swedish commanders needed to reopen the communications route disrupted by Potyomkin, but in light of the limited resources available, this was easier said than done. In early July, the Governor-General of Ingria, Gustav Evertsson Horn, sent 200 cavalry and 40 mounted infantrymen to Kaporie further to the east. It is unlikely that he expected this detachment to be able to regain the Karelian Isthmus, but he needed information on the situation there. However, at Kaporie the inexperienced Swedes were taken by surprise in a Muscovite night attack. Even though the attack was repulsed, the Swedes deemed they were too few to pursue, so they returned to Narva.[40] Henceforth, western Ingria became a contested territory, where Swedes and Muscovites engaged in small war against each other. It was accordingly up to the commanders in Finland to make the next attempt to reopen the route.

The Invasion of Kexholm County

Meanwhile, the Muscovite attack on Kexholm commenced as well. In mid July, Pushkin's men finally laid siege to the town. North of Lake Ladoga, small Muscovite units entered Finland, too.

The attack was delayed because Pushkin was unable to act with the speed of his colleague Potyomkin. In part, this was because of the conflicting orders which seem to have confused the schedule, but to an even greater degree the delay was caused by Chelishchev's arrogance. Chelishchev did not wait for Pushkin to conclude preparations. Instead, he moved out on his own against easier targets which presented opportunities for personal profit or entertainment. This included looting and random acts of violence but also tax collection in the name of the Tsar, which in reality seems to have been a ruse to fill Chelishchev's own coffers. Because of Chelishchev's activities, Pushkin's army reached Kexholm only well after the town had received warning that Muscovites were ravaging the area.

The first of Chelishchev's adventures involved the dispatch of his son Mikhail with cavalry and 105 streltsy to capture the Swedish border post at Salmis on the eastern shore of Lake Ladoga. The attack succeeded, and the Mayor of Salmis, Henrik Blanckenhagen, was captured with 12 of his 20 or so men. Only one Muscovite fell in the attack. Blanckenhagen, who since 1634 also served as the Swedish border inspector and thus head of the border guard, spoke Russian. He told Chelishchev that he could persuade Kexholm to surrender, so the Muscovite sent him to Pushkin in Olonets.

---

40 Fagerlund, 'Kriget i östersjöprovinserna', p.93.

Kexholm Castle. (Photo: Tommi Nummelin)

Perhaps the claim was a means to avoid torture at the hands of the notoriously violent Chelishchev. Pushkin, whose plans were already in ruins because of Chelishchev's activities, eventually came to believe Blanckenhagen (who nonetheless died in captivity).[41] Although there is nothing to indicate that Blanckenhagen either could, or would, persuade Olof Bengtsson, the commandant at Kexholm, to surrender, the discussions may have delayed Pushkin's operation against Kexholm yet further.

Kexholm consisted of a fortified town built on an island next to the north bank of the River Vuoksi (Swedish: Vuoksen), which in earlier centuries had constituted the Karelians' main sailing and trade route across the Karelian Isthmus from the Gulf of Finland to Lake Ladoga. In those days, and perhaps still at the time of the Deluge, it was possible to sail a river craft along this route all the way to Viborg. Next to the town, there was another island on which was built a small castle. In mid July, Pushkin's fleet entered Kexholm's port at night. Even though the defenders had received early warning of the Muscovite approach through the ill-advised activities of Chelishchev, they were still surprised by the sudden arrival. Pushkin did not immediately attempt to storm the well-defended Kexholm. Instead, he deployed two companies between the port and town and demanded the town's surrender. The commandant, Bengtsson, had no intention of giving up. His garrison consisted of some 100 infantry, including a few artillerymen under artillery lieutenant Daniel Larsson, but the townsmen and burghers were able to fight, too. Immediately upon the arrival of the Muscovites, Bengtsson sent men to burn the farm buildings on the south bank of the Vuoksi.

---

41 Lappalainen, 'Finland', p.21; Gullberg and Huhtamies, *På vakt i öster*, vol. 3, pp.91–3. The attack took place on 2 June (O.S.), only one day later than the originally planned invasion date. However, since Chelishchev ordered the attack as the immediate response to an intelligence report, the attack took place by chance, not according to the plan.

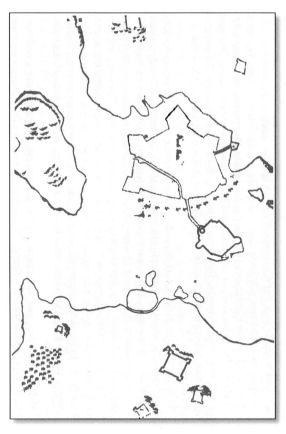

Contemporary hand-drawn sketch of what is believed to be the siege of Kexholm, 1656. (Swedish Military Archive (KrA), Finska handritade kartor, Kexholm nr 17)

Soon afterwards, Pushkin's men took up positions there, where they also built a redoubt, and on the next day they built a second redoubt on the north side of the river. While Pushkin initiated the siege at once, he had only one 4-pounder and some lighter artillery pieces, described as falconets. Kexholm was defended by six or eight cannons, most of them four-pounders. The Muscovite artillery's effect on the fortified town was minimal, so after about a week, Pushkin had his artillery moved at night to the rocky island of Kalliosaari, to the west of Kexholm. From this island, it was possible to fire into the town from above. He sent 50 streltsy and 29 levied Orthodox Kexholm peasants under a Captain Mikhaylov to carry out the operation. Realising the danger, Bengtsson ordered a party of 80 men under Gerhard Corving to row across the water, storm Kalliosaari, and evict the Muscovites. Corving carried out the order without difficulties. Losing five men of his own, Corving estimated the number of fallen Muscovites to have reached some 40, including Captain Mikhaylov. Corving's men also took eight captives. When questioned, they reported that Pushkin had 1,200 men, under himself and his subordinate Stepan Parfen'yevich Yelagin, in addition to 50 levied Kexholm peasants. Following the failure on Kalliosaari, Pushkin ordered the construction of a better redoubt on the north side of the river, for which logs were taken through the demolition of the wooden Lutheran church there. He also had two redoubts built on the south side. Then he settled down, awaiting the arrival of heavier artillery. Meanwhile, since neither side dominated the river, Bengtsson remained in communications with Viborg, 100 km away, which received information about the attack from a courier already on the day after Pushkin's arrival.[42]

The Karelian Isthmus and the Gulf of Finland

We have seen that Potyomkin despite his limited manpower now dominated the Karelian Isthmus, eastern Ingria, and the eastern shore of the Gulf of Finland. Without Nyen, the Swedes no longer had access to the overland route between Finland and Ingria. In western Ingria, the Swedish commander Gustav Evertsson Horn lacked the resources to go on the offensive towards the east. Although skirmishes continued in Ingria, Horn focused on holding the Narva line. Lacking trained soldiers, he called out the general levy of Estonia. This produced, Horn noted, a couple of thousand peasants who

---

42 Lappalainen, 'Finland', pp.54–6; Hedberg, *Kungl. Artilleriet: Carl X Gustafs tid*, p.104.

were expected to arm themselves, often with improvised weapons.[43]

Beyond a few isolated outposts, the main Swedish troop concentration in the region at this point in time was the fortified town of Viborg in Finland. The Viborg command was not idle. In late June, some 100 Viborg cavalry and dragoons under Berendt Gröön and Reinhold Johan von Hagen advanced upon the little Ladoga town of Taipale between Kexholm and Nöteborg. At first, they were accompanied by several hundred peasant levies. However, upon learning that the Muscovites at Taipale had brought a strong cavalry force, the levies were sent home. Instead, Gröön and Hagen proceeded on their own. They received intelligence that Potyomkin had returned to Nyen, leaving a garrison of only 80 men in Taipale to augment the remaining Orthodox town militia (who technically were Swedish subjects but now had sworn fealty to the Tsar). Gröön and Hagen accordingly attacked Taipale at night. They set fire to the town so as to push out both Muscovites and townsmen. The surprise attack was successful, and most of the defenders took to the boats, departing across the Ladoga. The rest, whether Muscovites or Orthodox townsmen, were massacred. While the killing of enemy captives and wounded was not a universal practice in the Finnish–Muscovite borderlands and some senior commanders took steps to prevent it, many officers on both sides made a habit of the practice. After the raid, the Viborg troops abandoned the ruined town, returning to Viborg. There was little else they could do there. As a result, in July Muscovite units again moved into the ruins of Taipale.[44]

The Viborg command then began to plan for an offensive to retake Nyen. However, when they received news about the siege of Kexholm, they instead sent the available units to relieve this town. Fortunately for Viborg, a veteran officer, Colonel Christopher Burmeister (c. 1600–1671), was in the area for the purpose of enlisting a new cavalry regiment. In late July, Burmeister led his 150 cavalry, 200 dragoons, and some 820 levied peasants in a relief expedition to Kexholm. On the way, they set up camp at Rautus, where there was a church. Making use of the church building, they fortified the camp, which was fortunate for the Swedes, since at 4:00 a.m. in the following morning, a Muscovite force under Sila Potyomkin attacked. Learning about the Swedish relief expedition to Kexholm, Pyotr Potyomkin had sent Sila Potyomkin's corps to shield Pushkin's siege of Kexholm from Swedish interference from the south. We do not know the number of men in Sila Potyomkin's corps, but they can hardly have been more than the Swedes. Burmeister and his men repulsed both the first and second attack. Potyomkin's Muscovites then retreated, pursued by Burmeister's horse. Although many Muscovites reportedly fell in the pursuit, Burmeister's men were too few for the battle to achieve any conclusive results. The Swedes captured four flags and drums and reportedly 250 muskets, which the retreating Muscovites probably abandoned. Swedish losses in dead were three officers, three corporals, and some 20 common soldiers. The wounded included another three officers and at least 58 under-officers and common soldiers. The losses suggest that the engagement was a major battle, even

43   Fagerlund, 'Kriget i östersjöprovinserna', p.94.
44   Lappalainen, 'Finland', p.52.

though neither side consisted of more than a few hundred regulars. The levied peasants seem not to have played any major role in the battle. Because of shortages in ammunition and, in particular, slow-match, Burmeister then returned to Viborg, after which the Muscovites again returned to their previous positions in the Karelian Isthmus.[45]

The battle of Rautus shows that Pushkin and Potyomkin had no difficulties in co-ordinating their operations. Certainly, the already described co-operation problems *within* Pushkin's command complicated his activities, but he and Potyomkin nonetheless operated in conjunction with each other. This was something that the Swedish commanders in Finland and Ingria had not yet been able to accomplish in the Karelian Isthmus. Perhaps they did not yet see the need, since they still enjoyed command of the sea in the Gulf of Finland.

However, Potyomkin's conquest of Nyen had opened the River Neva for the Muscovite inshore fleet in Lake Ladoga. In early August, Potyomkin brought additional river craft (rowing boats of the *lodja* type) into the Gulf of Finland, bringing the total up to some 50. The only Swedish naval vessel on duty was a small reconnaissance sailing vessel from Narva commanded by Erik Dansonwille, which since mid July had patrolled the eastern part of the Gulf of Finland. Dansonwille's vessel was armed with four falconets and, in addition to the sailing crew, carried 30 musketeers from the East Nyland Regiment. In early August, Dansonwille encountered Potyomkin's squadron at the island of Reitskär (Finnish: Retusaari; Russian: Kotlin) not far from Nyen. Wind conditions did not allow Dansonwille to escape, so a naval engagement took place. Early on, Dansonwille sank two of Potyomkin's rowing vessels with falconet fire. However, Dansonwille knew that he could not win a prolonged battle. Moreover, he knew that Ingrian peasants who had sworn allegiance to Muscovy held the shore. After throwing the falconets and everything else of value overboard, Dansonwille beached his vessel. However, the Ingrians and Muscovites killed or captured most of his crew as they attempted to make their escape through the forest. Dansonwille was captured, too. Potyomkin sent him to the Nöteborg camp as a prisoner of war. Eight of Dansonwille's captured men instead went into Muscovite service.[46] Potyomkin had won a flawless victory (and the battle, insignificant as it was, is traditionally regarded as the first victory of the Russian Navy). However, the battle had also exposed the vulnerability of his inshore vessels to even light artillery fire. After the battle, the Muscovites destroyed the village on Reitskär. However, five days later, rumours of the impending arrival of a Swedish war fleet persuaded Potyomkin to order his squadron back into the Neva, all the way to the Nöteborg area. It was a prudent precaution; warships carried both more and heavier artillery than what had been available to Dansonwille.

As noted, the Admiralty in Stockholm had appointed Vice-Admiral Gustav Wrangel commander of a relief squadron to the eastern Gulf of Finland. Wrangel's orders were to patrol the Viborg archipelago and the

---

45   *Ibid.*, pp.56–8.
46   *Ibid.*, p.59.

waters around Nyen for the rest of the year, until the Gulf of Finland was closed to shipping by ice.[47] His squadron consisted of three warships: *Jägaren*, *Näktergalen*, and *Danske Prinsen*. *Jägaren* (also known as *Gröne Jägaren*; 'Green Hunter') was the only real warship, 30 m long and armed with 20 or, more likely, 22 cannons. *Näktergalen* ('Nightingale') was a pinnace employed for customs duties with eight or, most likely, 10 cannons, while *Danske Prinsen* ('The Danish Prince') was a pinnace once captured from the Danes and since employed for customs duties, with only six cannons. A pinnace was a small full-rigged ship of a type that would later develop into the frigate. The squadron also included the kray *Björkö*, named after an island. A kray was a small square-rigged merchantman with two or three masts; the type was known in the Baltic as *kraier* or, in Swedish, *krejer* or *krejare*. In addition, Wrangel had two yachts (small, fast sailing vessels of the Dutch model with leeboards which enabled them to work to windward), one named *Sjöhästen* ('Sea Horse') and the other only referred to as the Admiral's Yacht. He also brought one longboat (*esping*) with a sailing rig and 22 rowing vessels of the *lodja* type. In August, Wrangel could add the kray *Ulfsund* (four cannons), named after a harbour, which served as the Admiralty's liaison ship. Ultimately, 96 sailors and artillerymen were raised, which was sufficient to provide the skeleton crews needed to sail the squadron to Finland, where additional crew could be embarked. Each *lodja*, for instance, was crewed by only two men during the voyage across the Baltic Sea. In addition, 136 men from the Uppland Regiment were ordered aboard to assist the sailors and to serve as marines.

In less than two weeks' time, Wrangel's squadron set out, bound for the Gulf of Finland. In mid July, the squadron reached Helsingfors (modern-day Helsinki). In early August, Wrangel's squadron arrived to the waters around Viborg and Nyen. By then, he had taken aboard additional men, increasing the crew's strength to almost 493 men. The squadron was also joined by two additional vessels of the *lodja* type and another longboat.[48]

Wrangel's arrival in the Gulf of Finland effectively prevented further Muscovite naval operations there. As a result, the Swedes in late August made the first attempt to co-ordinate their army units in Finland and Ingria. Gustav Evertsson Horn, who by then had received some reinforcements from Finland by sea, set out from Narva to meet and join forces with Field Marshal Lewenhaupt from Viborg and Wrangel's squadron from Stockholm. Their target was Nyen, and the goal was to reopen the land route. Somewhat delayed because of Muscovite activities at Wask-Narva (see below), Horn left Narva with 600 cavalry and 300 musketeers, advancing by way of Kaporie towards Nyen. However, upon approaching Nyen he learnt that neither Lewenhaupt nor Wrangel was in place. Wrangel's squadron had been at the appointed place but had already departed, while Lewenhaupt had returned to Viborg for infantry reinforcements. Wrangel's smaller vessels had indeed sailed up the Neva to Nyen, but without support from Lewenhaupt's army

---

47 *Ibid.*, p.81.
48 *Ibid.*, pp.80–81, 178; Askgaard, *Kampen om Östersjön*, pp.71, 75, 77. *Danske Prinsen* is identified as a pinnace in archive documents: *Ibid.*, p.539 n.158.

units, Wrangel after a skirmish with Sila Potyomkin returned into the Gulf of Finland.[49] Horn then changed his plans. Instead of advancing on Nyen without support, he attacked a Muscovite redoubt at Ingris (on modern-day River Izhora), south of Nyen. The redoubt had been established by Ivan Poltev, who had commandeered local peasants to build it (Poltev's original corps consisted of only 250 soldiers and cossacks[50]). Horn's attack failed, so he decided to retreat in order to re-establish communications with Wrangel at Reitskär. Soon after, Pyotr Potyomkin with some 200 cossacks arrived from Nöteborg. In light of the Swedish offensive, which so far had not been well co-ordinated but yet represented a significant force, Potyomkin ordered his men back to Nöteborg, leaving only a redoubt manned by 400 men half-way between Nyen and Nöteborg as a defensive measure.[51]

Soon afterwards, Horn and Wrangel made another attempt to retake Nyen and reopen the land route. This time, the attempt succeeded. In early September, Horn reached the abandoned Nyen, where he destroyed the newly established Muscovite palisade. Meanwhile, Wrangel attempted but failed to make it upriver because of contrary winds and the rapid water flow. He accordingly retreated to await the arrival of Lewenhaupt.[52]

Lewenhaupt's Expedition to Kexholm

Lewenhaupt had left Viborg in mid August with the Viborg Cavalry Regiment, about 100 dragoons, and some field artillery. Before advancing all the way to Nyen, he sent out Lieutenant Colonel Erik Pistolhielm with 300 horse to investigate the situation at Kexholm. Pistolhielm raided a Muscovite camp, captured a flag, and took some prisoners. His own losses were four dead and a few wounded. After interrogating the Muscovite prisoners, he had them hanged. After Pistolhielm's return, Lewenhaupt himself led 500 cavalry and 100 dragoons towards Nyen. After a skirmish with Sila Potyomkin, he concluded that he could not defeat the Muscovites without infantry. Moreover, Aleksandr Potyomkin's Don cossacks showed up in his rear, which resulted in another skirmish. Because of the marshlands in which the skirmishes took place, neither side could use its cavalry properly.

Instead of proceeding to join forces with Horn and Wrangel at Nyen, Lewenhaupt returned to Viborg to gather some infantry. He also hoped to discuss the campaign plan with Wrangel. In early September, Lewenhaupt again set out, but this time to relieve Kexholm. He brought some infantry from the Tavastehus Regiment.

By then, Pushkin had received two cannons from Novgorod, which enabled him to put yet more efforts into the siege of Kexholm. In addition to artillery and musket fire, he let loose burning rafts in an attempt to set the town on fire. However, Bengtsson found volunteers who in exchange

---

49 Lappalainen, 'Finland', p.82.
50 Gadzyatskiy, 'Bor'ba', p.25.
51 Lappalainen, 'Finland', pp.87–8.
52 *Ibid.*, p.88.

for ample vodka supplies were willing to undertake the dangerous work of building, under enemy fire, water barriers which prevented the rafts from reaching their destination.[53]

In mid September, Lewenhaupt finally reached Kexholm. This time, Lewenhaupt was prepared for anything. In addition to the cavalry and dragoons from Viborg and the Tavastehus infantry, he brought a field artillery train in the form of two 6-pounders, four 3-pounders, and two mortars (one 80-pounder and one 100-pounder). Moreover, with considerable difficulty his men managed to move a siege artillery as well in the form of two 24-pounders with the army. Lewenhaupt immediately sent the infantry and dragoons into action against one of Pushkin's redoubts, but he was unable to deploy the artillery. After three hours of combat, the Swedes retreated with serious losses. By then, Lieutenant Colonel Olof Lagercrantz, who had led the assault, had fallen, together with two other officers. The total number of dead and wounded was about 60. The assault party almost lost its colour, but it was saved by a drummer boy. In comparison, the Muscovites suffered very few casualties.

Even so, during the night the Muscovites abandoned the redoubt. It seems that they had seen the ongoing deployment of the two heavy cannons and drawn the conclusion that they could not withstand a second assault. It was probably not the artillery support as such which determined the Muscovite decision (we will see that the other redoubts could withstand artillery fire). Probably, the first redoubt was too isolated for it to receive support from the other two. As a result, Lewenhaupt managed to re-establish communications with Kexholm, even though combat with Pushkin's corps continued, with the Muscovites defending themselves from two other redoubts. Lewenhaupt did not attempt to storm either of them but instead ordered his siege artillery into action. Unfortunately for the Swedes, the intensity of fire turned out to be too high, so after three days, both 24-pounders shattered, first one, then the other. Lewenhaupt then decided to abandon the attempt to dislodge the Muscovites. He reinforced the Kexholm garrison with 40 infantrymen, sent in additional supplies including cattle and hops for beer-brewing, and evacuated the ill and wounded together with women and children. This left the garrison with supplies for nine months, enough to last throughout the winter. Lewenhaupt's men had taken 10 prisoners, mostly peasants, whom Lewenhaupt then had hanged, after which he departed for Nyen. The women and children were sent under escort to Viborg.[54]

Meanwhile, fighting took place elsewhere along the border as well. Ingria remained a contested territory. Prince Ivan Golitsyn, the commander of the Novgorod Army, in August dispatched a second Muscovite corps into Ingria, in addition to that headed by Potyomkin who operated on the Neva. The second corps, consisting of some 630 old-style cavalry, dragoons, streltsy, new formation infantry, and assorted other men under Semyon Tolbugin, deployed further to the south. Except for some limited raiding, Tolbugin's

---

53 *Ibid.*, pp.89–90.
54 *Ibid.*, pp.90–91; Hedberg, *Kungl. Artilleriet: Carl X Gustafs tid*, p.105; Gadzyatskiy, 'Kareliya', p.257.

main task was apparently to guard the Muscovite border. Tolbugin had no means to support Potyomkin on the Neva, which was too far away and difficult to reach because of the terrain.[55]

There was yet more naval activity in the Gulf of Finland, too. In July, King Charles had again written to the Council of the Realm in Stockholm. He requested the dispatch of a second naval squadron of three to four warships to the Gulf of Finland and also to the Gulf of Riga. King Charles wanted to establish a blockade system so as to prevent enemy ships from entering or leaving the Gulf of Finland, or approaching Riga. In late August or early September, the second squadron accordingly left Stockholm bound for the Gulf of Finland. Commanded by Captain Gustav Sperling, it consisted of the three ships *Salvator*, *Svan* ('Swan'), and *Falken* ('The Falcon') and had orders to patrol the western Gulf of Finland and ensure that the communications line between Finland and Livonia remained open. Sperling was also ordered to prevent any additional arms supplies to Muscovy through the Gulf of Finland. Ultimately, a *struts* named *Väktaren* ('The Guardian') with four cannons was also attached to Sperling's squadron.[56]

During the autumn, Wrangel's squadron, too, received further reinforcements, in vessels and men, until in September he commanded three warships, four merchant ships, 22 vessels of the *lodja* type, and one longboat. His total manpower was then 506.[57]

In mid September, Horn, Wrangel, and Lewenhaupt finally managed to concentrate their forces at Nyen. On the north bank of the Neva, Lewenhaupt gathered some 860 cavalry, 200 dragoons, and 300 infantry. On the south bank, Horn assembled 500 horse and 250 foot. Wrangel had brought most of his squadron upriver to Nyen. In total, the three officers commanded some 2,500 men, which constituted a significant force on the Karelian Isthmus. However, because of the poor roads and the fact that Potyomkin had destroyed the bridges, the three concluded that it was not feasible to relieve Nöteborg. Instead, they built a new bastion at Nyen, where they deployed some 130 men under Captain Johan Sabelhierta.[58]

In October, the three forces again separated. Wrangel returned to Viborg to lay up his squadron for the winter. This was a necessary precaution, since the Gulf of Finland generally was covered by ice in winter. This year winter had come early, and two of his vessels were already stuck in ice. Wrangel then returned to Stockholm in *Jägaren*.[59] Horn returned south to assist in a relief expedition to Dorpat. Leaving a garrison of 100 cavalry and 50 dragoons at Kaporie, Horn was back in Narva in mid October.[60] Lewenhaupt established a main camp in Rautus. It seems that the three commanders had concluded that the Neva line only could be defended from Viborg in Finland, not Narva.

---

55 Gadzyatskiy, 'Bor'ba', p.26.
56 Askgaard, *Kampen om Östersjön*, pp.79–80; citing a letter from the King dated 5 July 1656 (uncertain whether O.S. or N.S) ; Lappalainen, 'Finland', p.83.
57 Lappalainen, 'Finland', p.81.
58 *Ibid.*, p.92.
59 Askgaard, *Kampen om Östersjön*, p.78. Wrangel arrived in Stockholm with *Jägaren* during the night between 25 and 26 November.
60 Fagerlund, 'Kriget i östersjöprovinserna', pp.94–5; Lappalainen, 'Finland', pp.87–8.

Henceforth, it was Viborg which became the headquarters for operations in the Karelian Isthmus.[61]

Meanwhile, Chelishchev had continued raiding activities on his own. He was not the only one. Bands of independent Orthodox peasant raiders ravaged the borderlands, torturing and killing whoever they caught. They attacked Lutheran churches, vicars' houses, and noble estates, all of which they usually burned. Moreover, Chelishchev's son-in-law, a likeminded noble known as Sergey Zelyonyy ('Sergey the Green') took the raids all the way into Finland. He set up headquarters at a remote village named Villala, conveniently located with river access to many parts of inner Finland, where he gathered boats, supplies, and not the least, men who shared his and his father-in-law's buccaneering attitude to war, be they Orthodox locals or Muscovite soldiers. From this location, Sergey the Green threatened not only Savolax but Kajana as well. His band may well have included regular soldiers, although this is unknown. They certainly carried unit flags with them. However, it was not unheard of for peasants to bring flags of their own, so this does not necessarily signify that they were regulars. Be that as it may, the raiders systematically plundered the area, burning villages and devastating the harvest. In August, a raiding party was sufficiently strong to attack and burn the wooden town of Nyslott (Finnish: Savonlinna). The raiders reportedly used 50 large boats. There was a castle at Nyslott, manned by 10 retired soldiers and up to 40 burghers who managed to reach it in time to take refuge. Swedes and Muscovites apparently opened fire on one another, but the raiders were uninterested in the castle, and the small garrison could do nothing to prevent the destruction of the town.[62]

Lewenhaupt had dispatched a relief force of 50 men to Nyslott, but they arrived too late. However, a combined task force under the command of Major Erik Boije, consisting of 150 fresh cavalry from Wilhelm von Yxkull's Tavastehus Cavalry Regiment and 100 dragoons in September deployed to the area with orders to operate as a mobile counterinsurgency task force. In late September Boije's men surprised and destroyed part of the marauders who had raided Nyslott.[63]

As a result of the raiding activities, Finnish peasants in many locations self-mobilised. This was in part to protect their families and property, but also to reimburse their losses by doing some raiding on their own. In northern Savolax, Lutheran peasants began large-scale attacks on their Orthodox neighbours, causing what essentially was a civil war among themselves which was unrelated to the general state of hostilities between Sweden and Muscovy.[64]

Meanwhile, the siege of Kexholm continued. Already on the day after Lewenhaupt's departure from Kexholm in mid September, Pushkin received reinforcements from Pyotr Potyomkin's corps at Nöteborg. Nonetheless, Pushkin decided to abandon the southern bank of the river. Instead, the Muscovites built a new redoubt on the north bank. In early October, the

---

61   Lappalainen, 'Finland', p.93.
62   *Ibid.*, pp.84–5.
63   *Ibid.*, p.85.
64   *Ibid.*, pp.86–7.

Kexholm garrison attempted a ruse. Expecting the Muscovites not to have a good overview of the south bank, they in two hours' time made considerable noise, played their drums, and marched all the flags they had along the town wall, giving the impression that additional reinforcements had moved in from the south. The Muscovites fell for the ruse. During the night, they burned all redoubts except one. By design or ill luck, the six prisoners taken earlier perished in the fire (unlike so many others, Pushkin did not kill captives, but his subordinates may have been less merciful). The Muscovites then retreated, some by the land route north of Lake Ladoga, others by shipping out. Sergey the Green, who just had returned from a raid, was ordered south to reinforce Potyomkin at Nöteborg. Characteristically, the notorious marauder ignored the order, instead setting out to plunder peasants elsewhere. Exasperated, Pushkin dispatched a detachment to arrest Sergey the Green, but he could not be found. During the retreat, Pushkin took care to encourage and assist Orthodox peasants to relocate to Olonets. In part, this was to raise the peasant population in northern Muscovy, but in light of the ongoing civil war among Lutheran and Orthodox peasants in Finland, it was a prudent move to save the Orthodox population from retaliation. Most Orthodox peasants abandoned their homes and followed Pushkin's retreating corps.[65] Immediately upon his return to Olonets, Pushkin had two new redoubts built at the border with Kexholm County, at Rajakontu and Tulemajärvi. It was obvious that henceforth, he had a defensive strategy in mind. The direct reason was probably less his failure to take Kexholm than the supply difficulties brought on by the large influx of Orthodox migrants, all of whom must be fed. As usual in Muscovy, Pushkin had to send home most units over the winter, in particular the cavalry. Moreover, Pushkin's corps had suffered so many desertions during the campaign that by the end of the year, he had only some 440 regular infantry left (370 in Olonets, 30 in Rajakontu, and 40 in Tulemajärvi).[66]

Meanwhile, Nöteborg remained mostly cut off from other Swedish units (the occasional messenger still got through, although at great risk), but the stronghold was well supplied and quite safe. The commandant, Frans Grave, died of illness (probably the plague) but the new commandant, Johan Mårtensson Spiggh, remained defiant. Potyomkin's men could do little against its defences. Even the cannons eventually received from Novgorod could not be brought to bear properly. Potyomkin's corps also suffered from desertions. Don cossacks, in particular, seem to have caused particular problems, frequently deserting to plunder the surrounding peasant population, irrespective of whether they were Lutherans or Orthodox. In November, Potyomkin received orders from Novgorod to abandon the siege. He made several additional attempts to negotiate the stronghold's surrender, but to no avail. In late November, when the Muscovites celebrated a religious festival, Spiggh dispatched a sally party of some 20 men in eight small boats. The sally took the Muscovite artillery battery by surprise, overwhelmed the

65 *Ibid.*, pp.93–4; Gadzyatskiy, 'Kareliya', pp.257–9.
66 Lappalainen, 'Finland', p.100; Gadzyatskiy, 'Kareliya', p.261.

gun crews, nailed the cannons, and then returned with a prisoner. The only Swedish casualty was one man who was lightly wounded in the raid.[67]

With the onset of winter arose yet more difficulties for the besiegers. Realising that with frozen ground and rivers, it would be easier for a Swedish relief force to reach Nöteborg, Pushkin concentrated his units in one location. As a result, Spiggh attempted a ruse. First, he made a show by walking out on the ice with 10 men to test its thickness. Then, he had his entire force march across part of the ice, while all grown children and women of Nöteborg, dressed as men and armed with pikes and a makeshift flag, lined up on the town walls. The two formations then signalled to each other with the Swedish salute (two cannon shots in rapid succession), to give the impression that reinforcements had arrived. Although we do not know if Potyomkin fell for the ruse, the incident seems to have made up his mind. On the following day, his men destroyed the redoubts and those river vessels which were already stuck in the ice. They also destroyed significant supplies of ammunition and other supplies. Then, he abandoned the siege. Potyomkin took similar precautions as Pushkin with regard to the Orthodox peasants, most of whom were evacuated.[68]

---

67 Lappalainen, 'Finland', pp.95–7; Gadzyatskiy, 'Kareliya', pp.267–8.
68 Lappalainen, 'Finland', p.97.

14

Tsar Alexis Invades Livonia; the Siege of Riga

While Pushkin's and Potyomkin's primary objectives in the Ladoga region were to cut off Finland from the Baltic provinces and tie up the Finnish regiments so that they could not be used to reinforce Livonia, the bulk of the Swedish army in the Baltic territories was already deployed there before the outbreak of war between Sweden and Muscovy. In the summer of 1656, the Swedish army in the Baltic territories, most of which was in Livonia, consisted of 3,996 cavalry, 485 dragoons, and 7,683 infantry, in total 12,164 men.[1]

A month after the Muscovite offensives around Lake Ladoga began, the two planned offensives against Livonia were launched, too. One, from Pskov, was directed against eastern and northern Livonia with Dorpat as its first objective. Meanwhile, the other, and primary, offensive was launched from Polotsk and aimed to conquer Riga.

The war began with cross-border raiding. The first raiding party seems to have crossed the border in the vicinity of Rappin (modern-day Räpina) south of Lake Peipus in mid June. Some Orthodox peasants migrated into Muscovy, while others supported the Muscovite raiders. The second raid took place in the same place, at Rappin, but in mid July. Apparently, the raiding party consisted of seven banners and aimed for the territory around Neuhausen further to the south. The same evening, Major General Heinrich Streiff von Lauenstein led a small Swedish force into Muscovite territory, surprising the raiders in their camp at Pechory. He took prisoners, and it is possible that Lauenstein's decisive action disrupted and delayed the subsequent Muscovite offensive against Dorpat, since a prisoner told him that they actually belonged to the Muscovite advance party.

Nonetheless, the two Muscovite offensives in Livonia began in late July.

The Pskov Army (some 7,000 to 10,000 men) under Prince Aleksey Trubetskoy advanced from Pskov to Dorpat, the main town in north-eastern Livonia, to which they laid siege in early August.[2] Meanwhile, a detachment,

---

1 Fagerlund, 'Kriget i östersjöprovinserna', p.185.
2 Kurbatov, 'Rizhskiy pokhod'.

according to the Swedes some 1,200 men, moved against Neuhausen, which surrendered without a fight. The garrison, some 40 to 60 men, went into Muscovite service. Dorpat, with a garrison of 520 men including 100 cavalry under the governor, Lars Fleming, and the commandant, Wolmar von Ungern-Sternberg (1606–1667), was a tougher nut to crack.[3]

Muscovites at Riga

Meanwhile, further to the south, the Tsar led another, larger army through Commonwealth-held Lithuania towards Riga. The Tsar's main army, altogether 35,000 men, marched in two divisions: 20,000 under the Tsar and 15,000 under Prince Yakov Cherkasskiy.[4] The Tsar first took Braslau, where several Samogitian nobles greeted the Muscovite arrival. He then moved against Dünaburg, defended by a garrison of 350 men under Johan Willichman. Dünaburg fell in mid August. The Muscovites massacred the inhabitants, at which point the commandant, Willichman, reportedly grabbed the colours and threw himself into a burning building. Meanwhile, Tsar Alexis detached a contingent under Semyon Saknovich Tresnov which in late August advanced on Kokenhusen. Tresnov sent a trumpeter to demand the town's surrender. Kokenhusen was defended by Lieutenant Colonel Lars Sperling with some 300 men.[5] Perhaps Sperling had heard of the fate of Dünaburg and had no illusions of what a surrender might entail. In any case, the Swedish artillery in a flagrant breach of protocol immediately opened fire on the Muscovite trumpeter, killing him instantly. The Muscovites then stormed the town, killing everybody in retaliation.

---

3   Fagerlund, 'Kriget i östersjöprovinserna', pp.86–7.
4   Kurbatov, 'Rizhskiy pokhod'.
5   Fagerlund, 'Kriget i östersjöprovinserna', p.88.

Meanwhile, advance units of the army under Prince Yakov Cherkasskiy pushed on towards Riga, in constant combat with the retreating units of Major General Henrik von Thurn (d. 1656), commander of the small Swedish field army in Livonia. However, Thurn could do little to delay the Muscovites, who within days reached Riga.

There is no information on the size of Riga's garrison at the opening of the siege. By its end, the garrison consisted of 7,389 men, of whom 5,335 men remained fit for duty (1,975 cavalry, 360 dragoons, and 3,000 infantry). The rest were disabled by illness. Riga also mustered a burgher militia of almost 600 men. In addition, Riga had plenty of artillery: 144 cannons along the city walls and another 57 in the castle.[6] At first, De la Gardie seems to have been shaken by the arrival of the Tsar's great army. In some haste, he had his men burn the outlying areas of the town. Unfortunately for them, the defenders only afterwards realised that the buildings which they burned contained many of the supplies necessary for surviving a siege. The Swedes soon found themselves suffering shortages in clothes, food, and even ammunition.

Henrik von Thurn fell in battle outside Riga, and much of the field army withdrew into the city. While De la Gardie remained in overall command, it was fortunate for the Swedes that the experienced Helmfelt was available to assume responsibility for the defences of Riga. Helmfelt retained command even when he sustained a head wound due to splinters from a gun carriage shattered by enemy artillery fire. It was largely due to Helmfelt's skill and experience that Riga did not fall to Tsar Alexis's superior numbers.

True enough, the Muscovites made several mistakes during the siege. They lacked warships and other means to take Dünamünde (modern-day Daugavgrīva), the key strongpoint where the Düna reached the Gulf of Riga. As a result, the Swedes could continue to bring in supplies and reinforcements by sea to Riga throughout the siege. The Muscovites also reportedly handled tactics and siegeworks less skilfully than required to breach modern fortifications, even though their artillery and mortars were up to date. Perhaps this was more the result of Helmfelt's very aggressive defensive operations. He ordered numerous sorties, during which the Swedes captured supplies and inflicted casualties on the Muscovites. At one point, Colonel Alvendahl and Captain Zeddelman returned from a sortie with 17 captured standards. They also claimed to have killed 2,000 Muscovites (certainly an exaggeration).

King Charles had not forgotten Livonia, and he sent those men and supplies which he could spare. In mid September, Riga's defenders were accordingly reinforced by a regiment of 16 companies of foot (approximately 11,000 to 1,200 men) from the Swedish possession of Bremen-Verden. The regiment was commanded by Conrad Christoph von Königsmarck, whom we last met when he in 1655 massacred the surrendering garrison of Tenczyn in Poland. His regiment was shipped to Riga from Pillau. Königsmarck's men were brought into the city at night by river craft, together with large supplies

---

6   *Ibid.*, pp.90–91.

of sorely needed gunpowder. A little later, four companies of Scots (450 men) from Colonel William Cranstone's Regiment arrived, too.[7]

In late September, it was rumoured that an entire Swedish army was on its way to relieve Riga, perhaps under the personal command of King Charles. The origin of the rumour was probably Stenbock's army which in mid September marched from Danzig to Tilsit on the border between Prussia and Samogitia as a precaution against any Muscovite offensive from the east. From Tilsit, Stenbock advanced towards Memel on the Baltic shore which would enable him to continue north to relieve Riga, if so became necessary. At about the same time as these rumours were heard, a Swedish cannonball accidentally destroyed an icon of Saint Nikolay in the Tsar's camp, which his men reportedly regarded as a bad omen. In mid October, Tsar Alexis abandoned the siege. Like Danzig in the south, Riga was simply too hard a nut to crack open.

Swedish losses were small during the siege, but Muscovite losses were serious, according to one source some 14,000 men (again likely exaggerated), of whom 6,000 were killed by peasants in the surrounding area. Among those Muscovite commanders who died from wounds sustained at Riga was Prince Semyon Urusov. The Tsar's army withdrew to Polotsk. The Swedes lacked men to pursue.

However, while Riga was saved, Dorpat surrendered to Prince Aleksey Trubetskoy's Pskov Army within a week of the Tsar's retreat from Riga. The commandant of Dorpat, Wolmar von Ungern-Sternberg, lacked gunpowder and the burghers were unwilling to fight. The town's mediaeval fortifications were crumbling, and the garrison of 520 was reduced to 140 or 150. The Swedes were granted free departure, and they were allowed to bring their two 3-pounders with them.[8] However, since Dorpat was a key strongpoint on the main road between Riga in Livonia and Reval in Estonia, this cut the communications route between Livonia and Estonia and also left the countryside between them open for raids.

This was a problem, because in the same manner as in Lithuania, Poland, and even the much less devastated Finland, the ongoing war resulted in significant unrest among the peasants in Livonia. Already in November 1656, peasant insurgents began to loot camps and abandoned settlements. In late November, they managed to take all the horses of a Swedish cavalry unit. Attacks took place on the properties of nobles. While some of the unrest can be explained by the attachment to the Muscovite cause of many Orthodox peasants, other occasions were more likely the result of the general lawlessness caused by the war. Violence and extractions by Swedish soldiers certainly also contributed to the unrest. In March 1657 when reports of the difficulties finally reached King Charles, he ordered De la Gardie to maintain stricter discipline among his men, since any serious revolt might jeopardise Swedish rule in Livonia. De la Gardie faced particular problems with the enlisted Scottish units, which

---

7   Margus Laidre, *Schwedische Garnisonen in Est- und Livland 1654–1699* (Universität Tartu: Staatliches Historisches Zentralarchiv der Estnischen SSR /Tallinn: Valgus, 1990), p.16.

8   Fagerlund, 'Kriget i östersjöprovinserna', p.87; Hedberg, *Kungl. Artilleriet: Carl X Gustafs tid*, p.108.

rapidly turned predatory. Soon, Swedish commanders found it necessary to have the Scots accompanied by Swedish cavalry at all times merely to check their worst excesses.[9]

The Treaty of Wilno

Muscovy's declaration of war on Sweden in May 1656 improved the Commonwealth's strategic perspective significantly. First, with the invasion of Livonia Muscovy no longer had the resources to continue the advance into Lithuania, so most combat operations there ceased. Second, the declaration of war opened up for Commonwealth diplomats to offer the Tsar the Polish Crown in an attempt to create an anti-Swedish alliance. The presumption was, of course, that Tsar Alexis would succeed not immediately, but following the ultimate demise of King John Casimir. This was an easy promise to give, since the Commonwealth diplomats knew that the election of the Tsar was unlikely ever to be ratified (in 1658, parliament did elect Tsar Alexis as successor, but the election was immediately annulled following protests by representatives of the Catholic Church). Nonetheless, negotiations about an anti-Swedish alliance ensued between Muscovy, represented by the able Afanasiy Ordin-Nashchokin, and Commonwealth representatives.[10] As a result, on 3 November 1656 Muscovy and the Commonwealth concluded the Treaty of Wilno, an armistice agreed at Niemieża (modern-day Nemėžis) near Wilno. In return, the Commonwealth promised Tsar Alexis the Polish throne after the passing of King John Casimir.

The armistice did not resolve all issues between the parties. The future status of the Hetmanate did not form part of the treaty. Nor did the treaty result in a formal alliance against Sweden. Both sides would continue their separate campaigns against the common enemy. Nonetheless, the Treaty of Wilno meant that for Sweden, a separate peace with either the Commonwealth or Muscovy was no longer possible.

While Tsar Alexis's invasion of Livonia took considerable military pressure off the Commonwealth because the Muscovite armies deployed elsewhere, neither Muscovy's attack on Sweden nor the Treaty of Wilno did more than dent Sweden's capability to wage war on the Commonwealth. With the exception of the one or two regiments which King Charles sent to Riga, the Swedish north-east had to rely on the military resources already in place to stave off the Muscovite threat. While the remaining Livonian army in theory might have been useful against the Commonwealth, had there been no Muscovite attack, Charles never had the intention to denude Livonia of troops as long as tensions remained with Muscovy. The one significant component of Swedish military might which was not brought to bear on the Commonwealth in 1656 was the one least likely to impact the situation there: the Navy. We have seen that the main fleet was mobilised, but this

---

9   Fagerlund, 'Kriget i östersjöprovinserna', pp.107, 199.
10   Malov, *Russko-pol'skaya voyna*, p.20.

was in preparation for a possible Dutch and Danish attack on Sweden, not as a means to repel Muscovy (for which Vice-Admiral Wrangel and his little squadron manned by a skeleton crew would have to suffice). Nonetheless, had there been no Dutch and Danish threat, the Swedish fleet might conceivably have played a greater role in Prussia.

Furthermore, by this time the plague had begun to ravage the region. This arguably had a greater impact on Swedish military operations than the machinations of either Tsar Alexis or King John Casimir. Logistics grew yet more difficult, and sometimes this made extensive operations impossible. Moreover, the plague spared nobody, and one reason for Tsar Alexis's retreat from Riga was certainly the emerging outbreak of disease.

15

The Treaty of Elbing

After the Swedish victory at Warsaw in late July, King John Casimir's army had again retreated south. The Swedish army followed him south for a while, until Radom, which the Swedes took in mid August. However, like in the past, the Swedes could defeat the Poles in the field, but the Polish mobility meant that communications lines and outposts remained vulnerable. In late August Czarniecki and his army (4,000 horse) together with a strong force of Crimean Tatars (2,000 horse) first plundered a Swedish convoy at Rawa, and then defeated a Swedish corps (1,500 horse) under Hans Böddeker at Łowicz. Czarniecki had won another victory, but the engagement also displayed how dependent the Commonwealth forces were on experienced commanders. Czarniecki was wounded in the battle, so afterwards he had to withdraw to Lublin, in effect cancelling the raid.[1]

However, King Charles had more urgent problems to deal with, namely Tsar Alexis's invasion in the north-east. Ordering reinforcements to Riga, Charles for a while contemplated going there himself, but ultimately ordered the able Stenbock with an army from Danzig to Tilsit and Memel, which would have enabled him to continue north to relieve Riga if required (ultimately, this was unfeasible because of a successful Lithuanian–Crimean Tatar offensive into Ducal Prussia, but the venture also turned out to be unnecessary, since Tsar Alexis abandoned the siege of Riga).

Meanwhile, Frederick William accompanied King Charles as far as Nowe Miasto, but then he would go no further. Frederick William claimed the need to return to protect Prussia, and we will see that Ducal Prussia was vulnerable to Lithuanian raids from the east.

Moreover, Brandenburgian reinforcements were on their way from Brandenburg itself. In mid August, Georg von Derfflinger led an army of 5,000 men, mostly horse, from Brandenburg into Greater Poland from the west. After taking Bomst (modern-day Babimost), he placed Brandenburgian garrisons in several towns including Posen, replacing the Swedish garrisons already in place, after which he proceeded to Ducal Prussia.[2] The replacement was in

---

1   Wimmer, 'Polens krig med Sverige', pp.368–9.
2   *Ibid.*, p.371.

accordance with the Treaty of Marienburg, which transferred four provinces in Greater Poland from Sweden to Brandenburg. Having accomplished this, Frederick William was lukewarm to the idea of supporting further Swedish offensives in Poland. After all, his Brandenburgers had already replaced the Swedish garrisons in Greater Poland and he thus had secured his new territories. Perhaps Frederick William also saw little profit in furthering King Charles's power. Not very long ago, they had been rivals, and one thing that the previous wars had made abundantly clear to Frederick William was that things change.

King Charles and the Swedish army soon returned north, too. The victory at Warsaw had not decisively improved the strategic situation. It was not only in the Commonwealth that Sweden faced problems. In late August, Charles wrote: 'God knows how our things stand. I do not believe that our homeland has been in such a dangerous situation for many years.'[3] It was not the situation in the Commonwealth which was such a cause of concern. The battle of Warsaw had proven that neither Commonwealth nor Tatar armies could defeat the Swedish–Brandenburgian army in the field. However, Muscovy was carrying out major offensives in the north, into Finland, Ingria, and Livonia. Meanwhile, the Empire, the Netherlands, and Denmark demonstrated an increasingly menacing attitude. Earlier in the year, the Netherlands had sent an experienced military engineer, Peter van Perceval, to assist Danzig in planning its defences. In late July, a Dutch fleet of 42 warships under Lieutenant Admiral Jacob Obdam (1610–1665), the commander of the Dutch navy, arrived off Danzig to break the Swedish blockade. The Dutch also brought 1,187 soldiers to reinforce the Danzig Army for an agreed period of 14 months.[4] The Netherlands and Denmark had activated a defensive alliance to protect their trade interests in Danzig, and although King Charles did not know it yet, a Danish fleet of nine ships was on its way to Danzig to support the Dutch.[5] The King had cause to be apprehensive.

But there were ways of dealing with the situation. To reduce vulnerability from raiders like Czarniecki, King Charles withdrew the Swedish garrisons from the Sandomierz province. Instead, he reinforced the garrison at Cracow. King Charles then returned to Royal Prussia, where the Swedish Lord High Chancellor, Erik Oxenstierna, was in the process of negotiating an agreement with the Netherlands in Swedish-held Elbing. On 11 September, Sweden and the Netherlands signed the Treaty of Elbing which ended the Dutch intervention in the siege of Danzig. In return, Sweden guaranteed the Dutch free passage to Danzig as well as conceded free trade and navigation in the Baltic Sea. Danzig was offered to join in the treaty but refused. Oxenstierna had employed the rivalry between the Netherlands and Brandenburg to convince the Dutch to

---

3   Holm, *Översikt*, p.46.

4   Askgaard, *Kampen om Östersjön*, 49, 60, 69; Edmund Cieślak, 'Gdańsks militär-politiska och ekonomiska betydelse under polsk-svenska kriget 1655–1660', Arne Stade and Jan Wimmer (eds). *Polens krig med Sverige 1655–1660: Krigshistoriska studier* (Stockholm: Kungl. Militärhögskolan, Carl X Gustaf-studier 5, 1973), pp.131–55, on p.138. Note that Obdam in the following year acquired a title and henceforth was known as Jacob van Wassenaer Obdam.

5   Askgaard, *Kampen om Östersjön*, pp.49, 60, 69.

Lieutenant Admiral Jacob
Obdam. (Jonas Suyderhoef)

accept an agreement. The recent Swedish victory at Warsaw also helped to persuade the Dutch that, for the time being, peace was more profitable than war. The Treaty of Elbing was Erik Oxenstierna's last major diplomatic success; he died from the plague soon after.

The Raids in Ducal Prussia

In autumn 1656 the rivalry between Lithuanian Grand Hetman Paweł Jan Sapieha and Field Hetman Wincenty Gosiewski prevented any co-operation between them. The immediate cause of the rivalry was food distribution. Sapieha controlled the territory around Brest. Gosiewski's army, however, did not have a territory of its own. As a result, quarrels and confrontations between officers from the two armies were commonplace, and many local settlements were forced to accept requisition of supplies and contributions from both. Sapieha cancelled Gosiewski's orders and had some of his officers arrested, while Gosiewski issued threats to those towns which failed to provide him with supplies.[6] Since Sapieha found himself in the more comfortable position from a logistical viewpoint, he was far less interested in fighting the Swedes than his colleague Gosiewski, who did not have the luxury of remaining idle.

And Gosiewski soon got his chance. Correctly identifying Danzig and the Prussian coastal towns as the key to both his own political survival and defeating King Charles, King John Casimir drew up plans for an offensive to relieve Danzig, which remained under siege by the Swedes. The plans entailed two linked offensives, both of which would set out from the Lublin area. One would advance west of the Vistula towards Danzig. The other would advance straight to the north by way of Tykocin into Ducal Prussia, to persuade Frederick William to return to the Commonwealth side or at least to abandon Charles. John Casimir would lead the first, against Danzig. Gosiewski would command the offensive into Ducal Prussia, but he would not ride alone. The offensive would be carried out together with the Crimean Tatars under Subhan Ghazi Agha whom we last met in the battle of Warsaw.

We do not know whether it was Gosiewski or Ghazi Agha who dominated the coalition. Polish traditional historiography asserts that Gosiewski played the leading role, and that Gosiewski also provided more men to the coalition army than Ghazi Agha. Since no real evidence seems to be available, we will follow this assessment. However, in light of later events it is certain that Ghazi Agha not only followed his own counsel but also made sure that his interests took precedence over those of Gosiewski. It accordingly remains

---

6   Kotljarchuk, *In the Shadows*, p.175.

possible that it was Ghazi Agha, not Gosiewski, who dominated the coalition. Assuming that Gordon's assessment of 6,000 Tatars at Warsaw was correct, and assuming that most of them remained, Ghazi Agha's army was probably larger than Gosiewski's. Unfortunately, there seems to be no way of knowing for sure.

Be that as it may, the combined Lithuanian–Crimean offensive was highly successful. On 8 October, Gosiewski and Ghazi Agha defeated a combined Brandenburgian–Swedish army under Lieutenant General Georg Friedrich von Waldeck (in overall command) and Major General Israel Isacsson Ridderhielm at Prostken (modern-day Prostki). The battle, which is also known as the battle of Lyck or Ełk, was won by traditional Tatar tactics. With a feigned flight, Gosiewski and Ghazi Agha successfully incited the Brandenburgers and Swedes into leaving their prepared position. Although there is some uncertainty about the numbers involved in the battle, Gosiewski and Ghazi Agha had no less than twice as many men as Waldeck (perhaps 8,000 against Waldeck's 4,000[7]). It was a decisive Lithuanian–Crimean victory. Among those who fell into captivity was Ridderhielm but also Prince Bogusław Radziwiłł, who commanded a cavalry unit in the battle. Waldeck managed to escape.

Gosiewski and Ghazi Agha then advanced into Ducal Prussia, where they burned villages, towns, and Protestant churches. The carnage lasted for less than two weeks, yet substantial numbers of civilian Prussians, certainly several thousands, were carried off into slavery by the Tatars and in time sold in the Crimean slave markets. For Ghazi Agha, this was the primary objective of the operation. Gosiewski probably regarded the enslavement of Prussian Protestants as a necessary means to compel Frederick William to break the alliance with King Charles. He also gave the Swedish captives to the Tatars, but not Prince Bogusław Radziwiłł (presumably, Gosiewski did not wish to send a member of the influential Radziwiłł family to the Crimean slave markets; incidentally, this decision may suggest that Gosiewski negotiated from a position of strength towards Ghazi Agha, after all, even though the latter's opinion on the matter is unknown).

Having received what he came for, Ghazi Agha then abandoned Gosiewski. This was bad news for the Lithuanians, because at this very moment, the redoubtable Stenbock led a Swedish–Brandenburgian relief army of 6,000 men against Gosiewski. Arriving too late to rescue Waldeck at Prostken, Stenbock nonetheless defeated Gosiewski's Lithuanians (perhaps 5,000 in number after the departure of the Tatars) in the battle of Filipów on 22 October.[8] The battle began and ended with Swedish artillery fire, which

---

7   Sławomir Augusiewicz, *Prostki 1656* (Warsaw: Bellona, 2001), pp.73, 96. Swedish sources suggest higher numbers on both sides, but still with significantly superior numbers for Lithuanians and Tatars. Wimmer, *Polens krig med Sverige*, pp.369–70 suggests that Gosiewski's and Ghazi Agha's combined army included 11,000 men which would seem to support the possibility that it included more Tatars (5,000 to 6,000) than Lithuanians (5,000). On the other hand, unlike Augusiewicz, Wimmer assesses Gosiewski's Lithuanian Army as having consisted of 8,500 men, which means that he had 2,500 Tatars in mind. The only possible conclusion is that more research is needed to ascertain the number of men available to either side.

8   Augusiewicz, *Prostki*, pp.184–5.

soon caused the Lithuanians to recoil. Retreating, Gosiewski's men abandoned their camp and also the captured Brandenburgian supply train and Prince Bogusław Radziwiłł who was thus rescued from his captivity. Others were not so lucky; the two Swedish officers Israel Isacsson Ridderhielm (d. 1669) and Hans Heinrich Engell (1608–1679), from Bremen and in Swedish service since 1636, were already on their way to the Crimea and had to spend years in Tatar captivity before their release could be negotiated.[9]

After his defeat, Gosiewski retreated through Muscovy-held Lithuania (as permitted by the Treaty of Wilno). Soon, he turned north to attack the last remaining Swedish garrison in Samogitia, at Birze.

Meanwhile, the Commonwealth army under King John Casimir was more successful. Advancing into Greater Poland, King John Casimir stormed Łęczyca (German: Lentschitza) in mid October. Reinforced by 2,000 men under Jacob von Weiher, he then advanced into Royal Prussia, where he took Bromberg (modern-day Bydgoszcz) and Konitz (modern-day Chojnice). In mid November, King John Casimir made a triumphant entry into Danzig.

The Treaty of Labiau and the Raid into Neumark

Well aware of his value as a Swedish ally and disconcerted by the loss of property and population to raiders in Ducal Prussia, Frederick William increased his demands. As a result, Sweden and Brandenburg on 20 November renewed their alliance in the Treaty of Labiau (modern-day Polessk). This agreement was significantly more favourable to Brandenburg than previous treaties. King Charles had little choice in the matter, since Frederick William at the same time was negotiating with King John Casimir, who in turn was negotiating with both the Emperor and the Tsar. In the Treaty of Labiau, King Charles recognised Frederick William as *sovereign* ruler of Ducal Prussia and Ermland. Henceforth, Brandenburg's Prussia no longer owed allegiance to any King of Poland. In return, Frederick William in a secret addendum accepted Swedish claims to the entire Baltic shore between Prussia and Pomerania and between Prussia and Swedish Livonia, namely the relevant parts of Royal Prussian Pomerelia in the west and Samogitia, Courland, and Semigallia in the north-east.

Frederick William was right in being apprehensive about threats to this territory. It was not only his Prussia which became a target of attack. Brandenburg itself was at risk. In early November, Royal Prussian units under Jacob von Weiher moved into Kalisz after a long siege. Units of the Levy of the Nobility of Greater Poland under Piotr Opaliński had assisted

---

9   Ridderhielm was ransomed in 1661 for 20,000 Reichsthalers, and having returned to Sweden, he gave his heavy Tatar iron shackles to Nydala Church. The two brothers Hans and Joachim Engell had each enlisted a regiment for King Charles, who in a pun on their name sometimes referred to them as 'the two angels'. Incidentally, not only officers were ransomed from Tatar enslavement. The cavalryman Jöns Andersson was captured by Tatar raiders near Cracow in 1656. He managed to get home in 1669, after being held as a slave in Constantinople for 11 years. Reinhold Stenbock, *Kungl. Andra Livgrenadjärregementet 2: Östgöta kavalleriregemente 1618–1699* (Stockholm: Ivar Haeggström, 1927), p.229.

Weiher's men, and soon afterwards, some of them, under Opaliński, raided the Brandenburg territory of Neumark, the region west of Greater Poland and east of the River Oder. Meanwhile, units of the Levy of the Nobility from Pomerelia made a raid into Brandenburgian Pomerania near the Baltic shore. The Brandenburgers had almost no military force in the region, panic broke out, but lacking artillery and more than token infantry forces, the raiders achieved little and were unable to take any town. Even so, the devastation created sufficient fright to enable the 12 December Truce of Zielenzig, in which Neumark promised not to become the base area for any future attack on Poland. In addition, several small Brandenburgian garrisons were withdrawn.[10]

The Truce of Zielenzig (which was extended in March 1657) marked the first step in Brandenburg's exit from the war against King John Casimir. Through this truce, Brandenburg de facto left the Swedish alliance, regardless of the recently concluded Treaty of Labiau. Moreover, Frederick William had already on 4 October negotiated the Treaty of Riga with Muscovy. This treaty of neutrality, friendship, and trade was negotiated between the Brandenburgian representative Colonel Jonas Casimir zu Eulenburg and Tsar Alexis in the Muscovite camp at Riga, hence its name. In the treaty Brandenburg also promised not to support Sweden against Muscovy in exchange for Muscovite recognition of Ducal Prussia's neutrality.[11]

---

10 Wimmer, 'Polens krig med Sverige', p.371.
11 Theodor von Moerner, *Kurbrandenburgs Staatsverträge von 1601 bis 1700* (Berlin: Georg Reimer, 1867), p.209.

16

The Treaty of Radnot

Most combat operations ceased in the Ukraine as well, for the same reason as in Lithuania. But politically, the situation remained unstable. Bogdan Khmel'nitskiy's emissaries were not invited to the negotiations about the possible succession of Tsar Alexis as King of Poland, nor to the Treaty of Wilno. As a result, many cossacks felt that Muscovy was returning them to Polish rule. Moreover, the Commonwealth's offer of the throne to Tsar Alexis worried the cossack gentry – for constitutional reasons. As the Tsar's subjects, the gentry would no longer enjoy the cherished liberties of the Commonwealth nobility. They had been concerned about this ever since the Treaty of Pereyaslav, and now prospects seemed worse. Hitherto, the Hetmanate had maintained its own foreign policy, but now Moscow requested Khmel'nitskiy to cease his diplomatic contacts with Sweden and instead join Muscovy in the war against the Swedes.

All of this was bad news for Khmel'nitskiy, who much preferred to rule an autonomous Ukraine. Although he accepted the concept of the Ukraine as a protectorate under Muscovy (or under any other suitable power such as Sweden, the Crimean Khanate, or the Ottoman Empire), the ongoing war meant that Khmel'nitskiy no longer could maintain an independent policy but had to follow Moscow's instructions. It became difficult to remain neutral between Muscovy and Sweden. Khmel'nitskiy seems to have preferred an alliance with Sweden than with Muscovy, if for no other reason than because Sweden was the more distant country and accordingly less likely to interfere in Ukrainian domestic affairs.

The issue grew urgent when on 6 December 1656, Swedish and Transylvanian representatives signed the Treaty of Radnot (modern-day Iernut, Romania), agreeing on a partition of the Commonwealth between Sweden, Transylvania, Brandenburg, Lithuania, and Cossack Ukraine. Representatives of Frederick William and Khmel'nitskiy attended the meeting which took place in Transylvania. The alliance was not made out of the blue, because Sweden and Transylvania had been allies during the Thirty Years' War. King Charles promised Prince George Rákóczy of Transylvania most of Lesser Poland and Lithuania as well as recognition as King of Poland and Grand Duke of Lithuania. Brandenburg would receive the parts of Greater Poland already granted in the Treaty of Marienburg, while the cossacks would receive the Ukraine. Sweden would take Royal Prussia. Although Cossack Ukraine was not a signatory to the treaty, it certainly presented a great opportunity, in particular if the Swedish–Transylvanian coalition grew victorious.

For King John Casimir, the Treaty of Radnot was a nightmare come true. Suddenly, most of the Commonwealth's periphery, that is, Ducal Prussia, Cossack Ukraine, and Radziwiłł's pro-Swedish faction in Lithuania, united against its Polish centre. Considering that the rest of Lithuania by then was under the firm control of Muscovy, the formation of the new coalition speaks volumes of the cultural and geographical fault lines within the Commonwealth. But yet worse for the Polish King, the Treaty of Radnot also meant that the periphery henceforth received the support not only of one powerful neighbour, Sweden, but of another, Transylvania, as well.

For King Charles, the treaties of Marienburg, Labiau, and Radnot were means to an end: to gain allies and reinforcements for the outnumbered Swedish forces in the Commonwealth. Realising that he ultimately would not be able to gain more of the Commonwealth's territory than, at best, the Baltic shore, Charles readily negotiated away the rest of the territory. In return, he received badly needed reinforcements. He would have preferred to rely on the experienced Brandenburgian army, but he also knew that Frederick William's loyalty could not be taken for granted. The second-best choice was Transylvania, which could contribute a large army, even though Charles knew, from the Swedish experiences of co-operating with Transylvanian allies during the Thirty Years' War, that it was unable to carry out modern warfare, in particular during sieges.

Militarily, King Charles's major problem remained Danzig. Since King John Casimir in mid November moved into Danzig with his men, Danzig was stronger than ever. Moreover, the Polish King showed no inclination for a set battle. Instead, while John Casimir stayed in the city, his cavalry remained outside where it was hard to pin down. And on 1 December, the Emperor and the Commonwealth signed the Treaty of Vienna, according to which Emperor Ferdinand agreed to support John Casimir with 4,000 men from the Imperial army.

Winter in the North

In November Field Marshal Lewenhaupt ordered the Viborg Cavalry Regiment to return home, since it lacked winter clothes, except 50 men who would remain in the forward base at Rautus. However, the companies should be kept together so that the regiment could be deployed immediately, if needed. He sent the other units (Christopher Burmeister's recently enlisted and understrength cavalry regiment, the two companies of the Retinue of Nobles of Finland, Major Erik Boije's detachment from the Tavastehus Cavalry Regiment, the dragoons, and infantry) to Kurkijoki in northern Kexholm County, where his deputy, Major General of Cavalry Erik Kruse, had his headquarters. Northern Kexholm County was chosen because from Olonets, the Muscovites could easily advance into Karelia or even Savolax, unless this direction was blocked. In comparison, the Karelian Isthmus was devastated and presented less of an opportunity for a Muscovite offensive. Soon after issuing these orders, Lewenhaupt died of illness in Rautus. He was not yet 37 years old, probably dying in the same plague which killed off many of his soldiers. He was replaced by Kruse.[1]

In December, Lieutenant Colonel Erik Pistolhielm led 300 horse to the Ingris area south of Nyen. He encountered and defeated a Muscovite patrol of 48 men commanded by Pavel Afanas'yevich Gur'yov, who fell in the engagement. The Swedes also took some prisoners, who described how Pushkin lacked the men and supplies for a winter campaign. Fighting also took place at the Muscovite border north of Olonets. However, when Pushkin in late December learnt of the raid, he ordered Lieutenant Colonel Hindrich Hultz (or Goltz) and some 500 men, including new formation infantry, to advance across the border. Between Salmis and Sordavala (Finnish: Sortavala), Hultz in early January engaged Major Boije's cavalry. The battle was inconclusive, both sides suffered losses, and Hultz took prisoners who told him of the Swedish deployment in northern Kexholm County.[2]

By December, the Swedish field army in Finland consisted of some 2,230 men (1,690 cavalry, 360 dragoons, and 180 infantry). Of these, some 950 cavalry, at least 200 dragoons, and all 180 infantry were deployed in northern Kexholm County. In comparison to when Muscovy declared war earlier in the year, Kexholm County was now well supplied with men.[3] Defences had been improved in Finland as well. Peasant levies were raised in each parish, including men with skis for transportation, and additional blockhouses and redoubts were built, primarily of logs which was customary in the region. In Brahea and Nurmes, the redoubts were particularly large. Both had walls about 4.5 m high. The Brahea redoubt was 75 x 54 m in size, while the Nurmes one was 75 x 68 m.[4]

Everybody in the region knew that frozen ground facilitated movement. For this reason, the Swedish commanders also had to pay close attention to what happened in the Arctic. Johan Graan, the governor of Västerbotten and Österbotten provinces, feared that the Muscovites might launch an offensive from Kem on the White Sea or Kola on the Barents Sea into northern Finland or Sweden. Later, after the outbreak of war with Denmark (which will be described in Volume 3), King Charles feared a co-ordinated Muscovite and Norwegian offensive in the Arctic. To prevent surprise, the Swedes arranged to have Lapp (Sami) patrols in the region, and to rely on Sami reindeer convoys for the transportation of supplies. Sure enough, in March 1657 reports came in that the Muscovites in Kola had set out on their way to northern Finland (although they turned back before reaching their target). The support of the nomadic Sami could not be taken for granted, since they frequently crossed the borders between Norway, Sweden, Finland, and northern Muscovy and resented being taxed by every state official whom they might encounter, regardless of nationality. Nonetheless, Sweden had

---

1 Lappalainen, 'Finland', pp.101–2.
2 *Ibid.*, 105; Gadzyatskiy, 'Kareliya', p.261.
3 Lappalainen, 'Finland', p.102.
4 *Ibid.*, pp.103, 104.

an advantage over Muscovy since quite a few Swedish officials, including Governor Graan himself, were ethnic Sami and spoke their language.[5]

By then, the garrisons in Estonia and Ingria suffered greatly from the plague which caused serious losses among both soldiers and civilians. In November, the Swedish military in Estonia consisted of 1,250 cavalry and 826 infantry. However, already in December all field units in Estonia were ordered to join the planned relief expedition to Birze, which eventually set out in January 1657.[6]

The weakest point in the defensive line of western Ingria was Wask-Narva (Russian: Syrensk; present Vasknarva), an old derelict stronghold also known (in Swedish) as Nyslott (and not to be confused with its aforementioned namesake in Finland). Already in August, the Governor of Estonia, Bengt Horn, had sent an officer with six soldiers and 150 levied peasants to defend the position. Meanwhile, the Muscovites built a redoubt opposite Wask-Narva, which they used as a base of operations. In early September, a Swedish cross-border raid destroyed the redoubt. The situation grew yet more volatile when peasants on both sides of the border began to carry out cross-border raids on their own initiative. In mid December, Muscovite raiders unsuccessfully attacked Wask-Narva. Raiding continued, however, for instance when Colonel Leonhard von Vietinghoff-Scheel (d. 1657 at Narva), another Thirty Years' War veteran who had served since 1640, in early January 1657 led the Retinue of Nobles of Ingria and 100 dragoons in an effort to harass the Muscovite camps.[7]

The winter 1656–1657 was unusually cold and characterised by very heavy snowfall. For this reason, and because of the ongoing plague, large-scale fighting gradually ceased. To an even higher extent than before, the war became one of raids. There were two primary winter raiding seasons. In early winter, when the frozen ground facilitated travel and snow cover was less deep, it remained possible to move small units. In late winter, usually around March, the top layer of the snow melted in the sunshine but froze at night, which resulted in a frozen crust on which it was sometimes possible to walk. While either period usually was suitable for raiding, in-between, skis and sledges were often the only means available for transportation. The Swedish forces remained on the defensive, as ordered by King Charles, with whatever local resources could be raised. The Muscovites, too, had switched to a defensive posture. As usual, Moscow had to send home most men, since there were neither supplies nor money to feed them throughout the winter.

On the northernmost front, the Swedes in Finland and Kexholm County began the year by going on the offensive into Muscovy. As was often the case, snow conditions were more favourable in the dry and cold north than further south. True enough, the offensive began already in January. Planning was facilitated by the information provided by a Muscovite captive, who

---

5   *Ibid.*, pp.103–4, 107.

6   Fagerlund, 'Kriget i östersjöprovinserna', p.99.

7   *Ibid.*, 95. The attack on Wask-Narva is only mentioned in Swedish, not Muscovite, sources. Gadzyatskiy, 'Bor'ba', p.28. However, most raiding parties were small and not all raids were documented.

also guided the attackers around the Muscovite outposts. Major General Erik Kruse, who had replaced the late Lewenhaupt, led the invasion force, which devastated Muscovite territory until it reached 2.5 km from Olonets, which he found too well-fortified to attack. Kruse accordingly returned to Viborg. Kruse was both meticulous and ruthless; based on his own account he burned 11 churches, 66 villages with a total of 304 buildings, and 58 *lodja*-type vessels (24 large and 34 small). He and his men also killed all men, women, and children they found, as well as all cattle which they could not bring back. During the Thirty Years' War, Swedish strategy had at times involved wholesale devastation so as to deny an area's resources to the enemy, but the murder of non-combatants was strictly forbidden according to the military law introduced by King Gustavus Adolphus. Kruse's actions caused outrage, including among Swedish nobles and officials, and Per Brahe, the Lord High Justiciar, condemned his activities.[8]

By then, Prince Ivan Golitsyn in Novgorod had already ordered Aleksandr Potyomkin to bring reinforcements to Olonets. The reinforcements, approximately 830 in total, were men from different units, including two companies of new formation cavalry of whom some 100 were recently enlisted peasants from a monastery, 300 Don and other free cossacks, 50 Novgorod cossacks, 243 assorted streltsy and cossacks from other towns, and 37 old-style cavalry in the service of the Metropolitan of Novgorod. They remained in Olonets until March, when they returned to Lava.[9]

South of Lake Ladoga, reinforcements were also gathered around Lava and Ladoga Town, under respectively Prince Bogdan Grigor'yev Yeletskiy and Boris Dement'yev Tushin.[10] In the Arctic north, Muscovite units remained in position in Kola as well as, it seems, further to the south between Rokonvaara and Selki opposite Kajana.[11]

Kruse's offensive was not an isolated incident. Next Swedish offensive was carried out by Gustav Evertsson Horn, who following the death of Lewenhaupt was appointed the new commander-in-chief in Finland and Kexholm County. In February, he advanced into Muscovy from Finland through northern Kexholm County to attack and destroy the settlements east of Lake Ladoga. Taking advantage of the Orthodox Easter, some 300 horse under Lieutenant Colonel Erik Pistolhielm made a surprise attack on Tulemajärvi. He killed all the inhabitants and burned the village as well as those of its inhabitants who remained in their houses. The Swedes also burned several Muscovite supply depots and ravaged the Muscovite countryside as they moved through. It was a continuation of the strategy employed by Kruse.[12]

The Swedish strategy of extermination in the Lake Ladoga region with its focus on killing non-combatants was not representative of Swedish strategy elsewhere. Certainly, non-combatants lost their lives in the counterinsurgency

---

8   Lappalainen, 'Finland', pp.105–6; Gadzyatskiy, 'Kareliya', pp.261–2.
9   Lappalainen, 'Finland', p.100; Gadzyatskiy, 'Kareliya', pp.262–3, 272.
10   Gadzyatskiy, 'Kareliya', p.272; Gadzyatskiy, 'Bor'ba', pp.27–8.
11   Lappalainen, 'Finland', pp.100–101.
12   *Ibid.*, pp.106–7.

campaign that took place both in the Commonwealth and, soon afterwards, in parts of Denmark. However, such killings were the result of failure to distinguish between enemy fighters and the peasants among whom they hid or, at worst, individual acts of revenge. While some commanders, no doubt, looked the other way when murder took place, military law clearly forbid such acts and on occasion, the perpetrators were brought to justice. On the border between Finland and Muscovy, however, the strategy of extermination was sanctioned by senior commanders. We do not know what King Charles thought of this, if and when he finally received reports about the activities. The Ladoga region was far away, and as we have seen, the murder of captives remained commonplace on both sides and derived from a long tradition. It is probably fair to say that the laws of war as they were understood in Western Europe including Sweden had not yet reached the shores of Lake Ladoga. In comparison, Gustav Evertsson Horn comes across as a far more ruthless commander than his counterpart Pyotr Pushkin, who at least made attempts to sanction vicious subordinates such as Sergey the Green.

When Gustav Evertsson Horn succeeded Lewenhaupt as commander-in-chief in Finland and Kexholm County, his relative Christer Horn (1622–1692) was appointed Governor-General of Ingria. Christer Horn lacked military experience, and his promotion to major general was little but compensation for being replaced as governor of the far more comfortable Riga. For practical reasons, the two agreed that Christer Horn would be responsible for the defence of western Ingria only, up to Jama and Kaporie,

The Swedish army employed cyphers of various kinds to maintain security of communications. In this message dated 16 June 1656 (N.S.), Gustav Evertsson Horn informs King Charles of the first day of the siege of Nöteborg. This particular cypher was employed by many Swedish officers. Every figure signifies a letter, so for more sensitive information, other cyphers would be employed. (Swedish National Archives (RA), Livonica II, Vol. 173)

while Gustav Evertsson Horn took command of eastern Ingria as well as Kexholm County.[13]

The large snowfall in early 1657 prevented major operations in Ingria, even though a Muscovite raiding party in February devastated the area around castle Lais, which was burned down, before cavalry from Estonia could intercept the raiders. After this raid, Estonia found itself almost denuded of soldiers. The Swedish units were subordinated the Livonian army, while the Muscovites focused on other theatres.

While major operations may have been unfeasible, small raids certainly took place. Following standard procedures on both sides in the region, the Muscovites equipped at least one raiding party of 60 men with skis. Other units may have been supplied with skis, too, but the sources are silent on this. Both Swedes and Muscovites carried out several cross-border raids during the winter. The Swedes certainly also employed levied peasants for these tasks. The levies then operated together with regular units.[14]

In March 1657, when snow conditions had improved even in Livonia, De la Gardie attempted an offensive into Muscovy, advancing with several units of the Livonian field army against Pechory on Muscovite territory. He then turned south, to Marienburg. From this position, he sent out a raiding party which devastated a number of villages around Pechory. We do not know the strength of the raiding party. A full battle developed around the Pskov–Pechory Monastery, which was defended by a Muscovite corps from Pskov under Matvey Sheremetyev. We do not know the strength of the defenders either. Sheremetyev's full corps consisted of a new formation cavalry regiment, four *sotni* of old-style cavalry, a *sotnya* of Pskov cossacks, and a regiment of streltsy. Based on the post-battle casualty lists, it seems likely that the monastery primarily was defended by streltsy and cossacks, that is, infantry, and possibly some old-style cavalry. The outskirts of the monastery burned during the battle, but the Swedes failed to dislodge the defenders. The Swedish raiding party returned to Livonia in early April, rejoining De la Gardie at Walk (modern-day Valga). The campaign ultimately never became more than a raid. De la Gardie afterwards explained his lack of progress by the shortages of equipment and the great losses suffered from to the plague (which was true enough; in Helmfelt's house alone in Riga 21 people died, including three of his children).[15]

---

13 *Ibid.*, p.111.
14 Fagerlund, 'Kriget i östersjöprovinserna', pp.104–5.
15 *Ibid.*, p.104; Yakov Nikolayevich Rabinovich, 'Neizvestnyye stranitsy istorii Pskovo-Pecherskogo monastyrya i Izborska v Smutnoye vremya', *Vestnik Pskovskogo gosudarstvennogo universiteta* (2013), pp.47–62, on p.59.

17

The Battle of Konitz and the Rescue of King John Casimir

In the Commonwealth, the year 1657 began with King John Casimir and most of the Crown infantry and artillery bottled up in Danzig. Meanwhile, most Commonwealth cavalry were dispersed, not least because they lacked supplies. The poor discipline of the Commonwealth armies, and their propensity for plundering even their own territory, was the unfortunate outcome of the fact that they only rarely were paid. Formally, funds were solely provided by parliament, but no parliament had met since 1655. As a result, the Commonwealth units resorted to contributions, in the same manner as Swedes and Muscovites. Even with contributions, few common soldiers actually received their pay, so they accordingly had to live on plunder alone.[1]

On or about New Year's Day, Queen Marie Louise's and Czarniecki's cavalry moved into quarters at Konitz in Royal Prussia. They were on their way to Danzig, so that Marie Louise could rejoin her husband. King Charles had graciously offered her free passage through the blockade, but such an option was far from what Marie Louise desired. Instead, she and Czarniecki intended to break through by their own efforts. At Konitz, they were joined by Crown Grand Hetman Potocki and Crown Field Hetman Lanckoroński with their armies. As a result, it was very substantial Polish army which in early January camped in the vicinity of Konitz. King Charles was eager to confront them.

This resulted in one or more engagements which have become known as the battle of Konitz. The actual events are difficult to disentangle, since surviving accounts paint radically different pictures of the outcome. Even taking the possibilities of propaganda into account, it seems that more than one engagement took place. The first engagement reportedly occurred on the night between 2 and 3 January. A Swedish cavalry unit encountered the Polish camp, raided it so thoroughly that Queen Marie Louise had to find shelter elsewhere, perhaps in the town, and then, upon finding that the Poles greatly outnumbered them, made a hasty retreat, pursued by Polish cavalry.

---

1   Wimmer, 'Armé och finansväsen', p.79.

In this story, which is based on a pro-Polish source (Pierre des Noyers, Queen Marie Louise's secretary), the Poles inflicted numerous casualties on the retreating Swedes without suffering any losses of their own to speak of.[2]

The next engagement, unless the mutually opposed sources describe the same incident, apparently took place on the following night, between 3 and 4 January. On this occasion, the Swedish Colonel Rutger von Ascheberg led a task force of 750 men, supported by four 6-pounders, with the task to find the Commonwealth cavalry.[3] As they approached, Ascheberg's men snatched a courier with a letter which mentioned that the Crown cavalry, reportedly 10,000 men, had gone into quarters around Konitz. Ascheberg decided to attack. With the Polish cavalry taken by surprise, Ascheberg's men tore up the regiment (*pułk*) of Prince Konstanty Wiśniowiecki and the banners of Jan Sobieski and Koniecpolski. However, the combat gave sufficient time for other Polish units to form up, and faced with the greatly superior enemy numbers, Ascheberg sounded the retreat. The raid was a great success, and Ascheberg's men returned with captives, captured horses, and plunder.

Essentially, both sides claimed victory. Be that as it may, King Charles was very satisfied with Ascheberg's actions, offering him a rapier which he once had carried himself, some cash, and an estate in Prussia. Such a reward is unlikely to have been the outcome had the pro-Polish account been correct. For this reason, either the two accounts describe separate incidents, or the pro-Polish account has to be discarded.

After the battle of Konitz, the Polish cavalry retreated south, to Exin (modern-day Kcynia). Nonetheless, the battle had no decisive impact on Polish strategy. As before, the Polish cavalry army remained elusive. It could travel fast, since it carried little baggage and instead supplied itself through the exaction of contributions, or plunder, from the territories it moved through. At this point, Queen Marie Louise asked her commanders to retrieve King John Casimir from his semi-voluntary containment in Danzig. However, they refused, since their men had not been paid. The Queen then tasked Czarniecki to retrieve the King, offering him her personal funding and the choice of his pick of men from the entire Commonwealth army. Encouraged by the Queen's promises, Czarniecki accepted, picked 3,000 cavalry and dragoons, and set out. First, he moved to Thorn, with the dual purpose of intimidating Frederick William's Ducal Prussia and deceiving the Swedes as to his real objective. Then, remaining on the move, he evaded all of King Charles's units which attempted to intercept his corps, and moving through the Swedish lines, again returned to Danzig, from which he successfully retrieved King John Casimir. As a tactical operation, it was a spectacular success. Czarniecki had pulled off what most other Commonwealth commanders, and perhaps the Swedes as well, believed to be impossible. Unfortunately, Danzig would, or could, not advance the money promised by the Queen, so Czarniecki allowed his men to plunder the Werder suburbs just south of Danzig on the way out. By then, the plundering of Commonwealth territories had become

---

2   Noyers, *Lettres*, pp.289–90 (8 January 1657).

3   Pufendorf, *Sieben Bücher* 3, pp.191–2. Ascheberg's strength is often given as 950 in secondary sources.

routine when funding for the Commonwealth armies was not forthcoming, so for Czarniecki, this probably had more to do with standard operating procedures than any particular malice towards those Prussians who in fact remained loyal to the Polish Crown. By the end of the month, Czarniecki brought King John Casimir to Częstochowa and the relative safety of Greater Poland near the Imperial border.[4]

The rescue of King John Casimir was bad news for the Swedes, and more bad news arrived from Lithuania. In late January, Paweł Jan Sapieha captured Tykocin, south-east of Ducal Prussia. When Sapieha's Lithuanians stormed the town, the defenders, Swedes and mostly Protestant Lithuanians who remained true to their oath, blew up the castle and themselves. Both the Swedish commandant, Colonel Dietrich von Rosen, and his Lithuanian deputy, Vice-Colonel Johann von Ottenhausen, died in the explosion. Then, in early February, the Swedes lost Birze, further to the north near Swedish Livonia. It was Gosiewski's Lithuanian Army which, following the Treaty of Wilno, received free passage through Muscovite-held Lithuania in order to strike at the Swedes. The Swedes now had to expect that Lithuanians and Muscovites would join forces against them. Ultimately no such joint offensive took place, not because of the Swedes but because the two sides distrusted each other, and because the plague which ravaged the country prevented large-scale operations.

---

4   Wimmer, 'Polens krig med Sverige', pp.374–5.

18

The Transylvanian Invasion

King Charles spent the rest of the winter in quarters in the conquered towns of Prussia. In March 1657, he commenced a new offensive into southern Poland. Although there is some uncertainty regarding the forces involved, Charles's field army was not large: probably some 4,000 Swedes and around 3,000 Brandenburgers in four regiments under Friedrich von Waldeck. Charles ordered his field artillery and musketeers to be mounted on horseback so that they could keep up with the speed of the cavalry.[1]

This time, King Charles had two new allies: Prince George Rákóczy of Transylvania and Bogdan Khmel'nitskiy of Cossack Ukraine. The latter in February sent Colonel Anton Zhdanovich of Kiev with three cossack regiments to join forces with the Transylvanian Prince and the Swedish King. One of Zhdanovich's sub-commanders was the aforementioned Ivan Bogun, one of Khmel'nitskiy's chief lieutenants. Khmel'nitskiy had planned to join the campaign himself, but he fell ill.[2]

Prince George marched north with a large army divided into three divisions under respectively János Kemény (1607–1662), Péter Huszár, and Ferenc Ispán (with Huszár being a description and Ispán a title). Prince George Rákóczy was soon joined by the allied contingent of Ukrainian cossacks under Zhdanovich. However, both contemporary observers and modern historians disagree about how many men the Prince brought into the Commonwealth. Gordon, a contemporary, claims that the army consisted of 20,000 Transylvanians, 5,000 Wallachians, 5,000 Moldavians, 6,000 cossacks, and 30 cannons, with a supply train of 1,000 wagons.[3] Since the cossacks were allies, this leaves us with a Transylvanian army of 30,000 men. Erik Jönsson Dahlbergh (1625–1703), a military engineer and fortification officer who participated in the Transylvanian

---

1   *Ibid.*, p.378; citing King Charles's own words but without further references. Wimmer's estimate follows the traditional Swedish view (for example, Holm, *Översikt*, p.53) but is possibly too low. Hedberg, *Kungl. Artilleriet: Carl X Gustafs tid*, p.118, suggests a total of 6,000 Swedes and 3,000 Brandenburgers.

2   Kotljarchuk, *In the Shadows*, p.226, with reference.

3   Gordon, *Tagebuch*, p.94.

Prince George Rákóczy of Transylvania, in traditional dress and with a mace as his symbol of command.

campaign, notes the total strength of the Transylvanian army as 24,000.[4] He also mentions a cossack contingent of 2,000, but it is unlikely that this figure refers to the entire cossack contingent since it was this number which accompanied Prince George together with an honour guard of 3,000 Transylvanians to a meeting with King Charles.[5] In the same context, Dahlbergh reckons the total cossack army to have consisted of 35,000, but he may then have referred to the total number of fighting men available to the Hetmanate, not those in the contingent of Anton Zhdanovich.[6] The figure of 6,000 cossacks mentioned by Gordon does seem to correspond to the perhaps three regiments which Zhdanovich brought from Kiev. It then seems likely that the 2,000 cossacks

---

4   Dahlbergh, *Dagbok*, p.93. Although ennobled as Dahlbergh only in 1660, this well-known officer is here nonetheless referred to as Dahlbergh for consistency.

5   *Ibid*., p.91.

6   *Ibid*., p.93. Dahlbergh notes that he functioned as de facto senior quartermaster to the entire coalition army, and he displays some familiarity with the Transylvanian army. However, even though Dahlbergh certainly acted in a liaison capacity, he may have exaggerated his influence. Besides, even if the allied commanders informed Dahlbergh of their respective strength, he had no means to verify the figures, which were likely exaggerated.

Erik Dahlberg a few years after the Deluge. His armour displays certain characteristics which suggest that he acquired it in Poland, in particular the two Gorgon's head placques in the 'Sarmatian' style which at the time was growing increasingly popular with the Polish nobility. Dahlberg's sidearm, too, seems to be of Polish origin: a *karabela* sabre. The same can perhaps be said of the dress worn under the armour, a casack the origin of which was the oriental caftan. (David Klöcker Ehrenstrahl, 1664; Uppsala University)

observed by Dahlbergh constituted one of Zhdanovich's regiments.[7]

In his writings, Dahlbergh displays some familiarity with the Transylvanians, and he functioned as quartermaster and general liaison during the campaign.[8] Assuming that his assessment was correct, the conclusion must be that Prince George Rákóczy brought an army of 24,000 Transylvanians, Wallachians, and Moldavians. This army was then joined by 6,000 cossacks, which leaves us with a total strength of 30,000 men.[9]

The cossack participation was the result of Khmel'nitskiy's personal foreign policy. Technically, Cossack Ukraine remained the vassal of Muscovy, which in the previous year had concluded the Treaty of Wilno with the Commonwealth in return for a promise that Tsar Alexis would succeed King John Casimir. Now, a few months later, Khmel'nitskiy sent an army to provide direct support to Sweden, with which Muscovy was at war, and Transylvania, whose ruler claimed the Polish throne for himself.

The Transylvanians at first wanted to lay siege to L'vov, but they lacked both the equipment and experience for extensive siege operations. When Prince George received a request for support from Paul Würtz in Cracow, which already for five months was besieged by Lubomirski, he decided to move towards Cracow instead. Not wishing to engage in battle with the Transylvanians, Lubomirski retreated towards the north-east along the Vistula. Prince George followed him, until he in early April met up with the Swedish army in the vicinity of Sandomierz.

The combat efficiency of the Transylvanians was less than desired. Moreover, they moved slowly because of their huge supply train and poor ability to bridge rivers. When the two armies had to cross the Vistula in mid April, the Swedes had to build a pontoon bridge for the Transylvanians, since their own attempt at bridge-laying collapsed. During the construction of the bridge, Polish snipers harassed the Swedes. At one point, when King Charles, disregarding the warning about the snipers, moved closer for a personal look at the proceedings, one of the Poles in Swedish service

---

7   Modern historians tend to suggest that Zhdanovich's cossack contingent consisted of 10,000 men. Wimmer, *Polens krig med Sverige*, p.376. However, there seems to be no conclusive evidence in favour of this interpretation, and cossack numbers often appear exaggerated.

8   Dahlbergh went on to play a prominent role in King Charles X's subsequent war against Denmark and then again, under King Charles XI, in the Scanian War of 1675–1679. On these wars, see the third volume of this work and Michael Fredholm von Essen, *Charles XI's War: The Scanian War between Sweden and Denmark, 1675–1679* (Warwick: Helion, 2019).

9   This estimate tallies with Wimmer, *Polens krig med Sverige*, p.376, who suggests some 25,000 men.

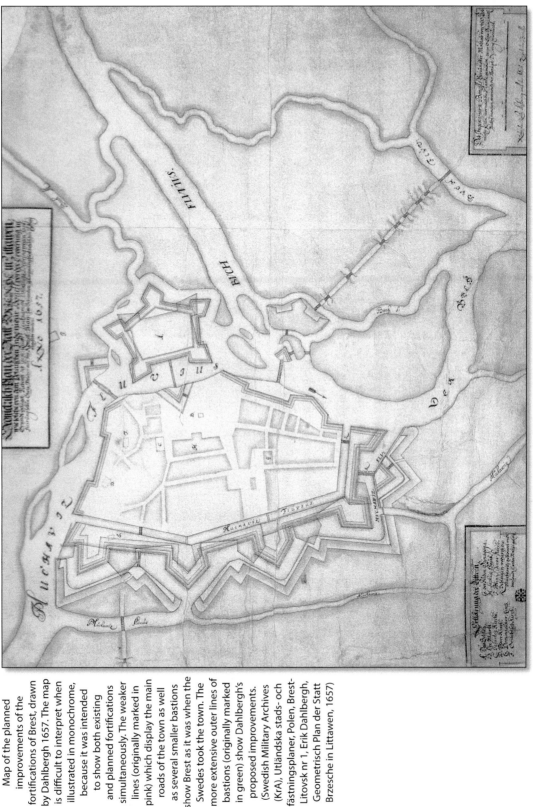

Map of the planned improvements of the fortifications of Brest, drawn by Dahlbergh 1657. The map is difficult to interpret when illustrated in monochrome, because it was intended to show both existing and planned fortifications simultaneously. The weaker lines (originally marked in pink) which display the main roads of the town as well as several smaller bastions show Brest as it was when the Swedes took the town. The more extensive outer lines of bastions (originally marked in green) show Dahlbergh's proposed improvements. (Swedish Military Archives (KrA), Utländska stads- och fästningsplaner, Polen, Brest-Litovsk nr 1, Erik Dahlbergh, Geometrisch Plan der Statt Brzesche in Littawen, 1657)

The Siege of Brest. (Erik Dahlbergh)

Prince George (centre, marked 3) and several Transylvanians discuss strategy with King Charles (right, marked 1) during the siege of Brest. (Erik Dahlbergh)

shouted to the snipers on the other side of the river that the King of Sweden had arrived, requesting them not to harm him. He also indicated King Charles with his hand. On the opposite river bank, the Polish officers ordered their men to cease fire, greeted the King with all the honours expected by a royal visit, and then retreated.

When the bridge was ready, it still took the Transylvanians three days to move all their units across the Vistula. King Charles sent Dahlbergh ahead of the army for reconnaissance, since intelligence was one of the quartermaster's tasks. Dahlbergh commanded a joint cavalry force, consisting of 120 men from the Swedish Life Guard of Horse (known as blackcoats), 100 Swedish cavalry, 200 Transylvanians under Ferenc Ispán, and 200 cossacks.[10]

Because of the tardiness of the Transylvanians, the Commonwealth forces easily refused battle. There was little that King Charles and Prince George could do but to follow their fast-moving adversaries. On 16 May, after some preliminary artillery fire, the Swedes took Brest, despite its modern fortifications and garrison of 2,000 under Castellan Melchior Sawicki.[11] Although offered free departure, a major part of the garrison, some 600 men,

---

10 Dahlbergh, *Dagbok*, p.95.
11 Wimmer, 'Polens krig med Sverige', p.381.

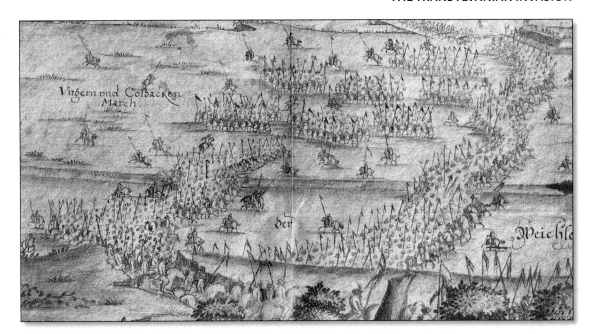

Vngern vnd Coßacken March.

der

Weichß

Transylvanian cavalry units at Zakroczym, March 1657. In comparison to the Swedish units in the coalition army, the order of march was as lax as the discipline. (Erik Dahlbergh)

instead chose to enlist in the Swedish army. The success of the siege was much due to the effort of Dahlbergh, who entered Brest in the guise of a junior member of a negotiation team for the purpose of assessing the fortifications. Even so, Brest ultimately surrendered without combat.[12] In accordance with the Treaty of Radnot, King Charles granted Brest to Prince George, who appointed a Transylvanian commandant, Colonel András Gaudi.

With regard to the combat efficiency of the Transylvanians, King Charles drew the same conclusion as the Swedes had done already during the Thirty Years' War. Although some Transylvanian units were dependable, most were irregular light cavalry or light infantry and, as noted, some served only for plunder, not pay. They were of little use in siege warfare. They also brought a huge supply train, not least to carry the loot, which they refused to leave behind. As a result, they were unable to march as fast as was required for a campaign in the Commonwealth, where fast-moving cavalry was the key arm. Moreover, Prince George could not be fully trusted. He refused to sign the treaties which he and King Charles had agreed to, and he carried out negotiations which he thought were secret with Polish commanders (which the Swedes nonetheless learnt of through their extensive intelligence network).

However, for King Charles the trustworthiness of Prince George soon paled in importance in comparison to other news. At Brest, he received news that the Danish parliament had granted funding for mobilisation. The King had no doubt that the intended target was Sweden. The information confirmed the suspicions of hostile Danish intentions which he and the Council had discussed already in 1654.

---

12   After the conquest, Dahlbergh reworked his sketches of Brest's fortifications into a plan for how to improve them. However, the improvement plan was never implemented, and it is currently preserved in the Swedish Military Archives (KrA), Utländska stads- och fästningsplaner, Polen, Brest-Litovsk nr 1.

Wallachian light cavalry officer in Commonwealth service. (Illustration by Sergey Shamenkov)

Meanwhile, the joint campaign with the Transylvanians had not lived up to expectations. Charles would have to see to his own possessions in the north, both those in Prussia and the Swedish core territories which now were under threat from Denmark. In June, the Swedish and Transylvanian armies parted company. Although the Swedish–Transylvanian alliance continued, for a short while, to play a role for the defence of Cracow, Prince George could do little on his own. Even though Prince George finally accepted the Swedish King's advice to abandon the campaign and return home, the Transylvanian army did not outlast July. Harassed by Polish and Tatar forces, the Transylvanians were defeated at Magierów, between Cracow and L'vov, and then again at Chornyy Ostrov (Polish: Czarny Ostrów) further to the east. In late July, Prince George agreed to a peace with the Commonwealth at Medzhibozh in the Ukraine. He then withdrew from the campaign, handing over command to his deputy János Kemény. Although successfully saving himself, Prince George's entire army was soon lost to continuous Tatar attacks. By then, Zhdanovich's men had already mutinied, abandoning the campaign. Kemény was captured at Trembovlya, with the rest of the army. He was only released in August 1659, upon the payment of a massive ransom.

19

The Imperial Intervention

For Emperor Ferdinand of the Holy Roman Empire, the Swedish invasion of the Commonwealth was bad enough. The subsequent Transylvanian invasion was possibly worse, since Transylvania was far closer to Vienna. However, what finally persuaded the Empire to intervene directly in the war was grand strategy unrelated to eastern Europe. For years, France had been at war with Habsburg Spain, the Habsburg Empire's key ally. In March 1657, France signed the Treaty of Paris with the English Protectorate of Oliver Cromwell. Both France and England were at war with Spain, and the Treaty envisaged joint operations against Spain in Flanders. The Habsburgs accordingly set out to establish a strong alliance of their own, against both existing and potential enemies. France had for some time attempted to persuade Sweden to join the war through an attack on the hereditary Habsburg lands of the Empire. Fortunately for everybody else, King Charles had been too astute to agree to such a scheme, which would have reignited the Thirty Years' War. However, the French plans ensured that in Habsburg eyes, Sweden without doubt belonged to the enemy camp. Besides, Sweden was the chief military threat in the north. As a result, the Empire on 27 May entered into an alliance against Sweden with the Commonwealth through the Second Treaty of Vienna: Since Emperor Ferdinand died shortly before, the Treaty was concluded by the heir apparent to the Holy Roman Empire Leopold, King in Germania, King of Hungary and Bohemia, and Archduke of Austria, who now ratified an agreement signed already on 30 March to send 12,000 troops and artillery, to be paid by the Commonwealth, to assist King John Casimir. In return, Cracow and Posen would be held as surety until the end of the war. In addition, Vienna would receive half the proceeds from the Wieliczka and Bochnia salt mines.

In late April and early May, before the treaty was signed, an Imperial expeditionary force under Melchior von Hatzfeldt (1593–1658) assembled at Oppeln in Upper Silesia.[1] During the Thirty Years' War, Hatzfeldt had spent almost a decade fighting the Swedish army, until he was captured in the 1645 battle at Jankow. Although in those years he had been matched against

---

1   Dzieszyński, *Kraków*, pp.187–9.

the very best Swedish field marshals, and accordingly lost most battles, he had nonetheless proved himself an able and very experienced commander. Moreover, his force contained a significant number of veterans from the Thirty Years' War.

As soon as the Treaty was signed, Hatzfeldt advanced into Lesser Poland, with Cracow as his first objective. Nobody was happier to see the Imperials arrive than King John Casimir, who after his escape from Danzig in March had set up a headquarters in Częstochowa, opposite Oppeln.

The Danish Invasion of Sweden

The Habsburg alliance was based on geopolitics and not religion. Their enemy France was a Catholic country. It was accordingly unsurprising that the Habsburgs, both in the Empire and Spain, at this point spent significant efforts on persuading Protestant Denmark to declare war on Sweden. This was not difficult, and Denmark eagerly declared war on 11 June 1657. The Netherlands, too, wanted the Danes to go to war against Sweden. In their case, it was because they were concerned that Swedish power was growing too strong, which would enable Sweden to control trade in the Baltic Sea.

The news of the Danish declaration of war reached King Charles on 30 June, at Thorn. The news confirmed what King Charles had long suspected and removed any remaining doubts from his mind. In 1654, the King's late Lord High Chancellor Erik Oxenstierna had reminded the rest of the Council of the Realm that a war with Denmark would be tough: 'We know what a job we had with Denmark last time, when we had the Netherlands on our side', he had said. King Charles had fought Denmark from 1643 to 1644 and knew that the Chancellor was right. He also knew that this time, the Netherlands, one of the two greatest sea powers in Europe, almost certainly would fight on the side of the Danes. The war in the Commonwealth, vicious as it was, never put Sweden at risk. The real struggle for national survival began here and now.

King Charles spent the next four days making necessary arrangements to safeguard his interests in the Commonwealth. Then, he led the Swedish field army towards the west. Any further conquests in the east would have to wait until he had defeated Sweden's primary enemy: Denmark.

To be continued.

Colour Plate Commentaries

Plate A

1. Sweden: Company Colour of Major General Claes Danckwardt-Lillieström's Regiment of Foot, 1647–1660

This colour was manufactured for the Life Company of then Colonel Claes Danckwardt-Lillieström's Regiment of Foot, which was enlisted in Germany during the Thirty Years' War. This regiment was disbanded after the war. The colours of the regiment were reused when Colonel Danckwardt-Lillieström enlisted a new regiment to serve as garrison in Danziger Haupt. This was one of four company colours from the unit, two of which remain preserved into the present. When Danziger Haupt finally no longer was defensible, Danckwardt-Lillieström, by then promoted to major general, negotiated an honourable surrender. According to the terms of the surrender, the Swedish soldiers marched out with full military honours, with flying colours of which this was one. After the war, the regiment was disbanded in 1660.

The colour is made of silk. It has a white field with painted motifs in the form of a royal crown in gold, flaming grenades, and a laurel. The Latin text, in gold, says FELICES NIMIVM! QVEIS SVB DIADEMATE TANTO CONTINGET IOVAE PACIS AMOENA QVIES ('Happy are those whose turn it is under this crown to enjoy the rest of God's peace'). Below, the date ANNO 1659 25 MAIJ is painted.

The colour has a breadth of 175.0 cm and a length of 208.0 cm (Army Museum, Stockholm; AM 068244).

2. Sweden: Company Colour of Unidentified Regiment of Foot, 1658–1660

Swedish company colour made by Peter Blom in Hamburg in 1658. Although the regiment has not been positively identified, several of its company colours remain in the Army Museum, Stockholm. This is the colour of the 1st (Life) Company (Army Museum, Stockholm; AM.067877). The colours of the other companies are similar, but with yellow fields and different text. The cypher of King Charles (C G R S, Carolus Gustavus Rex Sueciae) is painted on one side of each colour. The breadth is 185.0 cm and the length 165.0 cm. The colour of the Life Company carries the text CAROLO DUCE, while the other preserved colours, as far as can be determined, carry the respective texts ARMIS [ÆQVISSI]MI[S], [ROBORE JUSTO], and OMINE FA[U]ST[O]. The colours of the other companies are of similar but not identical size.

Plate B

1. Polish-Lithuanian Commonwealth: Polish Cavalry Standard

Some Polish cavalry units still fought under large banners reminiscent of the sixteenth century. This large cavalry banner of silk, depicting a white eagle on a red field, has a breadth of 160 cm and a length of 176–313 cm. The yellow wheat-sheaf on the eagle's breast dates the banner to the reign of the Polish Vasa dynasty. Believed possibly to have been taken at Cracow in 1655, the banner is of an early type and may accordingly have been significantly older, perhaps dating to the late sixteenth century. (Army Museum, Stockholm; ST 28:58).

2. Polish-Lithuanian Commonwealth: Privateer Ensign of the Danzig Navy

The Commonwealth had no navy. Its only maritime capacity was provided by Danzig, which employed a small number of privateer vessels against its Swedish opponents. The Danzig maritime ensign during the Deluge consisted of a red field with four white crosses, of the cross pattée type formerly associated with the Teutonic Order, each surmounted by a stylised crown in either silver or gold. It is possible that this type of standard also was used by the Danzig Army; however, it consisted of enlisted regiments of German type which carried regimental and company colours of the same basic types and motifs as other German regiments.

Plate C

1. Brandenburg: Cornet of Georg Friedrich von Canitz's Regiment of Horse

Several Brandenburgian cavalry cornets were captured by Czarniecki's units at Bromberg in February 1657. Based on contemporary published descriptions, the cornets were eight in number. They have been attributed to Georg Friedrich von Canitz's Regiment of Horse, under the assumption that the regiment received eight new cornets even though it consisted of only four companies. Four of the captured cornets must accordingly have been captured from the regiment's supply train (Daniel Schorr, *The Bromberg Trophies 1657*, Northern Wars web site (defunct), 2007). Part of the contingent which Brandenburg provided to the Swedish field army in accordance with the January 1656 Treaty of Königsberg, Canitz's Regiment of Horse was permanently transferred to the Swedish army by the end of the year. The Life Company cornet was, as usual, white, and it included the name of Frederick William of Brandenburg. On the other side was instead the name of Carl Æmil (b. 1655), the young Prince Elector. The cornets of the remaining companies each had a blue field. Each had a different coat of arms. The style, including the inclusion of the two names, one on each side, was otherwise similar.

2. Brandenburg: Guidon of Georg Friedrich von Canitz's Dragoon Regiment

Several Brandenburgian dragoon guidons were captured by Czarniecki's units at Bromberg in February 1657, on the same occasion as those in Plate C1. Based on contemporary published descriptions, the guidons were four in number (Daniel Schorr, *The Bromberg Trophies 1657*, Northern Wars web site (defunct), 2007). There is no consensus on which unit they belonged to. However, assuming that Georg Friedrich von Canitz's Regiment of Horse originally consisted of dragoons, it seems likely that these dragoon guidons were the original ones fielded by the unit, and that they remained in storage in the supply train even though the regiment had received new cornets when it was upgraded to cavalry status. Alternatively, the guidons belonged to dragoon companies which were attached to the cavalry regiment – a common practice during the Deluge.

Plate D

1. Muscovy: Colour of 1st Company, Jacob Leslie's New Formation Regiment of Foot (Belgorod Regiment), Belgorod Army, 1663

The first new formation regiments were modelled on the Swedish pattern, so it is possible that some also followed the Swedish custom of using a white field for the first, Life Company. Certainly, this is the colour of Leslie's first company, since the number of stars corresponded to the company's number. However, according to the reconstruction of Leslie's company colours on which this drawing is based (Babulin, *Kanevskaya bitva*), all companies within the regiment used white fields.

2. Muscovy: Colour of 4th Company, Osip Speshnev's New Formation Regiment of Foot (Karpov Regiment), Belgorod Army, 1663

The colour of yet another of the new formation regiments of the Belgorod Army. As in the previous case, the number of stars in the upper corner corresponded to the company's number. Several new formation regiments employed colours with red or reddish-brown fields, but other varieties existed, too (drawing based on Babulin, *Kanevskaya bitva*).

Plate E

1. Cossack Ukraine: Bogdan Khmel'nitskiy's Personal Banner

This reconstruction is based on Bogdan Khmel'nitskiy's personal banner which possibly was captured at Berestechko in 1651 and brought to Warsaw. In 1655, the banner was taken by Swedish units. The obverse and reverse are similar. The motif is a cross above a recumbent half-moon surrounded by ten stars and a circle on a white field. Outside the circle, the Cyrillic letters B, Kh, G, V, and Z signify *Bogdan Khmel'nitskiy Getman Voyska Zaporozhskogo* ('Bogdan Khmel'nitskiy Hetman of the Zaporozhian Host'). Inside the circle, the Cyrillic letters Ye, K, and MLO correspond to the Roman letters J K M

(*Jego Królewskiej Miłości*; 'His Royal Grace'), known from Commonwealth Royal Guard units. When read out in Ruthenian (*Yego Korolevskoy Milosti*) together with the previous text, the letters mean 'Bogdan Khmel'nitskiy, Hetman of His Royal Grace's Zaporozhian Host'. The banner's current breadth is 110 cm and its length 184 cm. However, the banner also had a red border, which is indicated by the present, broken stave which is 126.5 cm long and is believed to have corresponded to the breadth of the complete banner. Moreover, the original position of the letters suggests that the original intention of this banner was to use it as a hanging banner (*khorugv'*), in the style of religious banners used liturgically in the Orthodox church (Army Museum, Stockholm; ST 22:212).

Ukrainian Cossack flags came in a large variety of shapes, sizes, and colours. Numerous captured cossack flags or illustrations of captured cossack flags exist in archives and collections. Several of those earlier taken by the Commonwealth were moved to Stockholm during the Deluge, where they remain the Army Museum. However, most date from the cossack rebellion of 1648–1654 and in particular from the cossack defeats of those years. This means that the continued usage of the same flag patterns in most cases cannot be confirmed. Having said this, it seems unlikely that the cossacks radically would change their accustomed flag patterns after a defeat. Motifs which included a cross of some kind, stars, and occasionally a half-moon were very common, and the motifs on Khmel'nitskiy's personal banner are quite typical.

2. Tatar Khanate of the Crimea: Tatar banner, possibly of Crimean origin

This two-tailed banner is believed to have been captured from a Tatar unit in Poland, possibly in 1656 at the three-day battle of Warsaw. Depicting two crossed sabres and the Shahada (the Islamic declaration of faith, 'There is no God but Allah, and Muhammad is the Messenger of Allah') in white on a red field with a white border, the banner otherwise follows Western styles. It might, for this reason, have belonged to a Tatar unit in either Commonwealth or Muscovite service. However, it is equally likely that it belonged to a Crimean Tatar unit, since there were close cultural contacts between the Khanate and its northern neighbours. The Khanate's contacts with the Ottoman Empire were primarily political and religious in nature. (Army Museum, Stockholm; ST 27:275).

Further Reading (Volume 2)

As noted in Volume 1, the possibly most important contemporary source to the wars of the Deluge is Samuel von Pufendorf's history of the deeds of King Charles. The official Swedish history of the wars, it was first published in Latin so as to get maximum international exposure. It is perhaps most easily accessible to the modern-day reader in its German translation, which was published in 1697 as *Sieben Bücher von denen Thaten Carl Gustavs Königs in Schweden*. Pufendorf worked with primary sources and eyewitness accounts. Naturally, large number of source documents are also available in the national archives of the countries which participated in the wars. For the researcher who knows Swedish or Polish, most relevant sources are summarised and analysed in the Swedish Military Academy's series of studies on the wars of King Charles (*Carl X Gustaf-studier*) carried out by leading military historians of Sweden, Finland, Denmark, Norway, and Poland under the leadership of Arne Stade. The eight volumes, published between 1965 and 1979, provide detailed descriptions of most aspects of the campaigns. They also provide extensive archival citations, which make the volumes of the series invaluable sources on what is already known about the wars of the Deluge as well as the location of relevant archival documents. While all volumes were published in a form understandable to Swedish, Danish, and Norwegian readers, several were also translated into Polish and at least one into Finnish.

With regard to earlier Swedish histories of the wars, Johan Levin Carlbom's several works (1905–1910) are very detailed but suffer from a number of erroneous details, which because of the lack of notes sometimes are difficult to identify. Torsten Holm's *Översikt* (1927) offers an excellent overview of the campaigns and can still be read with great profit, even though this brief work is dated with regard to some details. Among the older regimental histories, *Kungl. Svea livgardes historia* 3:2 by Bertil C:son Barkman, Sven Lundkvist, and Lars Tersmeden (1966) remains a solid study. Intended to form part of the Swedish Military Academy project, it was published earlier and gives a for its time up-to-date interpretation of the battles in which the Life Guard took part, based on Swedish sources. Jonas Hedberg's *Kungl. Artilleriet: Carl X Gustafs tid* (1982) presents later research on the artillery not included in the project's volumes. For specifically the Brandenburgian and Imperial armies, the works by Curt Jany on the former (published 1901–1906 and 1928–1933) and those by Alphons von Wrede on the latter (published 1898–1905) are invaluable.

We mentioned in Volume 1 that all countries, or their modern successors, which participated in the wars of the Deluge at one time or another went through periods when historiography was coloured by nationalist ideas. Such views frequently affected the literature associated with the wars, and nationalist historiography to some extent still affects public and scholarly opinion. The impact of such views was described in Volume 1 and need not be repeated here. Fortunately, a more balanced attitude to historiography eventually emerged in all these countries. However, it is worth repeating that much less research has been devoted to those states which participated in the wars but either lack modern successors or find themselves represented by less formidable entities. Lithuania's part in the story is to some extent covered by Polish research, but the far greater geographical extent of Lithuania in the seventeenth century means that the Grand Duchy's history does not fit easily into the historiography of either modern-day Poland or modern-day Lithuania. Major parts of the territory in question now belong to Belarus, which of course has a historiography of its own which is only seldom consulted by historians elsewhere. Moreover, the voice of the Crimean Khanate is conspicuously lacking. The Khanate had already ceased to exist in the eighteenth century, and there is little current research on its military history. Since the attention of most military historians is drawn elsewhere, they usually take for granted that the Crimean Khanate played a subordinate role. Not so. We have seen that realities on the ground show that the Khanate was still a major power and that it often was the senior partner in any alliance.

Since most works on the wars of the Deluge are published in other languages than English, the following bibliography is limited to the works most frequently referenced in notes and most useful for continued research. Other works are only mentioned in the notes.

Bibliography

Contemporary Sources and Compilations

Abduzhemilev, Refat R. (ed.), *Dokumenty Krymskogo khanstva iz sobraniya Khuseyna Feyzkhanova* (Simferopol': Akademiyanauk Respubliki Tatarstan, 2017)

Anon., *The Swedish Discipline, Religious, Civile, and Military* 1–3 (London: Nathaniel Butter and Nicholas Bourne, 1632. Edited by William Watts. Reprinted in facsimile by Pallas Armata, Tonbridge, Kent, 1998)

Anon. [Pierre Chevalier], *Histoire de la guerre des cosaques contre la Pologne, avec un discours de leur origine, païs, mœurs, gouvernement & religion: Et un autre des Tartares Précopites* (Paris: Thomas Iolly, 1668)

Anon. [Pierre Chevalier], *A Discourse of the Original, Countrey, Manners, Government and Religion of the Cossacks, With Another of the Precopian Tartars, and the History of the Wars of the Cossacks against Poland* (London: Hobart Kemp, 1672. Translation of the above)

Anon. [Samuel Collins], *The Present State of Russia* (London: John Winter, 1671)

Beauplan, Guillaume Le Vasseur, Chevalier de, *Description de l'Ukranie depuis les confins de la Moscovie jusqu' auxlimites de la Transylvanie* (Paris: J. Techener, 1861. First published in 1651) This edition reproduces the revised and enlarged 1660 text)

Beauplan, Guillaume le Vasseur, Sieur de, *A Description of Ukraine* (Cambridge, Mass: Harvard Ukrainian Research Institute, 1993). Translation of the above by Andrew B. Pernal and Dennis F. Esar.

Bennigsen, Alexandre; Pertev Naili Boratav; Dilek Desaive; and Chantal Lemercier-Quelquejay, *Le Khanat de Crimée dans les archives du Musée du Palais de Topkapi* (Paris and The Hague: Mouton, 1978)

Dahlbergh, Erik, ed. Herman Lundström, *Erik Dahlberghsdagbok (1625–1699)* (Uppsala: Almqvist & Wiksell, 1912)

Ehrenstrahl, David Klöcker, *Certamen Equestre: Karl XI:s karusell inför samtid och eftervärld* (Stockholm: Byggförlaget, 2005. Facsimile edition of the original copperplates from 1672)

Erdmannsdörffer, Bernhard, *Urkunden und Actenstücke zur Geschichte des Kurfürsten Friedrich Wilhelm von Brandenburg* (Berlin: Georg Reimer, 23 vols, 1864–1930)

Evliya Efendi [Evliya Çelebi], *Narrative of Travels in Europe, Asia, and Africa, in the Seventeenth Century* (London: Oriental Translation Fund of Great Britain and Ireland, 1834 and 1850. Translation by Joseph Hammer-Purgstall)

Gordon, Patrick, ed. Dmitry Fedosov, *Diary of General Patrick Gordon of Auchleuchries 1635–1699* (Aberdeen: AHRC Centre for Irish and Scottish Studies/Aberdeen University Press, 2009–2016)

Gordon, Patrick. *Tagebuch des Generalen Patrick Gordon, während seiner Kriegsdiensteunter den Schweden und Polenvom Jahre 1655 bis 1661, und seines Aufenthaltes in Rußlandvom Jahre 1661 bis 1699* (Moscow: Prince M.A. Obolenskiy and M.C. Posselt, 1849). The traditional, but inferior, published version of the diary, easily available online but more of an edited summary than a translation.

Gordon, Patrick, *Passages from the Diary of General Patrick Gordon of Auchleuchries A.D. 1635–1699* (Aberdeen: Spalding Club, 1859. An earlier edition of excerpts in English.)

Haller, Gábor, ed. Károly Szabó, 'Haller Gábor naplója 1630–1644', *Erdélyi Történelmi Adatok* 4 (1862), pp.1–111. Gábor Haller's diary 1630–1644, including his military writings.

Jany, Curt, *Urkundliche Beiträge und Forschungen zur Geschichte des Preussischen Heeres* (Berlin: Grosser Generalstab, Kriegsgeschichtliche Abteilung II / Ernst Siegfried Mittler und Sohn, 1901–1906). Jany's work has been described as the most comprehensive treatise of the subject not only of its time but of all times, since many of the original army records he worked with were destroyed in an air raid on Potsdam in 1945.

La Chapelle, Julius Richard de, *Een Militarisch Exercitiæ Book eller Regementz Spegel, aff ett infanterie, hwaruthinnan författas huru ett regemente böör wara besatt medh officerare, sampt hwars och ens plicht och grad ifrån en gemen alt in til en öfwerste så och någre förslagh och påminnelser om ett och annat som böör observeras; jämpte alle simple och dubble exercitier, offensive och defensive fächtande medh en förmeradh skantz battalie, för Swerges blomstrande ungdom som lust hafwa till thet ridderlige och militariske wäsendet korteligen samman fattadt* (Stockholm: I. Meurer, 1669)

Montecuccoli, Raimondo, ed. Alois Veltzé, *Ausgewählte Schriften des Raimund Fürsten Montecuccoli* (Vienna: Kriegs-Archiv/W. Braumüller, 4 vols, 1899–1901)

Noyers, Pierre des, *Lettres de Pierre des Noyers* (Berlin: B. Behr, 1859)

Pasek, Jan Chryzostom, *Pamiętniki: Całość* (Cracow: Polska Akademja Umiejętności, 1929)

Pasek, Jan Chryzostom, *Memoirs of the Polish Baroque: The Writings of Jan Chryzostom Pasek, a Squire of the Commonwealth of Poland and Lithuania* (Berkeley: University of California Press, 1976. Translation by Catherine S. Leach)

Pastorius, Joachim, *Bellum scythico-cosacicum, seu, De conjuratione Tartarorum Cosacorum et plebis Russicae contra regnum Poloniae ab invictissimo Poloniae et Sveciae rege Ioanne Casimirio* (Dantzig: Georg Förster, 1652)

Pufendorf, Samuel von, *Sieben Bücher von denen Thaten Carl Gustavs Königs in Schweden* (Nuremberg: Christoph Riegel, 1697). Translation of *De rebus a Carolo Gustavo, Sueciæ rege, gestis commentariorum libri septem* (Nuremberg: Christophor Riegel, 1696)

Roberts, Michael, *Sweden as a Great Power 1611–1697: Government; Society; Foreign Policy* (London: Edward Arnold, 1968). Translation of numerous Swedish primary sources including records of the Council of the Realm.

Schildknecht, Wendelin, *Harmonia in fortalitiis construendis, defendendis & oppugnandis* (Stettin: Johann Valentin Rheten, 1652)

Troupitzen, Lorentz von, *Kriegs Kunst: Nach Königlicher Schwedischer Manier eine Compagny zu richten, in Regiment, Zug- vnd Schlacht-Ordnung zu bringen, zum Ernst anzuführen, zu gebrauchen, vnd in esse würcklich, zu unterhalten* (Frankfurt-am-Main: Matthaeus Merian, 1633)

Voget, Peter, *Wahrhaftiger und gründlicherBericht von Belagerung und Eroberung der Haupt-Schanze in der Danziger Nährung* (Danzig: David Friedrich Rhete, 1661)

Zetterstéen, Karl Vilhelm, *Türkische, Tatarische und Persische Urkundenim Schwedischen Reichsarchiv* (Uppsala: Almqvist and Wiksell, 1945)

Later Studies

Alm, Josef, *Blanka vapen och skyddsvapen från och med 1500-talet till våra dagar* (Stockholm: Rediviva, 1975. First published 1932)

Alm, Josef, *Eldhandvapen 1: Från deras tidigaste förekomst till slaglåsets allmänna införande* (Stockholm: Rediviva, 1976. First published 1934)

Alm, Josef, *Arméns eldhandvapen förr och nu* (Stockholm: Kungl. Armémuseum, 1953)

Alm, Josef, 'Flottans handvapen'. *Sjöhistorisk Årsbok 1953–54* (Stockholm: Föreningen Sveriges Sjöfartsmuseum i Stockholm, 1954: pp.67–147)

Asker, Björn, *Karl X Gustav* (Lund: Historiska Media, 2010)

Asker, Björn, 'Svenska uniformsförteckningar 1655–1683'. *Meddelande XXXVII Armémuseum 1976–77* (Stockholm: Armémuseum, 1978: pp.77–100)

Askgaard, Finn, *Kampen om Östersjön på Carl X Gustafs tid: Ett bidrag till nordisk sjökrigshistoria* (Stockholm: Kungl. Militärhögskolan, *Carl X Gustaf-studier* 6, 1974)

Augusiewicz, Sławomir, *Prostki 1656* (Warsaw: Bellona, 2001)

Augusiewicz, Sławomir, 'Skład i liczebność stałej armii w Prusach Książęcych w latach 1656–1660'. *Komunikaty Mazursko-Warmińskie* 243 (1/2004), pp.27–47

Babulin, Igor' B., *Smolenskiy pokhod i bitva pri Shepelevichakh 1654 goda* (Moscow: Russkiye Vityazi, 2018)

Babulin, Igor' B., *Bor'ba za Ukrainu i bitva pod Konotopom 1658–1659 gody* (Moscow: Russkiye Vityazi, 2015)

Babulin, Igor' B., *Kanevskaya bitva 16 iyulya 1662 goda: Zabytaya pobeda* (Moscow: Russkiye Vityazi, 2015)

Babulin, Igor' B., *Bitva pod Konotopom, 28 iyunya 1659 goda* (Moscow: Zeughaus, 2009)

Babulin, Igor' B., 'Sostav russkoy armii v Chudnovskom pokhode 1660', *Reytar* 28 (2006); available from *Oderint dum probent* blog (<www.rusmilhist.blogspot.com>)

Babulin, Igor' B., 'Vazhneyshiye pobedy Rossii v russko-pol'skoy voyne 1654–1667 gg.: Otvet retsenzentu'. *Istoriya voyennogo dela: issledovaniya i istochniki* 9 (2017), pp.375–397

Babulin, Igor' B., 'Oborona Glukhova protiv pol'skoy armii korolya Yana Kazimira v 1664 g. *Slavyanskiy al'manakh* 2019, pp.213–36

Barkman, G. Bertil C:son, *Gustaf II Adolfs regementsorganisation vid det inhemska infanteriet: En studie över organisationens tillkomst och huvuddragen av dess utveckling mot bakgrunden av kontinental organisation* (Stockholm: Meddelanden från Generalstabens krigshistoriska avdelning, 1931)

Barkman, G. Bertil C:son; Sven Lundkvist; and Lars Tersmeden. *Kungl. Svea livgardes historia 3:2: 1632 (1611)–1660* (Stockholm: Stiftelsen för Svea livgardes historia, 1966)

Bellander, Erik, *Dräkt och uniform: Den svenska arméns beklädnad från 1500-talets början fram till våra dagar* (Stockholm: Kungl. Armémuseum/P.A. Norstedt & Söner, 1973)

Belyayev, I.D., *O russkom voyske v tsarstvovaniye Mikhaila Feodorovicha i posle ego, do preobrazovaniy, sdelannykh Petrom Velikim: Istoricheskoye izsledovaniye* (Moscow: Universitetskaya tipografiya, 1846)

Bobiatyński, Konrad, *Od Smoleńska do Wilna: Wojna Rzeczypospolitej z Moskwą 1654–55* (Zabrze: Inforteditions, 2004)

Bobrov, Leonid A., Amet-han A. Sheykhumerov; and Alexey V. Salnikov, 'Stabbing Long-Shafted Pole Weapons of the Crimean Tatars and Nogais in 1440s–1650s: According to the Written Sources', *Bylyye Gody* 49: 3 (2018), pp.884–914

Bobrov, Leonid. 'Kalmytskaya konnitsa v Russko-pol'skoy voyne 1654–1667 gg.: Vooruzheniye, taktika, voyennaya strategiya', *Zbroyeznav* 2014, pp.47–63

Borcz, Andrzej, *Przemyśl 1656–1657* (Warsaw: Bellona, 2006)

Carlbom, Johan Levin, *Om Karl X Gustafs polska Krig och öfvergången till det 2:dra Sundskriget* (Gothenburg: Centraltryckeriet/Oscar Ericson, 1905)

Carlbom, Johan Levin, *Tre dagars slaget vid Warschau den 18, 19 och 20 juli 1656: Samt de föregående mindre fältslagen 1655 och 1656 – Ett tvåhundrafemtioårigt minne* (Stockholm: Varia, 1906)

Carlbom, Johan Levin, *Karl X Gustav: Från Weichseln till Bält 1657 – Tåget över Bält och freden i Roskilde 1658* (Stockholm: Fahlcrantz, 1910)

Cavallie, James, *De höga officerarna: Studier i den svenska militära hierarkien under 1600-talets senare del* (Stockholm: Militärhögskolan, 1981)

Cederström, Rudolf, *Svenska kungliga hufvudbanér samt fälttecken vid i Sverige, Finland och öfriga svenska provinser stående trupper förvarade i Kungl. Lifrustkammaren och Kungl. Artillerimuseum m. fl. in-och utländska Samlingar* (Stockholm: Meddelanden från Lifrustkammaren Nr. 2, 1900)

Chernov, A.V., *Vooruzhennye sily Russkogo gosudarstva v XV–XVII vv.: S obrazovaniya tsentralizovannogo gosudarstva do reform pri Petre I* (Moscow: Voyennoye Izdatel'stvo Ministerstva Oborony Soyuza SSR, 1954)

Cieślak, Edmund, 'Gdańsks militär-politiska och ekonomiska betydelse under polsk-svenska kriget 1655–1660'. Arne Stade and Jan Wimmer (eds), *Polens krig med Sverige 1655–1660: Krigshistoriska studier* (Stockholm: Kungl. Militärhögskolan, *Carl X Gustaf-studier* 5, 1973: pp.131–5)

Collins, Leslie J.D., 'The Military Organization and Tactics of the Crimean Tatars During the Sixteenth and Seventeenth Centuries', Vernon J. Parry and Malcolm Edward Yapp (eds), *War, Technology and Society in the Middle East* (London: Oxford University Press, 1975: pp.257–76)

Danielsson, Arne, 'Polska baner och gardesfanor i Statens Trofésamling'. *Meddelande 41–42 Armémuseum 1980–1982* (Stockholm: Armémuseum, 1984: pp.35–51)

Davies, Brian I., *Warfare, State and Society on the Black Sea Steppe, 1500–1774* (Abingdon, Oxon: Routledge, 2007)

Dzieszyński, Ryszard, *Kraków 1655–1657* (Warsaw: Bellona, 2019)

Englund, Peter, *Ofredsår: Om den svenska stormaktstiden och en man i dess mitt* (Stockholm: Atlantis, 1993)

Englund, Peter, *Den oövervinnerlige: Om den svenska stormaktstiden och en man i dess mitt* (Stockholm: Atlantis, 2000)

Ericson, Lars, *Krig och krigsmakt under svensk stormaktstid* (Lund: Historiska Media, 2004)

Fagerlund, Rainer, 'Kriget i östersjöprovinserna 1655–1661: Operationer och krigsansträngningar på en bikrigsskådeplats under Carl X Gustafs krig', Arne Stade (ed.), *Kriget på östfronten* (Stockholm: Militärhögskolan, *Carl X Gustaf-studier* 7:1, 1979)

Fredholm von Essen, Michael, *Muscovy's Soldiers: The Emergence of the Russian Army 1462–1689* (Warwick: Helion, 2018)

Fredholm von Essen, Michael, *Charles XI's War: The Scanian War between Sweden and Denmark, 1675–1679* (Warwick: Helion, 2019)

Fredholm von Essen, Michael, *The Lion from the North 1: The Swedish Army during the Thirty Years' War, 1618–1632* (Warwick: Helion, 2020)

Fredholm von Essen, Michael, *The Lion from the North 2: The Swedish Army during the Thirty Years War, 1632–1648* (Warwick: Helion, 2020)

Frost, Robert I., *The Northern Wars: War, State and Society in North-eastern Europe, 1558–1721* (Harlow, Essex: Pearson Education, 2000)

Frost, Robert I., *After the Deluge: Poland–Lithuania and the Second Northern War, 1655–1660* (Cambridge: Cambridge University Press, 2003)

Gadzyatskiy, S.S., 'Bor'ba russkikh lyudey Izhorskoy zemli v XVII veke protiv inozemnogo vladychestva', *Istoricheskiye zapiski* 16, 1945 (Moscow), pp.14–57

Gadzyatskiy, S.S., 'Kareliya i Yuzhnoye Priladozh'ye v voyne 1656–58 gg.', *Istoricheskiye zapiski* 11, 1941 (Moscow), pp.236–81

Gawęda, Marcin, *Połonka-Basia 1660* (Warsaw: Bellona, 2005)

Gembarzewski, Bronisław, *Husarze: Ubiór. oporządzenie i uzbrojenie, 1500–1775* (Warsaw: Nakładem "Broni i Barwy", 1939)

Gembarzewski, Bronisław, *Żołnierzpolski 1: Ubiór, uzbrojenie i oporządzenie od wieku XI do roku 1960* (Warsaw: Wydawnictwo Ministerstwa Obrony Narodowej, 1960)

Glete, January, *Navies and Nations: Warships, Navies and State Building in Europe and America, 1500–1860* (Stockholm: Almqvist & Wiksell International, Acta Universitatis stockholmiensis (Stockholm Studies in History) 48:1, 2 vols, 1993)

Grushevskiy, Mikhail [Mykhailo Hrushevsky], *Illyustrirovannaya istoriya Ukrainy* (Kiev: MPP Levada, 1997). Authorised translation of Hrushevsky's work into Russian, based on the author's 1913 edition with additional materials of his published 1921 in Vienna.

Gullberg, Tom; and Mikko Huhtamies, *På vakt i öster*, vol. 3 (np: Schildts, 2004)

Hahlweg, Werner, *Das Kriegswesen der Stadt Danzig 1: Die Grundzüge der Danziger Wehrverfassung 1454–1793* (Berlin: Junker und Dünnhaupt, 1937)

Hahlweg, Werner, *Das Kriegswesen der Stadt Danzig 1: Die Grundzüge der Danziger Wehrverfassung 1454–1793* (Osnabrück: Biblio-Verlag, 1982. Facsimile edition with additional materials)

Haratym, Andrzej, *Smoleńsk 1654* (Warsaw: Mówiąwieki, 2020)

Hedberg, Jonas (ed.), *Kungl. Artilleriet: Yngre vasatiden* (Stockholm: Militärhistoriska Förlaget, 1985)

Hedberg, Jonas, *Kungl. Artilleriet: Carl X Gustafs tid* (Stockholm: Militärhistoriska Förlaget, 1982 (1995 edition))

Hellie, Richard, *Enserfment and Military Change in Muscovy* (Chicago: University of Chicago Press, 1971)

Herbst, Stanisław, 'Tredagarsslaget vid Warszawa 1656', Arne Stade and Jan Wimmer (eds), *Polens krig med Sverige 1655–1660: Krigshistoriska studier* (Stockholm: Kungl. Militärhögskolan, *Carl X Gustaf-studier* 5, 1973, pp.255–93)

Holm, Torsten, *Översikt över Sveriges krig under 1600-talets senare hälft* (Stockholm: Militärlitteraturföreningen 148, 1927)

Hrushevsky, Mykhailo, *History of Ukraine-Rus'* (Edmonton and Toronto: Canadian Institute of Ukrainian Studies Press, 10 vols (in 12 books), 1997–2014). The final three volumes describe the cossack uprising.

İnalcık, Halil, 'The Khan and the Tribal Aristocracy: The Crimean Khanate under Sahib Giray I', *Harvard Ukrainian Studies* 3/4, Part 1: *Eucharisterion: Essays presented to Omeljan Pritsak on his Sixtieth Birthday by his Colleagues and Students (1979–1980)*, pp.445–466.

Jakobsson, Theodor, *Lantmilitär beväpning och beklädnad under äldre Vasatiden och Gustav II Adolfs tid*. Published both separately and as Suppl. Vol. 2 in Generalstaben, *Sverigeskrig 1611–1632* (Stockholm: Generalstaben, 1938)

Jany, Curt, *Geschichte der KöniglichPreußischenArmee bis zum Jahre 1807* (Berlin: Karl Siegismund, 4 vols, 1928–1933)

Keep, John L.H., *Soldiers of the Tsar: Army and Society in Russia, 1462–1874* (Oxford: Clarendon, 1985)

Köhler, Gustav, *Geschichte der Festungen Danzig und Weichselmünde bis zum Jahre 1814 in Verbindungmit der Kriegsgeschichte der freien Stadt Danzig 1: Bis zum Jahre 1734* (Breslau: Wilhelm Koebner, 1893)

Kotljarchuk, Andrej, *In the Shadows of Poland and Russia: The Grand Duchy of Lithuania and Sweden in the European Crisis of the mid-17th Century* (Södertörn University College, dissertation, 2006)

Kujala, Antti, 'Förrädiska ryssar och förrymda finnar: Flyttningsrörelserna från Ingermanland och Kexholms län under ryska kriget 1656–1658 och provinsens kolonisation efter kriget', *Historisk Tidskrift för Finland* 97 (2012), pp.469–98

Küpeli, Özer, 'Campaigns of the Crimean Tatars and Ottomans against Iran', *Zolotoordynskoye obozreniye (Golden Horde Review)* 2:4 (2014), pp.226–42

Kurbatov, Oleg Aleksandrovich, *Iz istorii voyennykh reform v Rossiivo 2-y polovine XVII veka: Reorganizatsiya konnitsy na materialakh Novgorodskogo razryada 1650-kh–1660-kh gg.* (Moscow, dissertation, 2002)

Kurbatov, Oleg Aleksandrovich, 'Russko-shvedskaya voyna 1656–58 gg.: Problemy kritiki voyenno-istoricheskikh istochnikov', *Rossiya i Shvetsiya v srednevekov'ye inovoye vremya: Arkhivnoye i muzeynoye naslediye* (Moscow, 2002), pp.150–66. Available from Vladimir Velikanov's *Oderint dum probent* blog (<www.rusmilhist.blogspot.com>)

Kurbatov, Oleg Aleksandrovich, '"Litovskiy pokhod 7168 g.", kn. I.A. Khovanskogo i bitva pri Polonke 18 iyunya 1660 g.', *Slavyanovedeniye* 4, 2003: pp.225–40. Available from Vladimir Velikanov's *Oderint dum probent* blog (<www.rusmilhist.blogspot.com>).

Kurbatov, Oleg Aleksandrovich, 'Polk Antoniya Granovskogo v pokhode 1654 g.: O polozhenii inozemnykh spetsialistov inzhenernogo i artilleriyskogo dela v pusskom voyske', *Inozemtsy v Rossii v XV–XVII vekakh: Sbornik materialov konferentsiy 2002–2004 gg.* (Moscow, 2006: pp.316–35). Available from Vladimir Velikanov's *Oderint dum probent* blog (<www.rusmilhist. blogspot.com>)

Kurbatov, Oleg, Organizatsiya i boyevyye kachestva russkoy pekhoty "novogo stroya" nakanune i v khode russko-shvedskoy voyny 1656–58 gg.', *Arkhiv russkoy istorii: Sbornik Rossiyskogo gosudarstvennogo arkhiva drevnikh aktov* 8 (Moscow, 2007), pp.157–97. Available from Vladimir Velikanov's *Oderint dum probent* blog (<www.rusmilhist.blogspot.com>)

Kurbatov, Oleg Aleksandrovich, 'Rizhskiy pokhod tsarya Alekseya Mikhaylovicha 1656 g.: Problemyi perspektivy issledovaniya', Rudol'f Germanovich Pikhoya (ed.), *Problemy sotsial'noy i politicheskoy istorii Rossii: Sbornik nauchnykh statey* (Moscow: RAGS, 2009), pp.83–88. Available from Vladimir Velikanov's *Oderint dum probent* blog (<www.rusmilhist.blogspot. com>)

Laidre, Margus, *Schwedische Garnisonen in Est- und Livland 1654–1699* (Universität Tartu: Staatliches Historisches Zentralarchiv der Estnischen SSR /Tallinn: Valgus, 1990)

Landberg, Hans, *Carl X Gustaf inför polska kriget: Kungamakt och statsfinanser 1655* (Stockholm: Kungl. Militärhögskolan, *Carl X Gustaf-studier* 4, 1969)

Lange, Ulrich, *Karl X Gustavs bror Adolf Johan: Stormaktstidens enfant terrible* (Stockholm: Medström, 2019)

Lappalainen, Jussi T., 'Finland och Carl X Gustafs ryska krig: Försvaret av den östra rikshalvan 1656–1658', Arne Stade (ed.), *Kriget på östfronten* *Stockholm: Militärhögskolan, *Carl X Gustaf-studier* 7:2, 1979)

Larsson, Lars-Olof, *På marsch mot evigheten: Svensk stormaktstid i släkten Stålhammars spegel* (Stockholm: Prisma, 2007)

Łopatecki, Karol, '"Szwedzkie napoje" czyli rzecz o wysadzeniu zamku w Sandomierzu w świetle grafiki *Gesta ad Sandomiriam* Erika Dahlbergha', W. Walczak and K. Łopatecki (eds), *Stan badań nad wielokulturowym dziedzictwem dawnej Rzeczypospolitej* 7 (Białystok: Instytut Badań nad Dziedzictwem Kulturowym Europy, 2017, pp.151–179)

Malov, Aleksandr V., 'Gosudarevy vybornyye Moskovskiye polki soldatskogo stroya: Kratkiy ocherk istorii i organizatsii', *Zeughaus* 13 (2001), pp.2–7

Malov, Aleksandr V., 'Gosudarevy vybornyye Moskovskiye polki soldatskogo stroya: Komandiry vybornykh polkov', *Zeughaus* 14 (2001), pp.2–7

Malov, Aleksandr V., 'Znamena polkov novogo stroya', *Zeughaus* 15 (2001), pp.6–10

Malov, Aleksandr V., 'Znamena polkov novogo stroya: Simvolika kresta', *Zeughaus* 16 (2001), pp.2–7

Malov, Aleksandr V., 'Russkaya pekhota XVII veka: Gosudarevo zhalovan'ye-sluzhiloye plat'ye', *Zeughaus* 17 (2002), pp.10–16.

Malov, Aleksandr V., '"Konnost', lyudnost' i oruzhnost" sluzhilogo 'goroda' pered Smolenskoy voynoy: Na materiale Velikikh Luk', *Zeughaus* 18 (2002), pp.12–15.

Malov, Aleksandr V., 'Gosudarev vybornyy polk Aggeya Shepeleva: Pervoye soldatskoye sluzhiloye plat'ye'. *Zeughaus* 20 (2002), pp.10–13.

Malov, Aleksandr V., 'Garnizon Borisoglebskoy kreposti: Gosudarevo sluzhiloye plat'ye, 1666', *Zeughaus* 21 (2003), pp.3–7.

Malov, Aleksandr V., 'Gosudarevo sluzhiloye plat'ye Pervogo vybornogo polka 1661 g', *Zeughaus* 22 (2006), pp.6–9.

Malov, Aleksandr V., 'Dukhovnaya simvolika znamen moskovskikh konnykh soten XVII v. (po dokumental'nym istochnikam)', *Patriotizm: Dukhovnyy sterzhen' narodov Rossii* (Moscow: Ekonomicheskaya literatura, 2006: pp.45–70)

Malov, Aleksandr V., 'Gosudarevo sluzhiloye plat'ye Vtorogo vybornogo polka v kontse 1650-kh–nachale 1660-kh gg', *Zeughaus* 24 (2007), pp.5–7.

Malov, Aleksandr V., *Russko-pol'skayavoyna 1654–1667* (Moscow: Zeughaus, 2006)

Manz, Beatrice Forbes, 'The Clans of the Crimean Khanate, 1466–1532', *Harvard Ukrainian Studies* 2: 3 (1978), pp.282–309

Munthe, Ludvig W:son, *Kongl. Fortifikationens historia 2: Fortifikationsstaten under Örnehufwudh och Wärnschiöldh, 1641–1674* (Stockholm: Norstedt & söner, 1906)

Nagielski, Mirosław, *Warszawa 1656* (Warsaw: Bellona, 2009)

Novosel'skiy, Aleksey Andreyevich, 'Ocherk voyennykh deystviy boyarina Vasiliya Petrovicha Sheremeteva v 1654 gody na Novgorodskom fronte', L.G. Dubinskaya (ed.), *Issledovaniya po istorii epokhi feodalizma* (Moscow: Nauka, 1994: pp.117–35)

Nowak, Tadeusz, 'Carl C Gustafs Kraków-operation 1655', Arne Stade and Jan Wimmer (eds). *Polens krig med Sverige 1655–1660: Krigshistoriska studier* (Stockholm: Kungl. Militärhögskolan, *Carl X Gustaf-studier* 5, 1973: pp.157–211)

Nowak, Tadeusz Marian, 'Det polska kronartilleriet före och under det polsk-svenska kriget 1655–1660', Arne Stade and Jan Wimmer (eds), *Polens krig med Sverige 1655–1660: Krigshistoriska studier* (Stockholm: Kungl. Militärhögskolan, *Carl X Gustaf-studier* 5, 1973: pp.103–129)

Ocakli, Sait, *The Relations of the Crimean Khanate with the Ukrainian Cossacks, the Polish–Lithuanian Commonwealth and Muscovy during the Reign of Khan Islam Giray III (1644–1654)* (University of Toronto, dissertation, 2017)

Opitz, Eckardt, *Österreich und Brandenburg im Schwedisch-Polnischen Krieg 1655–1660: Vorbereitung und Durchführung der Feldzügenach Dänemark und Pommern* (Boppard am Rhein: Harald Boldt, 1969)

Ostapchuk, Victor, 'Crimean Tatar Long-Range Campaigns: The View from Remmal Khoja's History of Sahib Gerey Khan', Brian J. Davies (ed.), *Warfare in Eastern Europe, 1500–1800* (Leiden: Brill, 2012: pp.147–71)

Ossoliński, Łukasz J.C., *Kampaniana Ukrainie 1660 roku* (University of Warsaw, dissertation, 1995, 2000)

Paradowski, Michał, *The Lithuanian Army 1653–1667* (Daniel Schorr's *Northern Wars* website (now defunct), 2008)

Penskoy, V.V., 'Voyennyy potentsial krymskogo khanstva vo kontse XV–nachale XVII v', *Vostok (Oriens)* 2, 2010: pp.56–66

Petri, Gustaf; with Erik Westman, *Kungl. Första livgrenadjärregementets historia* 2: *Östgöta regemente till fot 1619–1679* (Stockholm: P.A. Norstedt & Söner, 1928)

Podhorodecki, Leszek, '1659 års fälttåg i Kungliga (Polska) Preussen', Arne Stade and Jan Wimmer (eds), *Polens krig med Sverige 1655–1660: Krigshistoriska studier* (Stockholm: Kungl. Militärhögskolan, *Carl X Gustaf-studier* 5, 1973, pp.295–323)

Roessel, *Die erste Brandenburgische Flotte im Schwedisch-Polnischen Kriege 1658–1660 und ihr Kommandeur Obrist Johann von Hille* (Berlin: R. Eisenschmidt, 1903)

Romański, Romuald, *Cudnów 1660* (Warsaw: Bellona, 1996)

Sikora, Radosław, *Taktyka walki, uzbrojenie i wyposażenie husarii w latach 1576–1710* (Siedlce: Uniwersytet Przyrodniczo Humanistyczny, dissertation, 2010)

Sikorski, Janusz, *Jasna Góra 1655* (Warsaw: Bellona, 1994)

Skoworoda, Paweł, *Warka – Gniezno 1656* (Warsaw: Bellona, 2003)

Sowa, Marcin, 'Transylvanian Military in Mid-17th Century', Michał Paradowski and Rafał Szwelicki (eds), *The Deluge: Northern War 1655–1660* (Warsaw: Wargamer, 2015: pp.206–31)

Stade, Arne, *Erik Dahlbergh och Carl X Gustafs krigshistoria* (Stockholm: Kungl. Militärhögskolan, *Carl X Gustaf-studier* 3, 1967)

Stade, Arne (ed.), *Kriget på östfronten* (Stockholm: Militärhögskolan, *Carl X Gustaf-studier* 7, 1979)

Stade, Arne (ed.), *Carl X Gustafs armé* (Stockholm: Militärhögskolan, *Carl X Gustaf-studier* 8, 1979)

Stade, Arne; and Jan Wimmer (eds), *Polens krig med Sverige 1655–1660: Krigshistoriska studier* (Stockholm: Kungl. Militärhögskolan, *Carl X Gustaf-studier* 5, 1973). Published in Polish as Jan Wimmer (ed.), *Wojna polsko-szwedzka, 1655–1660* (Warsaw: Wydawnictwo Ministerstwa Obrony Narodowej, 1973)

Stevens, Carol Belkin, *Soldiers on the Steppe: Army Reform and Social Change in Early Modern Russia* (DeKalb: Northern Illinois University Press, 1995)

Stevens, Carol Belkin, *Russia's Wars of Emergence 1460–1730* (London: Routledge, 2013)

Syroyechkovskiy, V.E., 'Mukhammed-Gerayiyegovassaly', *Uchonyye- zapiski Moskovskogo gosudarstvennogo universiteta* 61 (1940), pp.3–71

Teodorczyk, Jerzy, 'Czarnieckis vinterfälttåg januari–februari 1656: Slaget vid Gołąb', Arne Stade and Jan Wimmer (eds), *Polens krig med Sverige 1655–1660: Krigshistoriska studier* (Stockholm: Kungl. Militärhögskolan, *Carl X Gustaf-studier* 5, 1973, pp.213–54)

Tepkeyev, V.T., '"Ot nego, krymskogo khana, pravdy i postoyanstva net": Nabegi kalmytskikh otryadov na Krym vo vremya Russko-pol'skoy voyny 1654–1667 rr.', *Novyy istoricheskiy vestnik* 4 (38), 2013, pp.9–28

Tersmeden, Lars, 'Carl X Gustafs armé 1654–1657', Arne Stade (ed.), *Carl X Gustafs armé.* (Stockholm: Militärhögskolan, *Carl X Gustaf-studier* 8, 1979: pp.163–276)

Tersmeden, Lars, 'Carl X Gustafs armé: En konturteckning mot bakgrund av kriget mot Polen', Arne Stade (ed.), *Carl X Gustafs armé* (Stockholm: Militärhögskolan, *Carl X Gustaf-studier* 8, 1979, pp.9–48)

Tersmeden, Lars, '"Manskapsersättningsproblematiken' vid det inhemska infanteriet under Carl X Gustafs krig', Arne Stade (ed.), *Carl X Gustafs armé* (Stockholm: Militärhögskolan, *Carl X Gustaf-studier* 8, 1979, pp.77–115)

Tersmeden, Lars, 'Värvningskampanjen 1655', Arne Stade (ed.), *Carl X Gustafs armé* (Stockholm: Militärhögskolan, *Carl X Gustaf-studier* 8, 1979, pp.117–62)

Tessin, Georg, *Die Deutschen Regimenter der Krone Schweden* 1: *Unter Karl X. Gustav (1654–1660)* (Cologne: Böhlau, 1965)

Ulfhielm, Hans; and Eric Granefelt (eds)., *Kungl. Artilleriet: Svenska Artilleriet i Östersjöprovinserna 1561–1721* (np: Militärhistoriska Förlaget, 2005)

Wennerholm, J. Bertil R., 'Svenska fantroféer i den ryska trofésamlingen', *Meddelande 41–42 Armémuseum 1980–1982* (Stockholm: Armémuseum, 1984, pp.53–97)

Wimmer, January, *Wojsko polskie w drugiej połowie XVII wieku* (Warsaw: Wojskowy Instytut Historyczny, Ministerstwo Obrony Narodowej, 1965)

Wimmer, January, 'Armé och finansväsen i Polen under kriget med Sverige 1655–1660', Arne Stade and Jan Wimmer (eds), *Polens krig med Sverige 1655–1660: Krigshistoriska studier* (Stockholm: Kungl. Militärhögskolan, *Carl X Gustaf-studier* 5, 1973, pp.41–101)

Wimmer, January, 'Polens krig med Sverige 1655–1660: Operativ översikt', Arne Stade and Jan Wimmer (eds), *Polens krig med Sverige 1655–1660: Krigshistoriska studier* (Stockholm: Kungl. Militärhögskolan, *Carl X Gustaf-studier* 5, 1973, pp.325–417)

Wrede, Alphons von; with Anton Semek. *Geschichte der K. und K. Wehrmacht: Die Regimenter, Corps, Branchen und Anstalten von 1618 bis Ende des XIX. Jahrhunderts* (Vienna: L.W. Seidel & Sohn, 5 vols, 1898–1905)

Zablocki, Wojciech, *Szable świata* (Warsaw: Bellona, 2011)